Transforming Youth Justice

Transforming Youth Justice

Occupational identity and
cultural change

Anna Souhami

Routledge
Taylor & Francis Group

LONDON AND NEW YORK

First published by Willan Publishing 2007
This edition published by Routledge 2012
2 Park Square, Milton Park, Abingdon, Oxon OX14 4RN
711 Third Avenue, New York, NY 10017

Routledge is an imprint of the Taylor & Francis Group, an informa business

ISBN-13: 978-1-84392-193-6 hardback
ISBN-13: 978-0-415-62808-2 paperback

British Library Cataloguing-in-Publication Data

A catalogue record for this book is available from the British Library

Project managed by Deer Park Productions, Tavistock, Devon
Typeset by TW Typesetting, Plymouth, Devon

Contents

Acknowledgements   *ix*

Introduction   1

1 Transforming youth justice   **11**
  Youth justice in disarray   12
  Origins   13
  Transforming youth justice   16
  Transforming youth justice social work   21
  Notes   25

Part 1: A Youth Justice Team   **27**

2 Experiences and problems of team membership   **32**
  'Not like social workers at all'   32
  Defining 'us' and 'them'   35
  Cohesion and change   37
  Understanding organisational culture   39
  Consensus, conflict and ambiguity: the complexity of team
    membership   40
  Notes   44

**3 Working in youth justice: the 'normal ambiguity' of
  social work**   **46**
  The police and social work: 'us' and 'them'   46
  Inter-agency conflicts   49
  What is youth justice social work?   50
  The 'normal' ambiguity of social work   62
  Ambiguity and the new youth justice   64
  Notes   69

4   An unrepresentative representative: being a police officer
    in a YOT   70
    Being a police officer   71
    Developing a police officer's role on the YOT   75
    Representing the police: 'a hardening of the shell'   79
    An unrepresentative representative of the police   84
    Notes   87

Part 2: Change and Ambiguity   89

5   **Joining an established team**   91
    Joining an established team   91
    Developing an inter-agency role   98
    Becoming a YOT   106
    Note   108

6   **Change, resistance and fragmentation**   109
    A changing team   109
    Practice, tradition and identity   113
    Introducing groupwork: ambiguity and innovation   116
    Resisting change   120
    Developing practice: the aims and values of youth
       justice work   125
    Notes   129

7   **Managing ambiguity and change**   131
    Looking for guidance   132
    Management, power and powerlessness   136
    Managing ambiguity: paralysis and creativity   143
    A disintegrating team?   152
    Notes   154

Part 3: A Youth Offending Team   155

8   **A youth offending team**   156
    Becoming 'settled'   156
    The changing nature of team membership   161
    The changing boundaries of team membership   164
    Becoming a YOT   175
    Notes   179

9   **Occupational identity and cultural change**   181
    Transforming youth justice social work   182
    Occupational culture and identity revisited   186
    Culture, policy and practice   188

Appendix: Researching a Developing YOT   **195**

References   *210*

Index   *218*

Acknowledgements

This book is based on doctoral research I conducted while in the Department of Criminology at Keele University. I am grateful to many people for their generous help throughout this process.

First, I would like to thank Richard Sparks, who supervised the thesis on which this book is based. I am hugely indebted to Richard whose insight, enthusiasm and encouragement has been strongly influential in shaping both this work and my wider career. Thanks also to Anne Worrall, my second supervisor, whose astute advice and support was invaluable throughout my time at Keele. Evi Girling, John Pitts and Tim Newburn have all read earlier drafts of this book in its various forms, and I am extremely grateful for their careful comments.

My thanks for the generous assistance of the Economic and Social Research Council who funded the original research, and the British Academy whose Postdoctoral Fellowship Award has given me the time to write this book. Thanks also to Brian Willan for his kind support and patience during its production.

I am enormously grateful for the invaluable advice and encouragement of numerous other friends and colleagues at LSE, Keele and elsewhere. In particular, I would like to thank my parents, Jessica and Robert Souhami, for their endless support and for putting up with me through all this.

Above all, I would like to thank the practitioners of the 'Midlands' Youth Offending Team for allowing me to do this research, and for offering me their hospitality, insight and trust. Although I frequently made significant demands on their time during an often uncertain and unsettled period I was met with unfailing warmth and kindness. I am deeply grateful to them.

Anna Souhami
LSE
December 2006

Introduction

In 1997, the newly modernised Labour party swept into power after nearly two decades in opposition, promising to make youth crime central to its priorities. It declared a 'radical overhaul' of the youth justice system. It would usher in a new era in the way in which youth offending was thought about and managed. It would change the culture of work with young offenders. And, perhaps most ambitiously, it would transform the structures through which youth justice services were delivered at both a national and local level.

Through the implementation of the Crime and Disorder Act 1998, Labour set in train the most extensive reform of youth justice services in fifty years (Goldson 2000c). The formation of inter-agency Youth Offending Teams (YOTs) for the local delivery of services was the cornerstone of the new approach. For the first time, the management of youth offending would become a multi-agency responsibility. YOTs were to replace the specialist teams of social workers in local authority social services 'youth justice' or 'juvenile justice' teams. They would not belong to any one department or agency, but were to consist of representatives from all the core agencies that worked with young offenders – social workers, probation officers, police officers, and education and health authority staff. Through inter-agency cooperation, it was envisaged that youth justice services would become more efficient and effective. Centrally, it would provide for a new and consistent approach among the different agencies who worked with young offenders. It would tackle an 'excuse culture' that was alleged to pervade the youth justice system and encourage the emergence of a 'common approach' to the delivery of youth justice services.

The reconfiguration of the services and structures of youth justice therefore brought about a major upheaval in the youth justice system. For the practitioners working within it, this produced a period of intense disruption, anxiety and uncertainty. Staff from all agencies were being asked to put aside their accustomed roles and ways of working in place of a new, shared approach that had yet to emerge. Practitioners were thus faced with a series of fundamental challenges to their sense of professional identity and vocation. They were forced to confront questions of the aims and scope of their work. What was the purpose of work with young offenders? How was it to be done? What were the values that should underpin this work? What were the appropriate roles for practitioners to adopt? And what was it to work in an inter-agency way? This was therefore a particularly important moment in youth justice services where core questions concerning the nature and purpose of contemporary youth justice work were at issue, and where wider issues of occupational identity and culture became of crucial importance.

This book explores the underside of the youth justice reforms in the everyday lives and experiences of those professionals whose task it was to enact them. Its focus therefore is not an evaluation of the implementation of the new youth justice measures (for which see, for example, Burnett and Appleton 2004; Holdaway et al. 2001; Crawford and Newburn 2003) but the changes they effected at the level of mundane professional practice. It examines the sweeping national reorganisation of the youth justice system through an ethnographic study of the formation of a single YOT in one locality. It follows a local authority social services Youth Justice Team through its transition into a multi-agency organisation, exploring the challenges this raised for practitioners as they carried out the delivery of youth justice services in the context of organisational change. In particular, it explores the effects of the transformation of the youth justice system on practitioners' sense of occupational identity, culture and vocation.

Occupational cultures in criminal justice

Although Labour's reforms put the occupational culture of youth justice work at issue, there has been little research in this area. However, there has been a long-standing interest in the occupational cultures of some other criminal justice agencies, in particular the police (e.g. Banton 1964; Bittner 1975; Skolnick 1966; Shearing and Ericson 1981; Reiner 2000; Chan 1996, 1997, 2003, to name but a few), and, to a lesser extent, prisons (e.g. Crawley 2004; Liebling 1992) and probation (e.g. McWilliams 1987, 1992; Nellis 1995a, 1995b). Much of the interest in culture in criminological writing focuses on the nature of these occupational cultures and their relationship with service delivery. For example, how do the particular tasks or working environments of an occupation affect the way members see the social world and their role within it? What are the implicit values and assumptions underlying practice? How does the culture of an occupation mediate practice? In the context of systems of social control, what are the implications for questions of justice and legitimacy? And how might occupational cultures impede organisational change?

Yet despite continued interest in these questions, there has been little critical engagement with the nature of occupational culture itself. Several common themes dominate the way culture is presented in much of this writing. Firstly, occupational cultures are generally understood as aspects of organisational life which are shared by occupational members. They are seen as common working assumptions, values and beliefs which are generated by the specific conditions or pressures arising from distinctive aspects of occupational life. As Reiner puts it in relation to the police, 'cop culture' is a 'patterned set of understandings that help officers to cope with and adjust to the pressures and tensions confronting the police' (2000: 87). The conditions of work facing members of particular occupations thus result in beliefs or responses which are 'general enough and similar enough to identify a distinctive "working personality"' (Skolnick 1966: 70).

The tendency to describe occupational cultures as 'monolithic' has been criticised, particularly in the context of policing (e.g. Reiner 2000). It has been argued that, while occupational members may share some broad aspects of their outlook, there are also significant variations. This is in part a consequence of research which has identified different 'subcultures' within occupations, generated by important differences in aspects of the working environment. For example, research on policing has identified subcultures generated by differences in structural pressures, such as the hierarchical divisions between rank-and-file 'street cops' and 'management cops' (Reuss-Ianni and Ianni 1983), different roles and expertise, like those between uniform officers and plain-clothes detectives (Reiner 2000) or those who undertake routine patrol and dedicated community officers (Fielding 1995), or different environmental conditions such as policing in rural or urban areas (Cain 1973; Shapland and Vagg 1988). These studies have thus focused on identifying variation in occupational life. However, while they are ostensibly studies of difference, they too are founded on the assumption that culture is something that is shared: subcultures describe similarities within particular groups (such as street cops or management cops). Conflicts between these groups are clear: subcultures are discrete and distinct.

For Waddington (1999), the multiplicity of subcultures that have been identified by researchers puts in question this understanding of culture. He argues that 'in the face of all this diversity, sub-culture – as a set of *shared* artefacts – almost disappears completely' (1999: 290 author's italics). Yet the 'near-infinity' (ibid.) of possible subcultural groups need not render them meaningless. There may be important shared experiences among occupational groups which are central to members' experiences. However, occupational members can instead be seen to belong to multiple, overlapping subcultures. So, for example, a police officer might be a uniform, 'street cop', white, woman, with children, working in a rural area, and so on. These different aspects of her identity provide her with important commonalities of experience with other subcultural members. Yet they are also potentially conflicting and contradictory. Different subcultural alliances may take on particular salience at particular moments. This begins to suggest that tensions, flux and ambiguities may also be a central part of occupational life, something which cannot easily be captured by prioritising a view of culture as those aspects of organisational experience that are shared.

Secondly, cultures are generally understood as those aspects of organisational life which are unique to particular professions. This leads logically from the understanding of culture as a set of shared responses to the specific pressures of particular occupational working environments. In exploring police culture for example, researchers have tended to prioritise and attempt to account for aspects of police officers' outlooks which seem different or unusual, such as an apparent suspiciousness, solidarity and so on. Of course, as some have argued, some aspects of occupational culture might be shared by other occupations which experience similar pressures. So, for instance, writing on police culture has drawn parallels with other hierarchical and potentially dangerous working environments such as those experienced in the military (Skolnick 1966).

A consequence of this understanding of culture is that it necessarily overlooks those aspects of members' experiences which are not a result of distinctive occupational pressures. Those elements of working life generally considered to be 'cultural' in much of this writing – such as working assumptions, values and beliefs – will clearly be shaped by numerous influences outside the boundaries of the organisation as well as those from within. So, for example, their extra-occupational identities and the pressures arising from the broader social, economic and political context may be intrinsic to members' responses to their working environment. So, for example, the gender and ethnicity of a 'street cop' are likely to be important in shaping her cultural outlook alongside her working routines and the danger she experiences. In other words, some parts of practitioners' cultural outlook may be shared outside occupations as well as across occupations. Yet because culture is rarely understood as transcending the organisation, these elements of occupational experiences tend to be overlooked.

Thirdly, research which explores individual practitioners' understanding and orientation to their working culture – which I describe in this book as their 'occupational identity' – has largely taken the form of identifying clusters of shared attitudes or perspectives. Thus, according to Reiner's typology, a police officer might fall within one of four broad types: an 'alienated cynic', a 'managerial professional', a 'peacekeeper' or a 'law enforcer' (Reiner 1978, see also, for example, Shearing 1981; Walsh 1977). However, some more recent work in the field of policing has implied a more fluid and dynamic relationship between practitioners and the way they see their occupational culture, arguing that police officers are not passively absorbed into the dominant culture but are active choosers in the way in which they employ cultural knowledge (e.g. Shearing and Ericson 1991; Chan 1996, 1997, 2003). This allows for the possibility that cultural knowledge may also be differently inter-preted, understood, unknown or ignored at different moments and in different contexts.

Lastly, the relationship between culture and change is something that has concerned much writing about criminal justice professions. There are two main and related strands to the way this relationship is envisaged. Firstly, 'culture' is often seen as a feature of organisations that can obstruct change, for example by reinforcing traditional ways of thinking and acting, or by promoting a resistance to innovation. For example, interest in 'police culture' in particular has arisen from concerns that such informal norms and values impede reform in the police service. Secondly, and in part as a result, attention has been paid to the way that 'cultures' change. An often-noted criticism of the dominant way of thinking about culture in criminological writing outlined above is that it gives little room to account for cultural change, or even acknowledge its possibility (see, for example, Reiner 2000; Chan 1996, 1997). If culture is seen, as Chan puts it, as 'all-powerful, homogenous and deterministic . . . insulated from the external environment' (1996: 112) it is indeed difficult to see how change to these informal values or assumptions could occur, or from where the impetus for change could come. Chan in particular has criticised this tendency in the context of policing, arguing that the changes in the broader external (social, political, economic and legal) context in which policing takes place shapes the way police officers understand and employ cultural knowledge (1996, 1997, 2003). But further, what Chan describes as 'cultural knowledge' and the ways it is employed can also be thought of in a state of change and flux, and similarly influenced and shaped by the external context of the organisa-tion.

In this book I take a different approach to questions of culture than that currently dominant in criminological writing. Rather than attempt-ing to identify a 'culture' of youth justice work, my focus is on the nature of occupational culture and identity itself. What does it mean to be a member of an occupation? What constitutes an occupational identity? In what ways do practitioners understand, account for and manage their sense of occupational identity and membership? How and why is this sense of identity disrupted? In attempting to engage with these questions, I have drawn on critical management literature – in particular the work of Martin and Meyerson (Martin 1992, 2002; Martin and Meyerson 1988; Meyerson and Martin 1987) and Parker (2000) – to explore different perspectives in the ways that occupational cultures can be understood, and through which the complexity, ambiguity, conflict and flux of organisational life can be captured. These perspectives are outlined in Chapter 2, and form the basis of the analysis throughout this book.

Research methods

Questions of culture and identity can only be explored by close observation. They are strongly grounded in the lived experience of organisational members. They emerge in the interactions, actions and behaviours of the practitioners involved, and the way these are understood, acted upon and managed in their working lives (e.g. Geertz 1973; Schein 1985; Schwartzman 1993; Van Maanen 1979). As Geertz (1973: 11) puts it: 'Culture is not a power, something to which social events, behaviors, institutions, or processes can be causally attributed; it is a context, something within which they can be intelligibly – that is, thickly – described.' An approach is thus required that allows these questions to be explored without artificially abstracting them from the context in which they emerge. Therefore my attempts to engage with these questions are closely grounded in an ethnographic exploration of the formation of a single YOT by one group of actors in a Midlands town.[1]

The book is the result of an intensive, 14-month period of fieldwork. It began in May 1999, when the Midlands team was still a local authority Department of Social Services Youth Justice Team, and ended in July 2000 when the new YOT appeared to have gained a degree of stability and the bulk of disposals mandated by the Crime and Disorder Act had become available to the courts.

The majority of this time was spent in observational research, talking to practitioners about their work, spending time with them in their offices, attending meetings and accompanying them on visits with young offenders. It became clear in the first months of research that the most useful data would be generated within the physical boundaries of the team's offices. This is where the practitioners spent most of their day (reflected in practitioners' association of the building with the team itself, as discussed throughout this book), and where the interactions between members and a large part of their work could be observed. My observations focused on how practitioners understood and talked about their work to me and to each other: the explanations, interactions, gossip and so on. There appeared to be three different types of talk which were loosely associated with different types of activity, though staff might suddenly switch between these. First, there were relatively formal, public discussions which took place when the team met as a whole. Practitioners often complained in private that this type of discussion was constrained: 'no one says anything'. The most important of these discussions were the regular team meetings, which, as described in Chapter 7, were the only point at which the whole team regularly met and were the main forum for the exchange of information, discussion, complaints and policy-making. They were also useful arenas for practitioners to negotiate their status and for conflict to be expressed and managed. More informal interactions, including the team 'banter', took place while practitioners performed the routine and mundane activities of office life such as doing the paperwork for cases, making phone calls, eating lunch. A third type of talk was marked by what Van Maanen (1992) describes as 'organizational time-outs', which represent a break from the ordinary rules of the workplace. They allow for chatting or gossiping about non-work topics, and 'allow for the expression of sentiments typically unheard (or hushed) during the pursuit of organizational purposes. In most ways, time-outs denote autonomy for the participants ... and a general sense of freedom from organizational constraint' (1992: 39). It was in these occasions that practitioners seemed least constrained in what they said, and where most of the gossiping, bitching and complaining took place. These 'time-outs' would sometimes be marked by a different location, such as moving into the kitchen or going outside to have a cigarette – the 'back places' (Goffman 1959) of the offices – or by an activity or ritual, such as bringing a pot of tea into the main office which would signal a break in the practitioners' work.

The observational research was supplemented by a series of loosely structured interviews to explore practitioners' expectations, preconceptions and anxieties about the shape their work would take. Interviews were conducted in private rooms in the team offices, and with permission (none refused) were tape recorded and transcribed. I intended to interview all team members. But as the team expanded and partnerships with outside agencies and individual consultants developed, the boundaries of the team blurred and the question of who constituted a team member became less clear. However, it appeared that some of these new members had a greater involvement and influence in the team than others. For example, as the first piece of multi-agency practice in the developing YOT the institution of groupwork became invested with practitioners' feelings about the change of identity in the team (Chapter 6). The role of the drama consultant hired to run the groups became of crucial importance, and it thus became important to interview him regardless of his temporary and transient status in the team.

The use of the research strategies in the setting was of course inextricable from the dynamics of the team and my position in it. A methodological account must therefore be to some extent a personal account. The appendix of this book describes some of the dilemmas and experiences of researching the developing team during a time of uncertainty and anxiety, and one in which the notion of team membership became of crucial importance.

The organisation of this book

This book is organised as a chronological account of the formation of the Midlands YOT in order to describe how a complex series of problems and processes unfolded as the team developed. Throughout I have attempted not to deviate too far from the empirical data, but have drawn on criminological literature and critical management theory to illuminate the text.

The first chapter sets the research in its policy context. What was the rationale behind Labour's strategy for the youth justice system? What were the nature of its reforms? And what challenges did this hold for practitioners within it? Chapters 2 to 8 follow the development of the YOT. The research is divided into three parts, marking points which were felt by team members to represent significant changes to the team.

In June 1999, the Midlands team was still felt to be a social services Youth Justice Team. Despite some significant signs of change, the transition into a YOT was not thought to have begun. Part 1 describes the last few months of the Youth Justice Team as staff anticipated the development of a multi-agency organisation. It considers the experiences, complexities and problems of being a youth justice social worker. How did practitioners understand their work, values and identity? What were the implications of the arrival of staff from partner agencies? Chapter 2 describes the problems and experiences of membership of the youth justice team and introduces some of the key ideas about occupational culture that form the basis of the analytical framework of the study. Chapter 3 explores the nature of youth justice social work. It argues that the aims, values and practices underpinning social work with young offenders are characterised by an essential ambiguity. Yet while this 'normal ambiguity' was held to be the essence of the team's practice, it was this that was both targeted by Labour's reforms and made it difficult to defend against innovation. Chapter 4 describes the experiences of the first police officer to join the team. As the first practitioner from a partner agency to join the team, and as a practitioner from an agency commonly felt to be 'in opposition' with social workers, his occupational identity was at issue. This chapter explores the nature of occupational identity and its implications for the problems and purpose of representing an agency on an inter-agency YOT.

In September 1999, the majority of staff from partner agencies joined the team and the transition to a YOT was now felt to be underway. The second part of the study describes the first months of the fully inter-agency team, as practitioners attempted to develop their roles and practice in the context of rapid change and widespread confusion and uncertainty. It explores the processes and problems of change, and the impact on practitioners' sense of identity and culture. Chapter 5 describes how new staff felt they were outsiders joining an unchanging, established team. It explores the difficulty of developing an inter-agency role, and the impact of the power relations in the team in the way practitioners' roles were shaped. Chapter 6 explores an alternative perception of change. It describes how the team was also in a process of considerable change, and calls into question the notion of established boundaries between social work staff and practitioners from partner agencies. Chapter 7 describes the problems of managing the team in a context of ambiguity and change. In particular, it explores the difficulties in negotiating the new relationships between the central and local governance of youth crime established under the Crime and Disorder Act.

On 1 April 2000 the YOT was officially launched, and the mood of the team appeared to change dramatically. Part 3 describes the first months of the Youth Offending Team. Chapter 8 explores the ways the team had changed from its incarnation as a Youth Justice Team a year previously. It discusses the nature of inter-agency working and the difficulty of forming a team in which the key element of identity is the incorporation of difference.

Chapter 9 draws together the arguments in this book. Why were the effects of organisational change felt so intensely by those practitioners working within it? What are the implications for wider questions of occupational culture and identity? What does it suggest about the purpose and nature of inter-agency working, in particular in relation to Labour's central rationale of developing a shared culture among youth justice practitioners? And how can questions of culture and identity contribute to an understanding of the dissonance between policy and practice?

Writing about the team

Lastly, a note about the way this book is written. The following account seeks to describe the processes involved in the formation of the Midlands YOT as they were understood by the practitioners involved. I have tried to refrain from attributing thoughts or beliefs to them, or elaborating or interpreting what they have left unspoken. As will become apparent, practitioners' accounts of events in the team demonstrated the ambiguity of their experience: they were at times confused, contradictory or conflicting. Following Martin (1992), I have tried to avoid the implications that the views of individuals or groups of practitioners are accurate descriptions of an 'objective' reality, by choosing phrasing that suggests that alternative interpretations are possible (e.g. 'some practitioners felt', 'many practitioners thought', etc.).

As the following chapters will show, the formation of the multi-agency YOT revealed a complex relationship between individual practitioners and their self-identity as representatives of their home agencies. I have therefore identified practitioners both by proper names and their occupational background (e.g. Duncan, social worker). Practitioners are referred to by the same name throughout the book to maintain a sense of the individual personalities of those involved and the diverse ways in which the unfolding events were experienced. However, I am aware that by separating team members and preserving this individuality the practitioners involved have become more easily identifiable. To try to preserve their anonymity I have changed their names (but not their genders) and excluded some quotations which may have identified them.

Note

1 At the time of the research, the total population of this town was approximately 250,000: the youth population (10–19) was about 60,000. There was a small Black and minority ethnic (BME) population (under 5 per cent), of which the largest minority ethnic groups were Asian and African Caribbean.

Chapter 1

Transforming youth justice

At the time this study began, the youth justice system was under intense political scrutiny. Youth crime had become a key issue in the 1997 general election. A series of serious and high-profile offences by young people had seen a recent 'repoliticisation' (Pitts 1999) of youth crime in which it was thrust into the centre of national attention and debate, most importantly following the abduction and murder of two-year-old James Bulger by two 10-year-olds in 1993 (Newburn 1998). At the same time, an increasing preoccupation with low-level incivilities or 'anti-social behaviour' by young people had become central to the concerns of the prized electoral constituency of middle-class, middle England (Pitts 2000). The run-up to the general election therefore saw the emergent Labour government attempting to reposition itself as the party of 'law and order'. Youth crime would be a 'matter of priority' (Labour Party 1996).

A series of consultative documents setting out their plans for a 'major reform of youth justice' (Labour Party 1996; Home Office 1997a, 1997b, 1997c, 1997e, 1997f, 1997g) and the establishment of a Task Force on Youth Justice (Home Office 1998b) were shortly followed by the White Paper *No More Excuses* (Home Office 1997d). This frenetic activity culminated the following year in the Crime and Disorder Act 1998: an ambitious and wide-ranging programme of legislative and organisational change, and one which set in train the processes described in this book.

This chapter sets the following research in its policy context and describes the climate facing youth justice professionals at the beginning of the study. What was the rationale behind Labour's strategy for the youth justice system? What were the nature of its proposed reforms? And what challenges did this hold for practitioners within it?

Youth justice in disarray

The government's assessment of the youth justice system was damning. The documentation surrounding the Crime and Disorder Act describes a system characterised by waste, inefficiency and complacency. In his foreword to the White Paper (Home Office 1997d), the then Home Secretary Jack Straw described an 'excuse culture' that had come to pervade the system and in which the practitioners and young offenders within it were colluding. The youth justice system 'excuses itself for its inefficiency'. It 'excuses the young offenders before it, implying that they cannot help their behaviour because of their social circumstances'. The system was infused by a culture of inactivity. Offenders were rarely 'confronted with their behaviour or helped to take personal responsibility for their actions'.[1]

Drawing closely on the newly published Audit Commission report, *Misspent Youth* (Audit Commission 1996), which formed the basis of the subsequent reforms, the government described a catalogue of failings. Three main strands of its critique are particularly salient to this discussion. First, the youth justice system was incoherent. It was 'in disarray. It simply does not work. It can scarcely be called a system at all because it lacks coherent objectives' (Labour Party 1996: 1). Instead, there was a profound confusion about its purpose. 'Concerns about the welfare of the young person have too often been seen as in conflict with the aims of protecting the public, punishing offences and preventing offending' (Home Office 1997d: 2.1). The structures through which the youth justice system was organised allowed for the perpetuation of these central tensions. At the centre, responsibility for youth offending was spread across different governmental departments, each with different priorities and approaches to youth offending. As a result, 'mixed messages' were conveyed through the Home Office's 'criminal justice' approach towards young offenders and the 'welfare' approach of the Department of Health (Labour Party 1996). Such incoherence was reflected at a local level. Youth justice professionals were confused about the principles that should govern the way in which they should work with young offenders, which 'creates real practical difficulties' (Home Office 1997d: 2.1). The Audit Commission found that the agencies which worked with young offenders had different views about what they were trying to achieve (Labour Party 1996: 16). This resulted in inefficient tensions and inconsistencies, with agencies working at different purposes. As a result, the youth justice system was confusing for both the practitioners and the young people within it.

Second, little was being done to address offending behaviour. The Audit Commission noted that 'all of the social services departments visited were committed to diverting transient young offenders (other than serious offenders) from the criminal justice system. But few offered alternatives which tackled offending behaviour' (1996: 17). Agencies were 'opposed in principle' to offering interventions to those who received cautions and thus there was even less effort made to tackle offending behaviour outside the court system (1996: 23).

In general, the documentation surrounding the Act described a youth justice system characterised by waste and inefficiency. The Audit Commission had argued that the youth justice system was becoming increasingly inefficient and expensive. It reached an excoriating conclusion:

> The current system for dealing with youth crime is inefficient and expensive, while little is being done to deal effectively with juvenile nuisance. The present arrangements are failing the young people, who are not being guided away from offending to constructive activities. They are also failing victims . . . And they lead to waste in a variety of forms . . . resources need to be shifted from processing young offenders to dealing with their behaviour. At the same time, efforts to prevent offending and other antisocial behaviour by young people need to be co-ordinated between the different agencies involved. (Audit Commission 1996: 96)

Reflecting the Audit Commission's analysis, the government could find little in the youth justice system to commend it. It was therefore in need of a 'radical overhaul' (Labour Party 1996). But how had this state of affairs arisen?

Origins

Neither the Audit Commission's report nor the documentation surrounding the Act situated their analysis of the operation of the youth justice system in its historical context. However, the features that it identifies for criticism are closely grounded in long-standing tensions and debates about the strategies, philosophies and principles that should govern work with young offenders.

Objectives

First, the 'incoherence' the government perceived in the objectives of the youth justice system describes a tension inherent since its inception. The development of a separate youth justice system for children was a response to the recognition that, because of the particular vulnerabilities of childhood and adolescence, children in trouble should be treated differently from adults. In other words, children should be dealt with in

separate institutions and according to different principles: the requirement to punish coexists with a duty to protect their welfare. However,
while these two objectives coexist, they are essentially incompatible
(Muncie 2004). They incorporate very different assumptions about the
scope and purpose of the youth justice system and the conception of
responsibility of the young people subject to its interventions. The
'welfare' approach sees crime as just one indicator of potential problems.
The criminal justice system is seen as a site of treatment: it attempts to
meet the 'needs' of the individual child, rather than addressing the
offence alone. In contrast, the 'justice' model emphasises criminal
responsibility and a focus on the offence rather than the young person.

Each of these approaches has dominated different periods in the youth
justice system in England and Wales.

For much of the twentieth century, the 'welfare' model dominated
youth justice in England and Wales. This approach culminated in the
Children and Young People's Act 1969, in which a philosophy of
'treatment' was so firmly entrenched that in effect it substituted 'the
principles and practices of child care for those of criminal justice' in
dealing with young offenders (Blagg and Smith 1989: 101). However, in
the 1970s welfarism came under attack from all sides, and the Act was
never fully implemented. It was argued that, through the guise of
'treatment' and 'welfare' objectives, young people frequently received
'justice' interventions which were not warranted by their behaviour
alone. They were subject to the discretionary power of the professionals
who assessed and supervised them and were denied full access to legal
rights. In addition, the language of welfare and treatment invited public
criticism that the youth justice system had become 'soft' on crime.
Consequently, a 'back to justice' movement argued for a return to
principles of due process and proportionality in sentencing, and for more
tightly defined, time-limited interventions that focused on the offending
behaviour rather than the young person themselves.

However, while the dominant approach to youth justice has swung
between justice and welfare philosophies at different moments, elements
of both approaches are visible at any one point. The tension between
'punishment' and 'welfare' objectives in the youth justice system – and
thus the 'incoherence' and 'confusion' described by the Labour government in its underlying principles – is inherent in a system whose
fundamental rationale is to take account of the particular needs and
vulnerabilities of children while punishing their offending behaviour.

Addressing offending behaviour

Second, the Audit Commission's observation that social services departments appeared opposed 'in principle' to rigorous programmes to

address offending behaviour reflects an influential movement that emerged the 1980s, in which it was held that the criminal justice system was not the appropriate place for intervention. Research seemed to show that welfare-focused criminal justice interventions had little impact on offending behaviour (e.g. Martinson 1974). But moreover, it was increasingly believed that formal intervention could do more harm than good. Drawing on labelling theory (e.g. Becker 1963; Lemert 1970) and informed by arguments that offending by young people is relatively 'normal' and, if left alone, young people would 'grow out' of crime (e.g. Rutherford 1986), it was argued that not only was state intervention unable to prevent reoffending, it had the potential to reinforce patterns of offending through the establishment of delinquent identities. Consequently it was argued that interventions by the formal criminal justice system had the potential to cause more harm than good and should thus be avoided or minimised wherever possible. As far as possible, therefore, it was held that more serious offenders should be diverted from custody and dealt with by tightly focused intermediate treatment programmes, and minor offenders should be dealt with by cautioning or other pre-prosecution disposals. In some areas, multi-agency diversion panels (such as the influential Juvenile Liaison Bureaux in Northamptonshire[2]) were established to recommend an appropriate course of action to the police, and as a site of informal intervention.

This emerging 'orthodoxy' among youth justice practitioners (Haines and Drakeford 1998) was encouraged and consolidated by official endorsement. It corresponded with the priorities of the (then) Conservative government by rationalising the reach of state apparatus while simultaneously allowing the government to appear 'tough' by concentrating resources on more serious or persistent offenders (Pitts 1999, 2005). Further, the pro-diversionary movement among practitioners was strengthened by its apparent success. During the 1980s there was a significant and sustained decline both in the numbers of children and young people entering the courts, and in the use of custody for young people (Smith 2003). The decade was therefore widely held by practitioners to have seen a 'successful revolution' in youth justice (Jones 1989). As the strategy of its success, diversion continued to dominate practitioners' thinking about youth justice interventions at the time of the Audit Commission's investigation in the mid-1990s.

Efficiency and effectiveness

The Audit Commission's emphasis on efficiency and effectiveness, and its report itself, is also situated in a particular way of thinking about youth justice. By the end of the 1980s, a further strategy for organising work with young offenders was developing which was not connected to questions of justice or welfare or particular strategies for intervention. Instead, and in line with a wider shift towards the 'new public management' (Hood 1991), an emerging 'corporatist' strategy (e.g. Pratt 1989) was concerned with managing the offending population as efficiently and effectively as possible. Its primary objectives were thus not transformative, such as, for example, the rehabilitation or treatment of the young person. Instead, policies aimed to make youth crime tolerable in the most efficient, economic way (e.g. Feeley and Simon 1992).

This approach was underpinned by a re-emerging optimism in the possibilities of the criminal justice system as a site for intervention. By the end of the 1980s, increasing attention was being paid to the 'what works' agenda, which emphasised the importance of evidence and outcomes in criminal justice interventions. Evaluative research appeared to show that, if directed appropriately, some forms of intervention could be successful in reducing offending behaviour for some young people (Muncie 2004). Thus in shaping policy options, moral questions about the purpose and process of intervention questions are side-stepped in favour of questions of cost-effectiveness and measurable, quantifiable outcomes (e.g. Muncie 2002, 2004). Actuarial techniques of risk assessment and classification became central to directing policy and practice.

The Audit Commission's emphasis on the benefits of multi-agency work can be understood in this context. Firstly, it is premised on the understanding that crime has multiple causes and effects. In other words, young people will present multiple problems, which may be connected to a range of factors related to, for example, their family, social, economic, health or education needs. A 'holistic' approach which can simultaneously address all of these in a package of interventions will therefore be more effective. Secondly, by consolidating the diverse expertise and resources of staff from different agencies into a single structure it allows for a better coordinated and more efficient use of resources. Thirdly, by coopting various professional and interest groups into a collective whole with consistent aims and objectives, the capacity for conflict and disruption between these agencies is reduced (Pratt 1989). In other words, multi-agency work attempts to 'design out' conflict (Pitts 2000: 9) between the different parts of the youth justice system to allow for its smooth running.[3]

Transforming youth justice

Through its reforms, the government hoped to put an end to these entrenched tensions and debates. The Crime and Disorder Act would 'draw a line under the past'. The new legislation would 'cut out the waste' in the system and 'refocus resources' through the professionals within it (Home Office 1997d). Centrally, it would 'resolv[e] some of the fundamental confusion between the relationship of welfare and punishment in dealing with young offenders at central and local government level' (Labour Party 1996: 8).

In order to accomplish this, the new arrangements for youth justice would provide a more coherent, more managed and more interventionist youth justice system. The government sought to achieve this through (i) establishing an explicit central purpose for the youth justice system; (ii) organising intervention through particular notions of risk, outcome and evidence; and (iii) consolidating the delivery of youth justice services through inter-agency cooperation at both the national and local level.

(i) Preventing offending

The Crime and Disorder Act established 'preventing offending by children and young persons' (s.37(1)) as the principal aim of the youth justice system, and placed a statutory duty on all agencies working within it to have regard to this aim. By this, the government hoped to provide 'unity of purpose and coherence of effort' to work with young offenders (Home Office 1997d: 2.5). The White Paper which preceded the Act argued that this overarching aim resolved the tensions between the underlying principles of welfare, protection and punishment in youth justice work. It accepted that the protection of the welfare of children and young people required protection from the criminal law. However, it argued that 'there is no conflict between protecting the welfare of a young offender and preventing that individual from offending again' (Home Office 1997d: 2.1). Indeed, not to intervene was viewed as harmful, and as allowing '[young people] to go on wrecking their own lives as well as disrupting their families and communities'. Preventing offending by intervention through the criminal justice system is therefore seen as a means of promoting the welfare of the young person. Formal intervention is presented as an enabling opportunity, even an entitlement (Muncie 2002). As such, intervention should be early: 'nipping crime in the bud' was more effective, and thus more beneficial for the child, than allowing offending behaviour to 'escalate out of control' (Home Office 1997d: 2).

This was an approach to the prevention of youth crime that stood in stark contrast to the dominant orthodoxy of youth justice work in the previous decades, outlined above. Instead of attempting to reduce the likelihood of establishing criminal careers by reducing contact with the criminal justice system, prevention was to be achieved by targeting young people thought likely to offend and by drawing them into the system at an early stage. Indeed, by putting an end to cautioning, the

Crime and Disorder Act effectively abandoned practices that divert young people from the formal criminal justice system (Goldson 2005). Through a raft of new disposals which the Crime and Disorder Act made available to the courts,[4] the youth justice system now became characterised by a 'robust interventionism' (Pitts 2001: 169) in which, for example, formal intervention now applies to children as young as 10, for second (or in some cases their first) offence, and pre-emptive measures provide for intervention with children below the age of criminal responsibility, including those who haven't committed an offence but are thought to be 'at risk' of doing so, or are thought by others (such as neighbours or police) to be causing trouble. Formal intervention was extended to their families through parenting orders. In this way, the elasticity of the aim of preventing offending and its implicit moral imperative for action provided for the wider and deeper penetration of the criminal justice system into the lives of young people in trouble and their parents. It extended the scope of the criminal justice system to younger children, including those below the age of criminal responsibility, and to an interest in disorderly as well as criminal behaviour.

(ii) Risk, outcome and evidence

Youth justice policy and practice now became directed explicitly through notions of risks, outcomes and evidence. Drawing closely on *Misspent Youth* (Audit Commission 1996), the delivery of youth justice services were now refocused towards selected 'risk conditions' associated with offending such as poor parenting, chaotic family life, truancy and school exclusion, and associating with delinquent peers (Home Office 1997d). These factors were derived from a particular literature on offending careers (e.g. Farrington and West 1990; Graham and Bowling 1995) that has now come to have a status of authority and certainty among policy-makers (Leacock and Sparks 2002). As Leacock and Sparks (2002) argue, these developments reflect an extension of the vocabulary of risk in current penal policy. Notions of risk no longer just describe 'riskiness' – the risks that young people who offend present to the public – but 'at-risk-ness': the ways in which young people might be at risk of offending, of being offended against or of social exclusion. In this way, the technical language of risk is fused with a highly moralised discourse about responsibility and obligation. Such notions therefore contain an obligation to intervene: risk factors become a 'checklist' of triggers to action.

At the same time, and in accordance with actuarial strategies, there was an increased emphasis on giving primacy to methods that can demonstrate efficacy (Audit Commission 1996) and continual monitoring and evaluation of new policy initiatives (Goldblatt and Lewis 1998).

Thus, as outlined below, the development of an 'effective practice strategy' has been central to the work of the newly created Youth Justice Board and interventions are monitored against a range of performance indicators. Central to this has been the development of Asset, a standardised assessment tool with which practitioners must rate from 0 to 4 the needs and 'risk factors' of all young offenders at the beginning and end of each programme of work. A change in Asset score is the primary measure of effectiveness by which programmes are judged. In this way, policies and programmes of work with young people must be shown to 'work' through evidence-based research; indeed, these are now the only ways in which they can be shown to work (Muncie 2002).

(iii) 'National leadership, local partnership': the new structures

The management of youth crime no longer belonged to any one department or agency. Instead, it now became a multi-agency responsibility at both the national and local level.

On a local level, the Act provided for the establishment of inter-agency Youth Offending Teams (YOTs) which now became responsible for the delivery of the bulk of youth justice services. YOTs replaced the specialist teams of social workers known as 'juvenile justice teams' or 'youth justice teams' which had been located in local authority social services departments. The formation of YOTs pulled together the various agencies which had been involved with young offenders (although, as Bailey and Williams (2000) point out, most had not been involved in post-sentence supervision of young people and thus will not tradition-ally have seen themselves as involved in youth crime). They must consist of at least one social worker, probation officer, police officer and education and health authority staff, and provide scope to involve practitioners from other agencies or organisations, such as the Prison Service, local authority youth services or voluntary organisations. These staff are usually seconded to the YOT in a full-time placement, or may be employed by the local authority specifically to work in the YOT, and are encouraged to take on work beyond their accustomed roles (Home Office et al. 1998). YOTs are 'stand-alone' teams, not belonging exclus-ively to any one department or agency. They are managed directly by a YOT manager, who can be appointed from any of the core partner agencies, and managed locally by multi-agency 'steering groups' and chief executive's departments where they can be linked into wider crime and disorder strategies. They are accountable nationally to the newly established Youth Justice Board, and through it to the Home Secretary. YOTs therefore exemplify the kind of partnership that Crawford (1997) terms 'inter-agency relations': in contrast to 'multi-agency' partnerships which form solely in relation to a particular issue and which operate within existing practices and structures, 'inter-agency' teams interrupt and interpenetrate the normal internal working relations of the collaborating organisations, usually resulting in new structures and forms of working.

On a national level, the Act created the Youth Justice Board for England and Wales (YJB), a new executive, non-departmental public body (NDPB) to oversee all parts of the youth justice system and advise the Home Secretary on its operation and standards for performance. The creation of the YJB thus consolidated the supervision of the youth justice system which had previously been shared across several government departments, and was intended to allow for the development of consistent standards and a coherent approach to the provision of services across England and Wales (1997a: para. 53).

The creation of these structures put into place a new set of relations between the local and central governance of youth crime, which Crawford describes as typical of the new administrative arrangements for local governance emerging in contemporary crime control (Crawford 1994, 1997, 2001). Rather than a conventional hierarchical relationship, the establishment of the YJB and YOTs put in place what Crawford terms a 'decentring-recentring dialectic' in which 'power and control are not resolved in any unilinear direction' (Crawford 1994: 503–4). Thus the relationship between the YJB and YOTs is described as one of 'partnership' (e.g. Youth Justice Board 2006a). The YJB's role is one of supervision and guidance rather than direct management.[5] It monitors the performance of YOTs against targets and standards, identifies and promotes 'effective practice', issuing guidance for practitioners accordingly. However, it is not intended to intervene directly in local service delivery. Responsibility for the management and delivery of youth justice services is instead devolved locally. Thus, while YOTs are charged with a series of centrally defined obligations, they are given considerable discretion and autonomy in the manner in which these are carried out. The membership of the teams, the partnerships created, the administrative structures in which they operate, the practices through which the required services are delivered, the funding of the YOTs and the allocation of budgets are not prescribed but are locally determined to fit local needs and arrangements. Yet this devolving of responsibility for the local delivery of crime control coexists alongside a tighter supervision of services at the centre. As Crawford (2001) puts it, the gulf created by 'governing at a distance' demands new flows of information to fill it. Thus the central monitoring and assessment of youth justice services has been strengthened by the establishment of the YJB, which requires detailed performance and delivery data in order to 'ensure the YJB's corporate aims and objectives for the youth justice system are delivered' (Youth Justice Board 2006b). So, for example, local authorities are required to submit an annual Youth Justice Plan to the YJB for approval, detailing the operation of each YOT, the services offered, and how these will be delivered, funded and managed. YOTs must provide performance data against a range of measures, currently including key performance indicators, National Standards and a self assessment framework to measure 'effective practice'. The YJB publishes the results, identifies 'effective practice' on the basis of which it allocates grants to local authorities to develop programmes, and issues guidance and training to practitioners. The effect is an 'unprecedented centralisation of control over the system' (Pitts 2001: 168).

Transforming youth justice social work

In this way, Labour's sweeping youth justice reforms promised to usher in a new way of thinking about and managing youth crime. For those working within the system, it would bring about new modes of practice that would be consistent throughout England and Wales, in which interventions would become more active, more focused and, through closer monitoring, more transparent. Above all, practitioners from all agencies would be in clear agreement about the overarching aim of work with young offenders and thus the principles that would govern their practice.

However, instead of bringing about coherence in the work with young offenders, the restructuring of the youth justice system introduced a new series of uncertainties in the practice and identity of youth justice social work.

Firstly, rather than clarifying the purpose of youth justice interventions, the elasticity of the central aim of 'preventing crime' instead allowed for the perpetuation of their central tensions. As Muncie argues, the term is so poorly defined that 'virtually any intervention, monitoring and scrutiny of young people's lives can be justified in the name of crime prevention' (Muncie 2002: 151). Thus, through the overarching aim of preventing crime, Labour's reforms provided for the introduction of diverse and potentially conflicting strategies in the delivery of youth justice services.

Three broad themes have been seen to underpin Labour's notion of prevention, each founded on a different rationale for intervention (e.g. Brownlee 1998; Downes 1998; Fionda 1999; Goldson 2000a, 2000b, 2000c; Haines and Drakeford 1998; Muncie 1999, 2000, 2002; Newburn 1998; Pitts 1999, 2000, 2001). First, the new measures prioritised deterrence and correction. In part, this reflected the climate surrounding the reforms, in which Labour had attempted to represent themselves as the party that would instigate the 'toughest' measures for dealing with youth crime (Brownlee 1998). The government's willingness to engage in such a battle for 'toughness' inevitably shaped their subsequent policy initiatives

(Newburn 1998). For example, custody not only retained its central position in the youth justice system though the introduction of Detention and Training Orders, a new custodial sentence (see Chapter 8), but was increased in its scope: DTOs increased the maximum period of detention for 15–17-year-olds for a single offence from six months to two years, and provided for the extension of custodial sentences to young people below the age of 12. Most significantly, the Act abolished the presumption of *doli incapax*, which held that because of their immaturity children under the age of 14 do not know the difference between naughtiness and serious wrongdoing. This move was perhaps the clearest declaration of Labour's punitive stance: a 'symbolic intervention' (Pitts 2001: 176). The presumption represented an assertion of the particular vulnerability of children and their need for protection from criminal justice sanctions. These measures in the Act therefore signalled a 'dejuvenilisation' (Pitts 1999, 2001) or 'adulteration' (Muncie 1999) of youth justice: an erosion of the special status of childhood in criminal law.

Second, alongside these authoritarian, exclusionary measures, the Act also introduced a series of explicitly inclusionary strategies. Apparently influenced by a particular form of communitarianism (e.g. Etzioni 1995), new measures were introduced which were founded on principles of reparation and restoration. So, for example, reparation orders focused interventions towards making young people face up to the consequence of their offending behaviour 'as a catalyst for reform and rehabilitation' (Home Office 1997d: para. 4.13), parenting orders were designed to 'help and support' parents to control their children (Home Office 1997d: 4.11), and the principles of restorative justice were confirmed and extended with the introduction of referral orders and youth offender panels under the Youth Justice and Criminal Evidence Act 1999 shortly afterwards.

Yet while these measures drew on the moral imperative of communitarianism or populist punitivism as a basis for intervention, others were governed by the amoral, administrative rationale of managerialism (Crawford 2001). Thus as well as providing for inter-agency coordination in order to fulfil the goals of the system, there was an emphasis on streamlining procedures and speeding up processes (see especially Home Office 1997b), specifying clear aims and objectives, creating performance indicators and monitoring information through the Youth Justice Board to improve the functioning of the system: all features consistent with a particular form of managerialism (Newburn 1998).

The government's sweeping youth justice reforms were therefore ambiguous. They sent out 'no clear message about new Labour's commitment to any political ideology on this subject' (Fionda 1999: 46). Or as Muncie puts it, the Act is defined by an 'all-pervasive political pragmatism': 'it is clouded in expediency, rather than intellectual integrity' (2000: 32).

The nature of the new youth justice system was no less ambiguous for those youth justice professionals working within it. The diversity of the new measures did little to provide coherence to their practice. But further, while the government had clearly signalled a change in the climate of youth justice, the ambiguity surrounding its reforms deprived practitioners of a means of making sense of it. Were they about to experience a change in the ethos in which the youth justice system operated? What would this mean for their practice and the professional values and principles that informed it?

Yet while the nature of the new youth justice system was uncertain, it was clear that the reconfiguration of its services and structures would bring about a period of major upheaval in the youth justice system, and a period of intense disruption for the staff within it.

The transformation of the youth justice system confronted practitioners with a series of fundamental challenges to their accustomed ways of working. Youth justice practitioners were faced with the implicit accusation that their prior practice had failed. It had been inactive, collusive and excusing and in need of whole-scale change. Important premises on which they had based their work were challenged by the demands of the new framework. The 'progressive minimalism' previously advocated by many youth justice social workers was overturned by the active interventionism of the new system. Principles of diversion, widely seen to represent a powerful 'practitioner movement' (e.g. Jones 1989; Haines and Drakeford 1998), were now effectively disparaged. The new demands of monitoring and audit threatened to undermine social work professionalism. The apparent shift in emphasis towards achieving quantifiable and cost-effective outcomes implied a move away from the individualisation, autonomy and discretion widely held to comprise the core of social work practice (e.g. Rojek et al. 1988; Nellis 1995a; Pitts 1999; and see Chapter 3). As Muncie put it, 'In no small measure social work professionalism is being replaced by a series of organisations whose performance is amenable only to measurable, quantifiable outcomes. "Success" or "failure" becomes a statistical artefact' (2000: 31).

But further, the restructuring of the youth justice system put at issue the nature of professional expertise itself. Firstly, transferring responsibility for work with young offenders away from social workers and social services departments to inter-agency teams not only required youth justice social workers to relinquish ownership of the work, but confronted them with the implicit claim that they were unable to manage youth crime effectively alone. As Crawford argues, the multi-agency perspective is 'premised on the belief that crime prevention lies beyond the competency of any one single agency' (2001: 60). A range of agencies are required to provide the holistic approach required by the multiple causes and effects of offending. In other words, this kind of working put at issue traditional notions of expertise and specialisation.

Secondly, the notion of youth justice as a distinctive area of expertise appeared to be further undermined by the nature of inter-agency relations required of YOT membership. Staff joining a YOT were required to undertake a full-time, long-term placement (often for several years) in a new organisation and work outside their home agency's traditional structures, roles and practices. To some degree they had to relinquish their core professional duties and take on new tasks and ways of working defined by the YOT. Practitioners were therefore required to transcend their accustomed organisational roles and identities. And crucially, the organisational relocation of youth justice work from the Department of Social Services to new stand-alone YOTs severed social workers' links from their home agency. What, then, would it mean to be a youth justice social worker? Could youth justice social work be seen as a distinct area of professional expertise, with its own knowledge base, training, values and skills (Goldson 2000a)? Would a YOT identity emerge in its place? And what would be the nature of this?

The merging of staff into inter-agency teams therefore threatened to disrupt practitioners' accustomed sense of occupational identity and membership. Yet at the same time, the extent to which staff retained a distinct professional identity within a YOT put in question the success of the reconfiguration of youth justice services. Without some degree of generic YOT identity, the absorption of staff from different agencies into a single team created scope for inter-agency conflict. Writing about multi-agency partnerships argues that the competing interests of participating agencies makes conflict central to partnership work (e.g. Crawford 1994; 1997; Crawford and Jones 1995; Gilling 1994; Pearson et al. 1992; Sampson et al. 1988). Important differences between the approach to work of different agencies are inevitable sources of tension. As Crawford and Jones explain: 'As a consequence of their different histories, cultures, and traditions, organizations engaging in multi-agency community crime prevention work pursue conflicting ideologies, strategies, and practices' (1995: 20). In other words, because agencies inhabit 'different assumptive worlds' (Gilling 1994: 251), they are likely to have different conceptions of the problems at hand and of the appropriate solutions to them. Indeed, Gilling argues that 'It is naïve to expect them [agencies] to act otherwise, or to cede to some higher mutual rationality' (1994: 254). Rather than bringing about unity in purpose, therefore, the incorporation of practitioners from diverse agencies into inter-agency YOTs instead created scope for inter-organisational conflict. For the practitioners within them, this raised the spectre of inter-agency conflicts within close working relationships. What would this mean for their working lives? How could the team cohere?

In June 1999, therefore, youth justice social workers were about to enter a period of intense disruption and anxiety. They were on the verge of a marked departure from the accustomed ethos of youth justice work, without a clear indication of what lay ahead. The formation of YOTs demanded the development of new, multi-agency practice, new routines and ways of working, with little guidance about what this would involve. They would simultaneously be more autonomous and more supervised than before. Practitioners would imminently merge into a new organisation with staff from different agencies who might have different approaches to work with young offenders. And, crucially, they were being asked to put aside their accustomed occupational identities in place of something as yet unformed and unclear. It was in this climate that practitioners in the Midlands Youth Justice Team found themselves at the beginning of this study.

Notes

1 As Leacock and Sparks (2002) point out, there is no tension acknowledged between the notions of 'confronting' or 'responsibilizing' and 'helping'. The way in which the government believes it has reconciled these discourses of care and control is discussed below.
2 The Northamptonshire Juvenile Liaison Bureaux were commended by Audit Commission as a model of multi-agency working (Audit Commission 1996) and may have influenced some features of the YOTs established by the Crime and Disorder Act. However, as discussed below, YOTs were to deliver a very different service: they were not created to divert young people from the formal criminal justice system but to enable more formal intervention.
3 Of course, this is a highly problematic process and one which occupies much of the following book. However, it raises a further question: is the 'designing out' of conflict appropriate? For example, Pitts argues that the negotiation of the conflicts between the different ethical, legal and administrative responsibilities of the various youth justice agencies is an essential feature of the youth justice system, which 'exists precisely to provide a site upon which conflict can be enacted': it is 'a place where the competing claims of rules and needs, guilt and suffering, justice and welfare can be confronted' (2000: 8).
4 The range of new measures introduced under the Act included 'pre-emptive measures' such as Anti-Social Behaviour Orders, Local Child Curfews and Child Safety Orders, which provided for intervention with children below the age of criminal responsibility; a reprimand and final warning scheme which replaced the police cautioning system and now required some form of intervention on a second offence; Action Plan Orders and Reparation Orders extended the range of non-custodial disposals; a new custodial sentence, the Detention and Training Order, was intended to represent a 'constructive' use of custody to address offending (see Chapter 8 for further discussion); and Parenting Orders extended preventive measures to the families of people

involved, requiring them to attend training and guidance sessions to help to keep their children out of trouble.

5 The exception to this 'arm's length' approach to the oversight of the youth justice system is the YJB's relationship with the range of secure institutions (young offenders institutions, secure training centres, youth treatment centres, secure children's homes, or any other secure accommodation), which now became known as the 'juvenile secure estate' (see Chapter 8). In 2000 it was given the statutory duty to purchase places for, and place, children and youth people remanded or sentenced to custody. The commissioning/purchasing relationship with the secure estate necessarily brings about a more direct intervention in the management and operation of these institutions.

Part I

A Youth Justice Team

In June 1999, the beginning of the transition to a Youth Offending Team was thought to be some months away.

Staff from partner agencies were scheduled to join the team in September, six months before the YOT's official launch, in order to be ready for its operation the following April. This would be the first time staff other than social workers would become team members, working in the offices alongside social work staff. The team would change dramatically, both in its composition and its working practices. For most team members, September marked the beginning of the YOT. Until this date, therefore, practitioners considered themselves members of a Youth Justice Team, belonging to a local authority Department of Social Services (DSS).

The team certainly looked like a Youth Justice Team. It comprised 14 social workers and was managed by social work staff. Mark, the YOT manager, had been in post for six months and had a background in youth justice social work, and Graham, the team leader, was previously a senior practitioner. The team was based in a social services building: Midlands House was owned by the DSS and was occupied by children and families services teams.

Further, the team still acted like a Youth Justice Team. The nature and distribution of work remained unchanged: practitioners supervised and administered court orders, visited young people serving custodial sentences, prepared pre-sentence reports (PSRs) for the courts, and shared routine duties such as acting as court officer or appropriate adult for the purpose of PACE interviews. Practitioners continued to meet in their traditional fortnightly team meetings in which they discussed particular problems in their work.

Yet despite this outward appearance of a social services Youth Justice

Team, there were clear indications that the team was already in a process of transition.

First, there was a fundamental reorganisation of the administrative and managerial structures of the team. The appointment of Mark, the YOT manager, was the first specifically concerned with the formation of the YOT. Two further management positions had been created, although were not yet filled: an operations manager, who had a strategic role, and a team leader, who would deal with the day-to-day management of the team. The current administrative staff had to re-apply for their posts and a senior administration manager for the YOT was appointed. The underlying organisation of the team was thus in a process of transformation.

Second, in early June the first practitioner from a partner agency joined the team. Mike, a police officer, was in post nearly three months before the rest of the new staff. Not only was the team now comprised of staff other than social workers, it consisted of a member of an agency thought to have a very different ethos to that of the Youth Justice Team. He was followed by a health officer, Karen, in August.

Third, it was becoming clear that the team would have to relocate. The arrival of staff from partner agencies would double the size of the team and the current offices would be unable to accommodate them. Midlands House was build as a children's home in the 1960s. Its design was intended to encourage a relaxing, secure environment for its residents: according to the practitioners who currently worked there, it had been designed to reflect the shape of a womb. This appeared to have suggested to the architect a symmetrical building, consisting of large, octagonal rooms linked by identical narrow curving corridors off which were smaller, irregular shaped offices. Four staircases led from the 'corners' of the building to a second floor, where the children's bedrooms once were. These were small, awkward shaped rooms and were at this time the offices of all other children and families units. The Youth Justice Team occupied a self-contained area on the ground floor. The overall structure appeared labyrinthine and confusing. The staff joked about getting lost in it and described it as a maze. But further, the large lobby areas and irregular shaped rooms would not allow for expansion or division of the existing offices. A YOT simply could not fit. It was impossible for the team to remain there and the YOT manager began to look for alternative premises.

Change and continuity

There were thus major signs of transformation among the team in this period. However, in practice they appeared less dramatic. There were few signs that the relocation of the offices was progressing: a suitable premises could not be found. Most of the new staff were either familiar – Karen, the new health officer, had a long working association with the Youth Justice Team and Graham, the acting Team Leader, had been a senior practitioner – or they were absent: Mark, the YOT manager, was based in social services head office and rarely visited the team. The appointment of a police officer, and someone unknown to the team, was the clearest evidence of change. However, the dominance of social workers meant that there was no tangible difference to their daily life or to the 'feel' of the team. As one social worker put it:

> It doesn't make any difference to me [that new practitioners are joining the team]. It's more difficult for them, because they're joining an established team with a strange culture. (Duncan, social worker)

In this way, practitioners' working lives in fact changed very little in these months. The changes underway were hidden from view. As one team member explained:

> It doesn't [feel like things are changing], until we have a meeting with Mark [YOT manager], and he gives us feedback of what's happening, and then you realise that things are going to be changing, and there seems to be lots of changes but it doesn't seem to be touching us. (Sally, social worker)

But in the context of these background indications of large-scale restructuring, the lack of tangible change in practitioners' working lives became a source of frustration and anxiety. Staff knew that the team was in a process of change but were unsure what these changes meant for their working lives. They had as yet had no training about the new orders that would become available to the courts in ten months time, and knew very little about what they would involve. They were unsure about what the roles of the practitioners from different agencies would be. But while they didn't know what they would be doing, they knew there would be more of it. Rumours abounded that pilot YOT sites that had been established six months earlier had experienced a large increase in their workload, often thought to be as much as 50 per cent.

As a result, some practitioners felt the team was worryingly un- prepared for the imminent changes. As one practitioner put it:

> The first team meetings in the last few months, I've said what are we going to do then, who's going to do what and when and how, what's being suggested, what's the time-scale, and everybody's looked at each other, and the answer from some of them, 'I don't

know, I've not thought about it'. So, I've given up worrying, I shall just go along with the flow. (Duncan, social worker)

Further, there was no way of resolving this uncertainty. As one social worker put it, the team were in 'limbo land'. Graham, the team leader, explained:

People are seeing a shape taking form, but it's a very kind of nebulous, Halloweeny kind of dark shape in the background because even though people know there's the new legislation, the new orders, they can't envisage how it's going to be, apart from they're going to be very busy. Doing what, they don't know.

In this context, declarations of change became increasingly salient. The name of the team became an important sign of progress: the continued use of 'Youth Justice Team' was seen as indicative of the inability of the team to develop:

I'm the only person who picks the phone up and says 'Youth Offending Team'. No one else has actually adopted the new name yet. Perhaps they will in September. But I can't see the reason for retaining the old name. It's just to get the mind round the fact that we are in the middle of change. (Mike, police officer)

The planned relocation of the team became a focus of practitioners' anxieties about the uncertainty facing their working lives. As Graham explained, the most basic aspects of practitioners' working lives – where they came to work – were facing imminent disruption and no apparent resolution.

So everywhere people are getting a bit anxious, a bit worried. Not sure what their work's going to be, not sure where they're going to be working from, because most things in most agencies boil down to, do you get paid for your mileage, and where do you work and how close is it to home, very simple things that mean a lot to people, and we don't have a resolve to them. (Graham, team manager)

By August, there was clearer evidence of the disruption to the team. Graham was not appointed to the permanent operations manager position. Although he had been acting in the post for eight months, he did not have the experience needed to be eligible for the post. This increased the team's feelings of insecurity: they no longer knew what to expect from the management of the team.

And people say 'oh you didn't get the job, I wanted you to get it because if you got the job I knew that I'd feel comfortable with what would be going on'. Because Mark's [YOT manager] an unknown quantity. (Graham, team manager)

So, throughout this period the team were aware that there would be significant changes to their working lives, but were uncertain about what these changes would mean or when they would occur. There was no source of resolution for these anxieties. There was no prior experience of changes of this kind and no permanent leadership in place to provide direction and reassurance. The team were thus in a state of ambiguity, where '. . . there is no clear interpretation of a phenomenon or set of events. [Ambiguity] is different from uncertainty in that it cannot be clarified by gathering more facts' (Feldman 1991: 146). Some practitioners said they found it exhilarating:

It's exciting. I like change. Some people don't . . . I'm an older worker so I'm used to change. (Duncan, social worker)

But the majority of staff described feelings of anxiety, stress and insecurity. This produced talk about the losses they might face with the transformation of the team.

This first part of the study describes the last few months of the Youth Justice Team as practitioners anticipated the transition towards a multi-agency organisation. It considers the experiences, complexities and problems of team membership. What did it mean to be a member of the Midlands Youth Justice Team? How did practitioners understand their work, values and identity? And what consequences did the introduction of staff from partner agencies have for the team and for the meaning of team membership?

Chapter 2

Experiences and problems of team membership

The Youth Justice Team was described by all its members as unusual. Unlike other social work teams that practitioners had experienced, staff were described as a tightly knit group in a happy and united working environment. Practitioners 'all felt comfortable with each other', were 'very sociable with each other'. The team was 'settled', 'gelled'. As such, the imminent disruption to the team and their working lives was felt to be particularly unsettling. However, the experience of team membership appeared to be more complex than the dominant presentation of the team suggested.

This chapter explores how practitioners described what it meant to be a member of the Youth Justice Team. It describes some of the ways in which team members appeared to construct a sense of shared identity and culture, and some of the more difficult problems and experiences that this obscured. Through this discussion, it introduces different perspectives in understanding organisational cultures, which form the basis of the analytical framework of this study.

'Not like social workers at all'

Although team members described themselves as social workers, they described important differences between youth justice social workers and other social work staff. As one practitioner put it, 'not like social workers at all, the Youth Justice Team aren't'.

In part, this difference was attributed to the nature of their work. Youth justice was thought to be significantly different in character from other areas of social work. Firstly, it required specialist knowledge and skills. The bulk of the team's work consisted of routines and practice that had little overlap with other areas of social work. The supervision of court orders, preparation of pre-sentence reports (PSRs), attendance at court and at PACE interviews and close liaison with the juvenile secure estate required a knowledge of processes and legislation particular to youth justice work. As one practitioner put it, youth justice was a 'specific job' and this was reflected in the experience of team members, most of whom had spent the majority of their social work careers in youth justice. Indeed, some staff had little experience of mainstream social work, having joined the social services as court officers and become part of the team. One team member explained:

> I mean, people here wouldn't even know, not to patronise them, that section 47 is the part of statute which gives to those family workers the duty [to investigate], but obviously our work is very different, we operate supervision orders, we know that legislation, but the two areas of work don't cross over much. (Duncan, social worker)

Similarly, youth justice work was generally not carried out by staff in other areas of the social services as they lacked the relevant specific knowledge. One practitioner who had recently joined the team from a residential social work team explained that Youth Justice Teams were seen as 'isolated' from other social work teams, 'something that you didn't really know that much about'.

The view that youth justice workers are specialist practitioners and as such distanced from other social work units appears contrary to the ostensibly generic thrust of the social services following the Seebohm report (1968), which intended to counter the previously fragmented delivery of services by specialist groups of practitioners with a generic, comprehensive service (e.g. Nellis 1995a; Worrall and Hoy 2004). The focus of their work and the knowledge and expertise specific to the team appears to have encouraged practitioners to have considered themselves specialists, regardless of their generic training.[1] However, the specialist work of the team appears to have brought about a further distancing from other areas of social work. Because of their expertise, youth justice practitioners felt they had a particularly nuanced understanding of offending behaviour and the problems experienced by the young people they supervised. As a result, their approach to these problems was thought to differ from other social work units. For example, one practitioner explained that the team occasionally had to refer young people to other social services teams. However, this was not considered 'ideal':

> I know and everybody else knows too because of the pressures upon them, you can make as many referrals as you like to the local

Children and Families Team, but it'll be a very low priority to them. (Duncan, social worker)

This perceived difference in the priorities of other units was thought to reflect a difference in attitudes and approach to offending behaviour. Duncan described the attitude of the children and families units towards a (hypothetical) 16-year-old drugs user who has been kicked out of home in the following way:

In their eyes a 16 year old is old enough to make some choices for himself, if they've contributed to it, so be it.

As this implies, it was thought Youth Justice Team members would respond differently to such problems. Because of their expertise it was felt they had a more sophisticated understanding of offending behaviour and underlying questions of responsibility and causation. It appears, then, that practitioners in the Youth Justice Team may have considered their work to be organised by different principles and priorities from that of other social work teams. As such, they had a different source of legitimating authority in their work. This was suggested by Duncan's explanation of the difference between the way social workers and youth justice workers 'see themselves':

We see ourselves as working as court officers in one respect, a social worker on a families team would never see themselves as officers of the court, they see themselves as local authority social workers, carrying out the demands of the Children Act, basically, they have a duty to investigate section 47, and that's what they see themselves as.

The Youth Justice Team's work as 'officers of the court' as opposed to 'local authority social workers' thus appeared to strongly influence team members' self-perception. They felt they were distanced from other social work units by more than the focus of their practice. Their professional separation also involved a perceived difference in the legitimating principles through which their work was organised.

The detachment from other social work teams was emphasised by other important aspects of members' experiences. Practitioners described youth justice work as having a 'culture' that was starkly different to the dominant culture of social work. Stereotypical social workers were described as middle-class women who tended towards a woolly, patronising attitude. As Mark, the YOT manager, joked to the new practitioners from partner agencies:

I don't want you to become social workers. If you were social workers you'd all be wearing sandals and jumpers.

Staff thought the Youth Justice Team members were markedly different to this stereotype. The team were predominantly male (only five out of 14 staff were women) and the majority appeared to self-identify as working class.[2] The profile of the team was sometimes associated with the particular focus of its work: for example, one male social worker argued that it facilitated a rapport with their service-users, most of whom were working-class boys:

> There's a bit more in youth justice teams of the male working-class attitude, and you could argue that that's better for the young people we're working with, you know, we can approach them more directly, without trying to patronise them [. . .] I feel more comfortable in a youth justice team, for that reason really. (Duncan, social worker)

Defining 'us' and 'them'

In this way, the Youth Justice Team was thought to be significantly different to other social work units in important aspects of team life. But the demarcation of these differences had a crucial function: they helped promote a view of the team as a cohesive, clearly defined group with a shared and distinctive culture. By describing the ways in which the team was not like others, staff were both delineating the boundaries of the team and describing its shared identity.

Parker (2000) argues that such claims about similarity and difference are the essence of organisational culture. As he puts it, 'Cultures [. . .] are not homogenous things, but contested processes of making claims about classification – about unity and division – suggesting that X is like us but Y is not' (2000: 86). In other words, 'Culture is an "us" and "them" claim, an identification, a boundary construction that suggests that an individual is like A but not like B' (2000: 94). They are thus the central way in which members construct their own sense of occupational belonging and identity: or as Parker describes it, 'the importance and inseparability of "us" and "them" as a way of constituting "we"' (2000: 5). The delineation of the ways in which the culture, composition and focus of the Youth Justice Team differed from other social work teams can thus be seen as a series of 'us' and 'them' claims: a means of defining and describing the identity of the team. Of course, claims about the classification of 'us' and 'them' can be a source of conflict and dispute. Parker argues that cultures should be understood as a contested, fluid process: 'a continually shifting set of claims and counter-claims' (2000:

225). As will be described in the following chapters, the ways in which the claims about 'us' and 'them' became contested and disrupted were of crucial importance as the YOT developed. Yet at this stage, the claims of similarity and difference that defined the team were presented as clear and uncontested.

Within the boundaries of team membership, the team was presented by almost all practitioners as an exceptionally cohesive and happy group. This was often attributed to an unusually low turnover of staff. Most practitioners had worked with the Youth Justice Team for a considerable time, some for as long as ten years.

> Its quite nice because inevitably in social work teams change so quickly, and you don't get a very settled staff group, get new workers coming in monthly, six monthly, but here is very settled. (Jenny, social worker)

The cohesiveness of the team was associated by almost all practitioners with the social atmosphere in the offices. Jokes flew up and down the large open-plan team room, usually about other team members and generally involving copious swearing. The swearing itself became a joke: practitioners instigated a 'swear box' and rang a bell each time someone swore in a team meeting. Practical jokes were frequent: rubber band fights, stapling practitioners' jacket sleeves to their desk, filling their shoes with 'confetti' from a hole-punch. As one practitioner described it:

> [The team are] brilliant, very, very good atmosphere, lots and lots of humour [laughs]. They're all mad, lots and lots of humour, and you get all this abuse flying around, bad language, I'm just as bad as everyone else. (Sally, social worker)

This banter appeared to be valued as an integral and important part of practitioners' experience. Some staff explained that it was important for the functioning of the team. Most commonly, it was understood as an important survival mechanism in a particularly stressful job: a function that has been described in other occupational contexts where professionals are dealing with difficult, emotional and pressured situations, for example such as medical staff or the police (see, for example, Meerabeau and Page 1998; Sims et al. 1993). As one practitioner explained:

> You know, you need that humour in this job, you really do. It's a life saver sometimes, it relieves stress, you know, somebody will come in who's had a really bad visit or whatever, and straightaway someone's taking the piss ... and that alleviates your stress straightaway, I think it's really important. (Sally, social worker)

However, it seemed that the social atmosphere had particular significance in the team. It was thought to be unusual, and as such indicated that there was something unusual about the team.

> It isn't like that on all social work teams, you know, I've done placements at different places, and some of it isn't like that at all, there's a lot of bitchiness and you get a lot of . . . you get some people who are so serious, you know. (Sally, social worker)

The banter seems to have been understood by practitioners as evidence of a particularly happy and unified team. Much of it consisted of 'office jokes': a common parlance among the whole team. So, for instance, one end of the team room where the more senior members of the team sat was known as the 'antiques corner'. There were common jokes about individual team members – they way they spoke, their clothes, their inability to give up smoking and so on – which were described (even by their victims) as good natured teasing and appeared to be considered part of the shared language of the team. As Sims et al. (1993) point out, such jokes require a social relationship and common understanding, and as such become 'a sign of trust and intimacy . . . affection and esteem' (1993: 163).[3] The banter appeared to be a source of pride as well as enjoyment: proof of an unusually cohesive team. Team members talked of the 'camaraderie', how the team have 'gelled together so well', how 'comfortable' with each other and 'sociable' the team were.

Cohesion and change

The value placed on the cohesive atmosphere in the team gave the forthcoming changes heightened significance. The 'settled' nature of the team and the 'camaraderie' among team members were understood to be interdependent:

> It does feel like things are changing. I think we're telling more because we've been such a settled team for such a long time [. . .] because you feel as though the team that you've got is a safe environment, know each other very well, we know our faults, we know the positives and negatives, we know how each other works. (Julie, social worker)

Some practitioners were concerned that the forthcoming large-scale changes to the team would result in the loss of its cohesion and thus threaten the 'safe environment' of the team and the atmosphere among its members. As one team member explained:

Because they're such a good team, you don't want that to change, and you're frightened that you'll lose something by bringing a lot of new people in. (Sally, social worker)

These concerns were reflected in the team's anxieties about the changes to their physical environment. The current offices reflected and rein-forced the feeling of a cohesive team with clear boundaries. The team were physically separated from the other teams in the building, occupying a whole side of the ground floor in self-contained facilities. Team members therefore had no physical point of contact with the other social services teams. But in addition, practitioners currently shared one large, communal team room, and this was thought to be a major contributor to the team's atmosphere. It was assumed that when the team relocated staff would be separated into different rooms. Practi-tioners felt this would destroy the current atmosphere.

We will split up, I assume, [. . .] I don't know how big the offices will be, but undoubtedly we'll be split, whereas we've got the big team room, haven't we, and that's why I think the banter's so good. I mean we've got the antiques corner that we call it at the top end [laughs], and then we've got us down the bottom like, and the banter that goes to and fro there, you know . . . (Sally, social worker)

In fact, the increase in the size of the team meant that the team had to 'split up' before the relocation took place. As more members of the team arrived, two social workers were asked to move from the main office into a smaller room to make more space. While one of these practitioners said he was quite happy to have a quiet place to work in, the move appeared to become a focus of many of the staff's anxieties about the loss of the atmosphere in the team: rumours circulated about how unhappy the two practitioners were to move, how isolated they felt. In other words, it appeared that the anxieties of some practitioners about the losses they might face as the team expanded were such that even this minor and not wholly unwelcome move became seen as a first manifestation of the inevitable collapse of team cohesion.

In this way, the social atmosphere in the team appeared closely associated with the nature of membership of the Youth Justice Team. It was felt to be produced by and evidence of an unusually cohesive group, demarcated by clearly defined boundaries. As such it was threatened by the influx of practitioners from outside agencies.

However, this presentation of the team as a cohesive group was problematic. While the strong sense of 'team feeling' appeared to be an important part of practitioners' experiences of team membership, there were other, complex aspects of these experiences which it obscured. This complexity is brought into focus by an exploration of different ways of thinking about organisational cultures.

Understanding organisational culture

Martin and Meyerson (Martin 1992, 2002; Martin and Meyerson 1988; Meyerson and Martin 1987) have identified three interpretative frameworks or 'perspectives' that have tacitly come to dominate thinking about organisational cultures. Each of these perspectives represents a set of seemingly conflicting and competing assumptions. The 'integration' perspective understands culture as 'what people share'. Studies attempt to look beneath the diversity of occupational life to find common underlying assumptions. Culture is seen the same way by most people in the organisation. Deviations or conflicts with this organisation-wide consensus are seen either as unrepresentative of the 'real' essence of the culture, disagreements that must be dug beneath to reach the true consensus, or a sign of a lack of culture. As Schein puts it: 'only what is shared is, by definition, cultural . . . If there is no consensus or if there is conflict or if things are ambiguous, then, by definition, that group does not have a culture with regard to those things' (1991: 247–8). In contrast, the 'differentiation' perspective emphasises difference and conflict. Organisational culture is understood as a nexus of competing, overlapping subcultures. Within the boundaries of these subcultures culture is shared and there is clear agreement; between subcultures there is inconsistency and clear disagreement. In other words, culture is not homogenous: diversity and disagreement is at its core. In this understanding, conflict is clear and dichotomous. In contrast, the 'fragmentation' viewpoint gives centrality to the ambiguities of cultural experiences. It prioritises those aspects of organisational life that are neither clear, nor clearly inconsistent or dichotomous. An organisational culture is understood as a web of loosely connected individuals for whom particular subcultural identities and coalitions become salient at specific moments and over specific issues. Rather than ignoring the ambiguities and flux of organisational life, it gives them centrality. Ambiguity is not the absence of culture: it comprises its essence.

These three perspectives do not represent descriptions of different types of organisational culture that could be objectively observed in different organisations. Instead, they are subjectively imposed frameworks that are imposed on the process of collecting and analysing cultural data. All three perspectives are therefore available in any cultural setting. As Martin writes:

> If any cultural context is studied in enough depth, some things will be consistent, clear, and generate organisation-wide consensus. Simultaneously, other aspects of the culture will coalesce within subcultural boundaries and still other elements of the culture will be fragmented, in a state of constant flux, and infused with confusion, doubt, and paradox. (Martin 1992: 4)

Consequently, each perspective is associated with its own distortions and exclusions. For instance, an 'integration' study that emphasises unity and clarity is likely to ignore the ambiguities and conflicts within that organisation; a 'differentiation' study may exclude similarities between subcultures or confusion within them. For this reason, they argue that organisations should be studied from a multi-perspective viewpoint, in order to avoid the 'usual blind spots' (Meyerson and Martin 1987: 643) inherent in adopting a single perspective.

However, one of the perspectives may seem the most obvious, accurate or appropriate way to view a particular culture at a particular time – for example, if one organisation appears to be characterised by consensus or by conflicting factions between its members. The majority of members of the organisation may also adopt this perspective.[4] Martin labels this the 'home perspective'. Yet although most members might agree that this 'home perspective' is the most appropriate way to view their organisation, the other two perspectives remain available, even if they are hidden. As Martin argues, 'It is not correct to conclude . . . that the two excluded perspectives offered "less accurate" descriptions of these contexts. When one perspective seems to be the "best" way to regard a context, the other two, forbidden perspectives, may be particularly useful sources of insight' (1992: 177).

Consensus, conflict and ambiguity: the complexity of team membership

These different ways of thinking about organisational culture indicate something of the complexities of practitioners' experiences as members of the Youth Justice Team. As described above, many staff described the team as a cohesive, unified whole. They were bound together by a closeness and camaraderie that was unusual among social work teams. While there is a complex relationship between the dominant theoretical perspectives in organisational culture research and the perspectives adopted by the members of those organisational cultures, the 'home perspective', or the dominant presentation of the team by its members, appeared to have a considerable amount in common with the 'integration' perspective described by Martin and Meyerson. As Martin puts it, integration studies 'tend to define culture as that which is shared and, usually, that which is unique to particular contexts' (1992: 56). The prioritising of the description of the team as an unusually 'settled', 'sociable' and 'tight' unit seems to promote such a view of the team's culture as unique and shared by all its members. The emphasis on a familial closeness among team members is also typical of the way consensus tends to be understood in an integration perspective. As Martin argues, such emotional closeness 'leaves no room for dissent' (1992: 47).

However, the inherent difficulty with the adoption of such a view is that it promotes elements of culture that are seen to unify and devalues those which differentiate. It excludes the possibilities of diversity and conflict. It thus tends to downplay or exclude the voices or interests of those who deviate from the supposedly dominant viewpoint. Similarly, as might be expected, despite the dominant presentation of the Youth Justice Team as a cohesive, happy, settled organisation, other interpretations and experiences of team membership were also evident.

Banter and team membership

The possibility of alternative experiences of team membership was evident in some practitioners' description of the banter in the team. Although this atmosphere of friendly joking was presented by many social workers as an important shared experience among its members, and thus evidence of a shared and cohesive culture, it was apparent that it was also a source of considerable discomfort for some staff.[5]

The banter in the team was clearly gendered, both in its manner, boisterous teasing and practical joking, and sometimes in its content, with the use of sexist language, flirting and innuendo. This was explicitly acknowledged by both male and female workers, who described the language, and the team itself, as sexist. For example, as Duncan put it (as above), there were not only more men than women in the team, but there was 'a bit more of the male working-class attitude'. He explained that as a working-class man, 'I feel more comfortable in a youth justice team, for that reason really'. In this way, the banter in the Youth Justice Team reflected the gendered nature of the team's dominant ethos. But for this reason it was also problematic. As Martin (1992) says, the assumption of a consensus of views or attitudes in an organisation is likely to reflect the power relations in the organisation. As she puts it, 'Because unanimous agreement is unlikely, organization-wide consensus is bound to entail the imposition of someone's authority on someone else' (1992: 68). Thus the shared language that underpinned the office jokes both reflected and reinforced the power dynamics in the team. Consequently, while the banter enabled some practitioners to 'feel more comfortable', it made other members uncomfortable. For example, one woman who had only joined the team a year previously described the working environment in comparison to others she had experienced:

> You know, at times there's lots of sexist remarks flying around. I know when I was asked to come here, people were saying you know it isn't very PC, and I had just come off the courts, with PC thrust down my throat, and I considered myself very PC, and for the first few days I didn't know how to take it, and I thought I'm going to have a problem here. (Sally, social worker)

Some women indicated that the pervasive sexism in the team had compromised their team membership. One described how her experience as a team member had only become tolerable after a 'struggle' to tackle the sexism among her colleagues:

> I think it's taken some struggling to be on the team, and move things forward, you know, it's far different than when it was a few years ago [when it was] very male dominated, I mean the team hadn't got a very good reputation in the areas, it's you know, males, and male chauvinist, and what not, but we have turned it round. (Julie, social worker)

Women practitioners described a variety of strategies for coping with the sexism in the team, which were similar to those adopted in other organisational environments in which discrimination is felt to be pervasive (e.g. Foster et al. 2005). For example, one practitioner explained that while she initially found the sexism on the team difficult to manage, she now took part in it: 'we're just as bad as anybody else now. Got sucked into it'. Another practitioner said she was able to manage her discomfort with the sexist behaviour in the team because, in her view, there was an implicit understanding that underneath the banter, staff actually shared a professional respect and commitment:

> I realised that you know, you hear all the sexist remarks, but then underneath all that people are very committed to their work, and very respectful, really, even though you've got this sexist banter going around, and I could see how committed the workers were on the team, obviously I'm talking about the men now, talking about sexist attitudes, and how committed they were and how hard they worked that I thought well that doesn't matter so much, it did at first but it didn't matter later on. (Sally, social worker)

In this way, while the banter in the team was prized as reflecting a strong sense of 'team feeling', it also revealed the possibility of conflict that was denied by the presentation of the team as a unified, cohesive group. The ambivalence and tensions this created for some practitioners indicated their more complex experiences of team life. So, for example, there was an inconsistency between the 'respect' Sally perceived as fundamental to team membership and the behaviour of her colleagues. Similarly, it was clear that such sexist or discriminatory behaviour would be considered unacceptable outside the boundaries of team membership. For example, Sally said the team were 'worried' about the absorption of a police officer into the team, because they would have 'different values'. In particular, she thought that police staff had a greater acceptance of discriminatory behaviour, 'like racist attitudes':

> You don't really hear any of that in the office, and I think that will be challenged anyway. I mean sexist attitudes, some people would argue are just as serious and challenging, and I'd argue that, but . . . the stereotype of police is that they're racist.

In other words, 'challenging' views outside the boundaries of the team were considered unacceptable, but within the team were tolerated, however uncomfortably. Such tensions and inconsistencies indicate that the banter was in fact a highly contested aspect of team life.

The diverse experiences of this prominent feature of team life indicated the possibility of divergent views about the imminent changes to the team. Some practitioners envisaged that when the boundaries of the team were challenged with the introduction of new practitioners, this disputed area of their working life would also be challenged. For this reason, rather than wholly resisting the expansion of the team, some staff welcomed the possibility of redefining its membership. Some hoped that the change in the profile of the team would bring about a change in its sexist culture:

> I think it's quite good because it's always been predominantly male, the team. But slowly, women are coming in, which is good. (Sally, social worker)

Indeed, despite the espoused consensus to the contrary, it appeared that some staff welcomed changes to those elements of team life most closely associated with the Youth Justice Team – including their offices – because they hoped it would bring about a change in ethos. For example, one practitioner said:

[The team is] very male and white [. . .] I think changing the office will help that, and changing management will help that hopefully as well [. . .] I think it needs to be done from the top. (Tom, social worker)

However, while some team members thought that a change in culture had to be driven by the management staff, as one practitioner noted, all the short-listed applicants for the (then unfilled) management positions were male:

[I'm] disappointed that there was no females who've applied, and that doesn't surprise me because youth justice for many years has been very male dominated, you know, I mean I just see the structure as being you know, we've got a male YOT person at the helm, and we'll have a male operations manager, and we will have a male team leader, and I just find it really frustrating. (Julie, social worker)

In other words, by replacing the male managers with other men, the dominant ethos of the team was unlikely to be challenged.[6]

In this way, the presentation of the banter among practitioners as evidence of and created by a unusually cohesive group was at issue. As well as being an important part of practitioners' experience, the banter also reflected and reinforced the dominant gender relations in the team. Thus, while it was seen to demonstrate and reaffirm the cohesive nature of team membership, at the same it was felt to compromise the membership of some staff. These positions were held simultaneously: for some practitioners the banter appeared to be a celebration of team membership as well as a source of considerable discomfort. The promotion of the social atmosphere of the team as an unproblematic demonstration of the team's cohesion thus denied the tensions, inconsistencies and conflicts that it also created. This indicates that, despite the dominant presentation of a unified, cohesive team, the experiences of team membership were in fact divergent, ambiguous and complex.

The following chapter explores further questions concerning the complexity and ambiguity of team life. How did practitioners understand their work and the values which informed it?

Notes

1 Of course, the restructuring of the youth justice system reinforced both the specialist nature of youth justice social work and its distance from other areas of social work by shifting the responsibility for work with young offenders from local authority field social workers to stand-alone YOTs (Pitts 1999).

However, as described in the following chapters, these promised to be different forms of separation and specialism. 'Specialists' were now drawn from a variety of occupational backgrounds, thus putting the nature of specialist expertise at issue. Further, as described in Chapter 6, there appeared to be an important difference between self-distancing and severance imposed on the team. The team were being separated from their home agency somewhat reluctantly and without a clear sense of their new identity. Therefore, rather than delineating the boundaries of the team, these new developments represented a series of challenges to its identity and that of the professionals working within it. These are discussed further in later chapters.

2 In addition, all team members were white and none were openly lesbian, gay or bisexual. See note 5 for further discussion.

3 However, the definition of the 'common language' on which the teasing was based was in fact contentious and reflected the power relations in the organisation. This is discussed below.

4 As Martin (1992) says, there is a complex relationship between the three perspectives described here and the perspectives of cultural members. The perspectives described by Meyerson and Martin are theoretical viewpoints developed by organisational culture researchers. These were derived inductively from extensive empirical research. There is thus likely to be some congruence between the theoretical perspectives and the viewpoints of cultural members. However, this congruence is partial and sporadic. Cultural members may say things that do not fit within one of these perspectives. They may also fluctuate between perspectives, even in the course of an utterance. As Martin argues, 'Perhaps because cultural members are not trying to leave a coherent, publishable written record of their perceptions, they feel freer to sacrifice conceptual consistency if it is necessary in order to capture the complexity of what they want to say' (1992: 15). At the most, then, these perspectives 'capture some of the major conceptual . . . dimensions of agreement and disagreement among studies of cultural members' (1992: 15).

5 As the following discussion makes clear, questions of sexism appeared to be particularly problematic in the team. It was notable that, in contrast, other aspects of staff diversity such as race or sexuality were rarely at issue. This undoubtedly reflected the composition of the team: all team members were white, and none were openly lesbian, gay or bisexual. As such, gender became the issue around which questions of power and membership were most markedly contested.

6 This is congruent with what has been termed 'homosocial reproduction': the process in which those in the top levels of an organisation tend to hire similar others who share their values, thereby maintaining the dominant culture of the organisation (Martin 1992; Ferguson 1984).

Chapter 3

Working in youth justice: the 'normal ambiguity' of social work

Social workers' worries about the imminent arrival of new practitioners were not solely concerned with the expansion of the team and the disruption it was envisaged this would cause, but about the different occupational backgrounds of the new staff. Many staff described Youth Justice Team members as sharing a common way of thinking about their work. They had broadly similar understandings of the aims and values underlying their work which derived from their common occupational background. Practitioners talked about 'social work values', what social workers are 'like', what they 'tend to do'. Some team members were concerned that staff from partner agencies might have a different approach to youth justice work. As one social worker put it, new staff would have 'other agendas': 'different ways of thinking, different rules, different values'. This allowed for the possibility of conflicts in these fundamental aspects of practice.

This chapter explores the nature of youth justice social work, and critically assesses the notion of conflicts between agencies. What were the values, goals and practices shared in the team? In what ways were these thought to conflict with other agencies? How else might such conflicts be understood? And what were the implications of the transformation of the youth justice system for the culture and practice of social work with young offenders?

The police and social work: 'us' and 'them'

Practitioners' anxieties about conflicts with collaborating agencies were brought into focus in June, when Mike, a police officer, joined the team.

Mike's arrival caused a considerable degree of unease among many of the Youth Justice Team. In part, it seemed that as the first member of a partner agency in post, he had become a focus for their anxieties. His appointment was the first obvious sign of the disruption and change facing a team that its members considered 'very settled'. It was also indicative of the uncertainty surrounding these changes. In contrast to other partner agencies, the team had not previously had a close working relationship with the police. Graham, the team leader, explained that the police had not been 'interactive with other agencies'. Although practitioners might meet on a managerial level or at case conferences, at an operational level the police 'stand alone'. Practitioners therefore had no context in which to place this new working relationship. Some admitted they were confused about the purpose of the police's inclusion in the YOT.

> Well, Mike's the police officer on the team, isn't he, really, he's the police officer on the team. I don't know what his role is. (Tom, social worker)

But, moreover, many practitioners could not see how it would be appropriate to form a close working relationship with the police.

Many social workers felt there was a fundamental incompatibility in the ethos of the two agencies:

> We all thought, police, oh god, what are we going to do with a policeman and you just think, police have got their view, social services have got their view, it's miles apart. (Jenny, social worker)

Such incompatibility was rooted in a markedly different understanding of the aims of work with young offenders. Social workers described themselves as trying to protect the welfare of the young people they supervised; in particular, they tried to keep young people away from custody. In contrast, the police were perceived as being interested only in 'nicking' or 'criminalising' young people:

> Well the police are out to lock them up, aren't they [laughs], when quite often I think we try and keep the kid out, out of lock up. (Jenny, social worker)

The punitive ethos of the police was thought to be reflected in the aggression of its staff. Social workers described a gendered machismo (see, for example, Reiner 2000) that was wholly inappropriate for work with young offenders:[1] they talked of police officers 'setting up' or 'beating up' young people, a 'cells culture', a 'cop culture'. For example, the YOT manager jokingly described the role of the police in a YOT in the following way: 'well, the police can beat confessions out of people.' In general, practitioners described a traditional relationship of mutual suspicion (see, for example, Thomas 1986). As one social worker put it:

> The police have always seen social workers as in league with the service-user. Social workers have always seen the police as bastards who are locking them up. (Gary, social worker)

Some staff thought these perceived conflicts in occupational norms would make it impossible for the team to cohere. These concerns crystallised around the issue of confidentiality and the disclosure of illegal activity. Some staff explained that despite their official obligations to do so, social workers tended not to act on information about offences that might come to light during supervision in order not to compromise their work. 'Colluding' with the young person or 'turning a blind eye' was crucial not to destroy their trust. Disclosing information to the police was considered 'grassing them [young people] up' or 'dropping them in it', and was harmful:

> We've always had the remit there that we should have told the police. But, there are so many grey areas. How can you work with drug users if they can't tell you what they're up to? [. . .] It is most important to keep the trust of the young person that you're working with. If they were to lie to me about their drug taking, about the offences that they're doing, I can't understand what's going on so I can't help them alter their behaviour. The honesty bit is important. (Gary, social worker)

It was assumed that this tacit practice could not continue with the introduction of a police officer to the team. Staff were certain that the police officer would not only routinely report any offence that came to light, but would have no qualms in doing so. As Tom, a social worker put it, 'I can't imagine a police officer turning a blind eye like we do'. In other words, confidentiality became the focus of concerns about the incompatibility of the ways in which police and social workers approached work with young offenders. The introduction of a police officer would compromise the entire work of the team:

> If I know about [service-user's] drug use I can minimise it and change his pattern of offending. Now I'll have to tell him to shut his mouth. The whole philosophy has changed. (Gary, social worker)

The extent of practitioners' concerns about Mike joining the team indicated how important a shared orientation to youth justice work was felt to be. A common understanding of underlying principles and goals of their practice was considered an essential part of team membership. It helped denote the categories of 'us' and 'them' that delineated the boundaries of the team. The punitive ethos of the police placed them firmly outside:

> I think looking at it from the youth justice team's side, to have a police officer sitting alongside you is quite unusual because it is a them and us situation in the past. (Gordon, social worker)

How then could the team accommodate a practitioner who apparently subscribed to such an incompatible approach to work with young offenders? Or, as one social worker put it, 'how can we actually become a tight team?'

Inter-agency conflicts

The problem of conflicts in the cultural norms and assumptions of different agencies – in particular between the police and social workers – and their implications for inter-agency working is a central theme in writing about inter-agency partnerships (e.g. Crawford and Jones 1995; Gilling 1994; Pearson et al. 1992; Sampson et al. 1988), and one which has been explored specifically in relation to the formation of YOTs (e.g. Burnett and Appleton 2004; Bailey and Williams 2000). However, as the following pages describe, while there was a strong sense of inter-agency conflict in the team, the nature of this appeared to be more complex than the perceived difference in occupational values.

Indeed, social workers' understanding of a conflict in the 'agendas' of the team and the police revealed some questionable assumptions about the nature of occupational values. Underlying this idea is the assumption that practitioners understand and embody a set of occupational norms and values, and so differences in these will therefore be played out among staff from those agencies. In other words, in the case of the conflicts anticipated by the Youth Justice Team, first that both police officers and social workers have a clear and agreed understanding of what the values underlying the work of their respective occupations are, and second that they are wholly and unambiguously attached to these. However, these assumptions are problematic, and particularly so in the context of youth justice social work and the kind of inter-agency relations required in the YOT.

The following pages explore the question of shared occupational values and practices in the Youth Justice Team. While team members strongly felt that social workers were bound by a shared way of working and thinking about their work that differentiated them from other agencies, the values and practices of youth justice social work were in fact complex and contested. This chapter considers three key aspects of the work of the team. What is their position in the criminal justice system and the relationships with other criminal justice agents? What is the purpose of their work and the values that inform it? And what is it that youth justice social workers actually do?

What is youth justice social work?

The Youth Justice Team and the criminal justice system

Many team members described the Youth Justice Team as clearly separated from other parts of the criminal justice system. The work of the team was seen as both distinct from other criminal justice agencies and in tension with it. Indeed, many practitioners described themselves as protecting young people from 'the system'. As one social worker explained, this was a key principle of youth justice work:

> I suppose that's where youth justice comes from, you take the kids from the system, and eventually they'll grow out of it [crime]. (Tom, social worker)

Practitioners' concerns about Mike joining the team exemplified this position: the police were concerned with drawing young people into the criminal justice system, 'nicking', 'criminalising' and 'locking them up', in contrast to the social worker's own aim of keeping young people away from it: 'keeping them out of lock up'.

This understanding of the Youth Justice Team's position in relation to the rest of the criminal justice system reflects the historical preoccupations of juvenile justice social work, in which children in trouble were segregated from adult offenders and treated according to principles of welfare rather than punishment. As the 'trained experts' in dealing with children (Worrall and Hoy 2004), the allocation of responsibility for young offenders to social workers reaffirmed both the separation of young people from the adult criminal justice system and the difference in the principles that governed their intervention. Similarly, the Youth Justice Team members described a stark ideological separation from the rest of the criminal justice system. As social workers, they were professionally bound to act in the best interest of children in trouble, whom, as Pitts (1999) points out, are defined by the Children Act 1989 and the UN Convention on the Rights of the Child as 'children in need'. As he comments, there is a conflict between this aim and other possible criminal justice outcomes, for example protecting the community. To act in the interests of the welfare of the young people they supervised involved keeping young people away from the criminal justice system as far as possible. In this they differed starkly from other, punitive criminal justice agencies. This contrast was described by one social worker:

> It's important to understand that person [. . .] rather than just being in there as another agency that's to do with pushing them through a system that's about ultimately them being punished and locked up. (Gary, social worker)

In this way, practitioners appeared to define the Youth Justice Team against the 'system'. They positioned themselves outside a set of interrelated agencies who worked together with a common purpose ('punishing' and 'locking up'). However, this understanding in fact obscured a more complex relationship between the Youth Justice Team and other criminal justice agencies.

Firstly, despite practitioners' espoused commitment to protecting young people from other criminal justice agencies, the Youth Justice Team was both integral to and interconnected with other parts of the criminal justice system through its statutory duties. Its primary duties were the administration of court orders. It thus had a central position in the network of agencies that comprised the youth justice system, and had the duty to direct young people to other agencies or formal structures such as the courts, despite any potential ideological conflicts.

Secondly, potential differences with other parts of the criminal justice system may have required social workers to alter their approach in order to avoid conflict. This was particularly evident in practitioners' accounts of their dealings with magistrates. Many social workers felt that magistrates' decisions were informed by wholly different principles to the work of the Youth Justice Team. Their sentencing decisions were felt to be punitive, unpredictable and seemingly capricious: they were a result of 'stupidity', 'they dish out justice blindly . . . not on the fact of the offence, but just how they feel'. However, while social workers felt wholly detached from the ethos and decision-making process of the magistracy, the relationship between the two groups was more complex. For social workers to exert any influence in the sentencing process, they must win credibility with magistrates (Brown 1991). For example, Tom, a social worker, said that his expertise gave him authority with the magistrates, which meant that his recommendations were taken serious- ly: 'I've built up experience over the years. I have quite some influence'.

However, such credibility is dependent not simply on practitioners' professional skills, but their ability to work within the same terms as the magistrates. Their recommendations are likely to have more impact if practitioners relate the arguments in a pre-sentence report to the concerns of the sentencer and the issues that they think important (Pitts 1999). But further, practitioners' recommendations must reinforce the dominant ethos of the magistrates' sentencing tendencies. As Brown (1991) argues, social workers are seen as credible to the extent that their recommendations fall within the limits of what magistrates already consider 'sensible' or 'realistic'. Conversely, practitioners who repeatedly recommend disposals outside the range of those which magistrates consider appropriate are likely to be labelled 'idealistic' and their recommendations ignored. Thus, while some Youth Justice Team members described a perceived conflict with magistrates in their approach to work with young offenders, they also understood a need to predict and reinforce magistrates' preferences to ensure that they retained some degree of influence. This was evident in the concern of management staff when one practitioner, already known for the disparity between her recommendations and the sentences passed, recommended a conditional discharge for one young man who in fact received a custodial sentence. The credibility of all the practitioners in the team as well as the social worker involved was seen to be in jeopardy.

In this way, not only were practitioners required to interact closely with other agencies and structures in the criminal justice system, they also needed to adapt to the concerns of the more powerful actors in the system. There was thus a conflict in the espoused values of the team (detachment) and their actual practice (integration and assimilation).

The aims and values of youth justice work

Practitioners described youth justice social workers as sharing a common understanding of the purpose of their work and the values that informed it. In contrast to other agencies, the Youth Justice Team was not concerned with punishing young people. Instead, many practitioners described its overarching purpose in terms of 'helping' the young people they supervised. This distinction was illustrated by one social worker, who described an incident in which Mike, the police officer, had responded to the disruptive behaviour of a young service-user by suggesting he should be taken to a police station and charged:

> I'm thinking more about well this child needs help [. . .] [Mike]'s like you know he wants lifting [. . .] whereas I think social workers will tend to come from the point of view that well, this child needs help as well. (Sally, social worker)

The understanding of the team's work as 'help' appeared to describe a number of ideological and professional positions reflecting the underlying obligation to the best interests and welfare of the young person. It was this shared orientation and ethos that practitioners felt differentiated social work from other agencies, and it was thus a crucial element of the identity of the team.

However, while team members strongly felt they shared a common orientation of 'helping' young people, the notion of 'help' in fact obscured ambiguous goals.

Firstly, the opposition that the team described between the 'helping' approach of the team and the 'punishing' roles of other agencies masked a more complex position. Social work inevitably involves the exercise of power and control, both through the use of professional skills and authority to influence service users, and in the profession's obligation to ensure compliance with social policies (e.g. Bailey and Brake 1975; Cohen 1975, 1985; Parton 1996; Payne 1996). So, while social workers might have explained their role as that of caseworker or enabler, it was also one of social control. As Thomas (1986: 8) puts it, 'The local authority social worker is circumscribed in all his work with a host of statutory obligations which put him into the "policing role", whether he readily accepts it or not'. This was acknowledged by one practitioner on the team, discussing the move to joint working with the police:

> Social workers have always been social policemen in a way, but this seems to be formalising our role. It's only a matter of time before we have to wear uniforms. (Gary, social worker)

While the tensions between the 'helping' or 'enabling' aims of social work and its exercise of power and control underlie all forms of social work, they are perhaps particularly overt in youth justice social work. Social workers acting within the framework of the criminal justice system are more obviously and directly involved in the apparatus of social control. Their 'policing role' – such as in the supervision of court orders and invoking sanctions for non-compliance – is thus explicit. Further, not only does the rhetoric of 'welfare' and 'help' not preclude the coercive nature of their interventions, it allows for a vastly increased level of intervention and supervision (e.g. Cohen 1985; Garland 1985; Morris and Giller 1979; Platt 1969). Consequently, rather than removing young people from the punitive reach of criminal justice agencies, social work with young offenders has been seen to represent a more insidious and potent penetration of the criminal justice system, an 'extension and multiplication of the judicial gaze' (Garland 1985: 239).

These tensions were acknowledged by practitioners and were a source of ambivalence and discomfort. Far from simply being 'social control agents', practitioners described feeling deeply uncomfortable about the contradictions between their own views about how to work with young people and the policies to which they had to persuade their service-users to conform (see also Cohen 1975, 1985). For example, some Youth Justice Team members felt the disposals of the Crime and Disorder Act and the increasingly stringent National Standards would require them to impose standards of compliance on the service-users which was 'totally out of kilter with what we'd like to work on the street', ' setting up a young person to fail'.

Yet as youth justice social workers, team members were especially vulnerable to such contradictions. Perhaps more than other forms of social work, social work with young offenders is shaped and constrained by its legal framework and the guidelines and standards for practice that follow (Smith 1998), and, due to the politicisation of youth crime, particularly subject to the vagaries of the political climate. Consequently, staff were particularly likely to find themselves operating within structures and demanding compliance with policies with which they felt uncomfortable. Thus some practitioners felt the Crime and Disorder Act heralded a shift in ethos towards a more punitive youth justice, and one in which the controlling aspects of their role would become more overt, despite their own sense of occupational values. For example, one practitioner said:

> It seems we're moving to be a statutory agency whose bottom line is preventing crime, not looking at the well-being of [young people], and the hard line is that the young people we get are usually very damaged individuals, I feel that will be missed out. I have the worry that we will become far too proactive in just punishment. There's very clear literature about what we're there to do, and this is underlined as to reduce offending. And that will be our bottom line as I understand it [. . .] if that means locking them up than that's what we'll be more likely to do. (Gary, social worker)

In this way, the contrast between the 'helping' work of the team and the 'punishing' roles of other agencies, while strongly felt, in fact obscured a far more ambiguous position. But further, although social workers described themselves as sharing a common orientation of 'helping' young people, the aim of 'help' itself embodies ambiguities. As Meyerson (1991) argues, '. . . in different contexts, to different audiences, or at different times, social workers vary in their beliefs about their [. . .] orientation, how to 'help', and even what it means to "help"' (1991: 132).

In the case of youth justice social work, what it means to 'help' is particularly problematic. Addressing offending behaviour demands an engagement with some of the underlying questions of causation. Why did the young person commit the offence? To what extent can they be held responsible for it? What should be done in response? As these questions are at the heart of most debates about crime, it is unsurprising that there was considerable disagreement and confusion about them within the team.

Understanding 'help' and offending behaviour

There were some common ideas that emerged in practitioners' accounts. Most team members thought that the external circumstances of young people's lives were integral to their offending. Offending behaviour was understood in the context of issues such as the chaotic lifestyles of families and peers, drug abuse, mental health or trauma:

> I've worked with young men who are shoplifting, drug-taking, the majority are sexually abused. (Gary, social worker)

These factors were often understood in a wider, structural context: they were shaped by socio-economic factors such as school exclusions, unemployment, poor housing:

> My feeling is that they [service-users] have got major major problems, young people excluded from school, living on huge rambling estates and they've formed a subculture of their own. (Julie, social worker)

In turn, these were inextricable from the political climate. The needs of young people in trouble were thought not to be understood or a priority for the government, and there were inadequate resources to help young people out of an offending lifestyle:

> This country's very backward compared to Europe [...] you can chuck the money around as much as you want to, but they're not channelling it into the drugs areas, sex education ... (Julie, social worker)

But although most practitioners seemed to be in agreement that social, structural and political factors were important in understanding young people's offending behaviour, these prompted further complex questions about what it was to be a youth justice social worker.

Firstly, an understanding of the importance of the wider context in shaping offending behaviour raised a series of questions about the scope of the work of the team and the roles of the practitioners within it. As social, structural and economic conditions are integral to offending behaviour, should these properly be the concern of social work rather than, for example, a therapeutic approach that focuses solely on the individual? At what level should social workers address their attempts to bring about change? For example, should they aim to empower individuals, or communities, or bring about broader structural and political change? These questions have been the subject of considerable debate, and formed the basis of a radical critique of social work in the 1970s (e.g. Bailey and Brake 1975). However, as Huntington (1981) points out, they lead to very different definitions of occupational identity: are practitioners clinicians, social reformists or revolutionaries? These definitions do not sit alongside each other easily but are competing and conflicting. As Huntington puts it: 'it is difficult to see just how long any one occupation can contain this kind of tension in its definition of itself, with its accompanying threat to consensus and cohesion' (1981: 103).

Secondly, an understanding of the ways in which structural and social circumstances shaped and constrained the behaviour of young people raised further fundamental questions about the nature of offending behaviour. To what extent could or should young people be held responsible for their offence? As Pitts puts it, young offenders 'have often been denied the means to become the authors of their own lives. Their social position, having granted them responsibility for nothing, effectively renders them irresponsible.' (1999: 72). Among the team, this was often couched in terms of young people being 'victims' of their circumstances. For example, one practitioner said:

> I think that the people that get involved in crime are victims for other reasons. Because they're seen as grotty individuals they're not seen as victims and it's that pain of being sexually abused and stuff that they're carrying with them. (Gary, social worker)

In addition, their age was thought to mediate the extent to which young people could be held responsible for their behaviour. As one practitioner put it, 'we are dealing with children and children are different':

> I think there is a general thing going on within our society now where we are not accepting that these are children offending, they are children until they offend and then we're trying to see them as adults, and make them very adult about their offences, when in a lot of cases we're dealing not only with young children but immature young children, a lot of them are very damaged and are a couple of years under their maturity. (Tom, social worker)

Some practitioners thought a common understanding of these issues was something that described and defined the team. Social workers shared an understanding of the responsibility of young people for their actions which demarcated them from practitioners in other agencies, notably the police (and, as described in Chapter 2, from some other social work teams as well). For example, one team member, Gary, tried to explain the difference in the police and social workers' attitudes to one of his service users, who had refused to cooperate with two supervision orders and had since been given a custodial sentence. Gary thought a custodial sentence could have been avoided if the abuse that lay beneath his offending behaviour had been more thoroughly explored. He explained that Mike, the police officer, didn't share his view. For Gary, this was indicative of a broader difference in approach between the police and social workers:

> I don't feel that the police necessarily would understand that, whereas I feel that it has got significant bearing on the case, in that area we're coming from two different perspectives. (Gary, social worker)

However, this polarisation of the beliefs of practitioners within the two agencies in fact obscured a diversity of opinion within the Youth Justice Team. As Gary continued, it became evident that Mike's views about how far the child's abusive background mediated his responsibility for his offending were also shared by some social workers:

> The police officer's saying he's had enough chances he's got to go and he believes that, as do some of the social workers on the team, they believe that as well, whereas I'm saying well hang on a second I don't believe we've dealt with the issues of his abuse.

In fact, it was clear there was a diversity of opinion among team members about the responsibility of young people for their offending behaviour. For example, Alan, a social worker, explained that he probably had a much more stringent view about this issue than some of his colleagues: 'Other social workers are more lax. As I say you know, it's black and white with very little grey for me.'

In this way, while social workers described a strongly-felt 'welfarist' orientation to their work, there was no clear shared understanding of or approach towards offending behaviour. Instead, as one practitioner acknowledged, there was a wide range of attitudes towards offending among Youth Justice Team members:

> We all work in exceptionally different ways ... some people have almost a punitive attitude, others ... work in the other extreme, very liberal, it's a very wide sort of range of attitudes. (Duncan, social worker)

What do social workers do? The 'functional territory' of social work

Lastly, the practice of the team itself was clearly crucial to the way practitioners understood their approach to work with young offenders. Indeed, Huntington (1981) argues that the primary or central tasks claimed by an occupation, its 'functional territory', is an important component of its identity. But what is the 'functional territory' of social work with young offenders? What do youth justice social workers actually do?

The difficulty in defining the technologies of social work has been well documented. In part, the 'vastness and vagueness of the social work task' (Goldberg and Warburton 1979) may reflect the lack of a coherent and explicit knowledge base for social work, which has resulted in a wide range of potential approaches, none of which has become dominant (Munro 2004). In the Youth Justice Team, the bulk of practitioners' work with young offenders took the form of casework. This generally consisted of a series of interviews agreed between the social worker and the young person in accordance with the requirements of the court order. Various types of structured work might take place within these interviews, such as anger management sessions or offence-focused work. However, practitioners found it difficult to articulate what it was that they did.

Some staff explained that this indeterminacy was in part a result of a key principle of social work. Practitioners stressed the importance of understanding the uniqueness of the personalities, circumstances and needs of each young person and adapting their interventions appropriately. As Rojek et al. (1988) say, 'Individualisation is indeed regarded as an essential value of social work. Students are taught to see clients as unique, special, and different' (1988: 33). Consequently, practitioners explained that they had no 'standard' way of working, and that it was impossible to predict how to approach the supervision of each young person. Instead, practitioners needed to adapt constantly their work to the responses of the young people involved:

> What works with that kid won't work with the next one I work with. Everyone's different I work with. [. . .] To effect any change, I think we have to work on their level. We have to work out the way they're functioning. (Tom, social worker)

But the difficulty in articulating what their work involved also arose from the nature of the social work task itself. In essence, social work involves the purposeful use of interpersonal relationships between the service user and the practitioner. Thus most team members described the development of a relationship as the essential aspect of their work and the central mechanism by which they attempted to bring about change in the young people they supervised. For example, one social worker described how he worked with a boy serving a custodial sentence:

It's sort of part of my role, to build that relationship up with him, and I can work with him in a positive way now, because I've been up there a lot visiting, I've got a certain amount of influence with him now because I know him quite well. (Tom, social worker)

The relationship was described as crucial for developing trust with the young person, which was essential for productive work to take place.

It is most important to keep the trust of the young person that you're working with. If they were to lie to me about the offences what they're doing I can't understand what's going on so I can't help them alter their behaviour, the honesty bit is important. (Gary, social worker)

The relationship with the young person was also productive in itself: staff explained that through it they were trying to 'build up [young people's] self-esteem', 'slowly build up confidence', 'broaden [their] experience', 'be a good role model'. As one practitioner explained, social workers were trying to let young people know they were supported:

I think we need to be regularly seeing young people. I think they need to know there's someone they can contact [. . .] we're trying to keep them out . . . they need to know that people are looking out for them . . . that gives a good message to them, a positive message. (Duncan, social worker)

However, while practitioners were able to describe the importance and functions of a good relationship with the young people they supervised, they found it difficult to describe what developing such relationships involved, or how they were used. This reflects a fundamental dilemma in social work. As the relationship between the practitioner and client is the primary tool of practitioners, this relationship – and the interview through which it is formed – become the 'technology' of the occupation (Huntington 1981). But the nature of human relationships makes it extremely difficult to define or explain their development. As Huntington (1981) points out, social work is left attempting to render technical precisely those aspects of human functioning that are considered indefinable and indeterminate in other professions. Indeed one classic casework text argues that prescription is impossible:

The pervasiveness of the relationship in the casework process gives it an elusive quality; no explanation or definition can do justice to a living thing, words have a certain coldness, while a relationship has a delightful warmth. (Biestek 1961: viii)

Social work is thus a practice which cannot be made wholly explicit. The skills, knowledge and styles of working that practitioners develop are in part private and personal, and applied in intuitive and tacit ways (Munro 2004). As Pitts puts it, youth justice workers need to be 'sensitive opportunists', trusting their instincts:

It is important to try, as far as possible, to do what *feels* right. There is no instruction book to explain when and how to engage a young person in counselling but we do have intuition, and we should listen to it and trust it. (Pitts 1999: 89, own italics)

Or as one social worker explained, working with young offenders involved relying on the intuition that comes with experience:

I've been doing it so long, you know what to look for. (Tom, social worker)

Practice and outcomes

The difficulty in describing the work of the team was further complicated by its elusive connection with outcomes. Many staff explained that the key outcome of their work was defined as 'reducing offending'.[2]

I mean our main role is reducing crime, we're told so many times it's reducing crime. (Tom, social worker)

However, many team members were disparaging about this as a measure of the work of the team. The complexity of human behaviour and the situations with which youth justice social work is concerned made the impact of interventions both unpredictable and difficult to assess. As one practitioner explained, the effects of his work might not be immediately apparent.

It [impact] might happen in another ten years, it sort of clicks in ten years later [. . .] it's not like teaching and you've got a result at the end of the day. It can happen two or three years later. (Tom, social worker)

Further, as young people's behaviour was influenced by many factors other than the work of the team, their role in bringing about any change in offending was hard to establish. For example, experimenting with offending behaviour was thought by some practitioners to be a normal part of growing up: stopping offending could therefore be a result of 'growing out of crime' (Rutherford 1986) rather than the work of the team. Similarly, the impact of social work was mediated by factors beyond the control of the practitioner. Staff explained that, however skilled their work, they were limited in the extent to which they could tackle the structural and social conditions that might underlie offending behaviour. One practitioner said:

> I don't know whether any of us have got the ability to work effectively with families, so often we see a single parent or a couple doing their best to confine and offer sensible routines and controls to their children, and the kids have got other things going on in their life, they take more notice of their mates than their parents. I can't imagine that anything that we're already doing, that there's any-thing else out there that we can do. (Duncan, social worker)

Crucially, the success of an intervention depended on the participation of the young person. Practitioners explained that they could not stop young people offending. Their job was to help young people decide to stop offending:

> The child has got to want to change first. You've got to find something that clicks with that young person. (Tom, social worker)

> You can't change somebody, they've got to want to change themselves. (Sally, social worker)

This unclear relationship between practice and outcome made the nature of the team's work appear intangible. As Meyerson puts it, 'technologies seem ambiguous because what one does as a social worker [. . .] is only loosely connected to what results' (1991: 136). Indeed, the difficulty in demonstrating the impact of interventions has resulted in long-running debates about the method and purpose of social work, where there is wide disagreement about the efficacy of particular types of intervention, or whether any intervention actually helps at all (e.g. Fischer 1973; Goldberg and Warburton 1979). These questions were brought into focus in relation to youth justice work in the 1970s, when research appeared to show that social work did not reduce recidivism (e.g. Pitts 1999; Worrall 1997; Morris and Giller 1979). For the Youth Justice Team, the intangible connections between practice and outcomes raised further difficulties in defining their work. If the impact of social work on offending behaviour could not be clearly demonstrated, what was the role of a youth justice social worker? What was it they were actually doing? And was it of any use? As described below, these questions became of crucial importance in the climate of change now confronting the team.

The 'normal' ambiguity of social work

In this way, key aspects of the working life of the Youth Justice Team were complex and unclear. Practitioners' relationships with criminal justice agencies and the state, and the values, aims and technologies of their work were inherently ambiguous. Thus, instead of being an occupational group which is clearly defined by a shared set of values and practices, the Youth Justice Team appeared to exemplify what Meyerson (1991, 1994) describes as an organisation with a culture in which ambiguity is 'normal'. Practitioners in the Youth Justice Team felt they had a shared culture. They shared a common overarching purpose and a common orientation. They shared comparable experiences and problems. But these experiences and purposes accommodated multiple beliefs and meanings. As Meyerson puts it, 'members do not agree on clear boundaries, cannot identify shared solutions, and do not reconcile contradictory beliefs and multiple identities' (1991: 131). How common experiences and problems are interpreted and enacted may vary to such an extent as to make what is shared seem meaninglessly abstract. Ambiguity is thus 'normal': it comprises the 'essence of their cultural community' (ibid.: 132).

The 'normality' of ambiguity in youth justice social work was implicit in the practice of the team. Practitioners' accounts of youth justice social work prioritised individualisation, intuition and the loose connection between practice and outcomes. Instead of indicating a lack of cohesion in the work of the team, acceptance of these ambiguous aspects of practice was an essential cultural cue of their work. The recognition of the subjective and idiosyncratic nature of practice made implicit claims about the working assumptions of the team: it 'reveals and reinforces beliefs about control, the social nature of the client condition and the subjective and diffuse nature of proper social work practice' (Meyerson 1994: 647). It was thus a consequence of the essential nature of their work that practitioners were unable to specify a 'technology' of their practice. The indeterminacy, individualisation and subjectivity that typified the work of the team was itself a defining characteristic of youth justice social work. As one practitioner put it:

> My old boss used to say, be very wary of people that have got answers, because there aren't any answers to this. (Tom, social worker)

The importance of 'us' and 'them'

In the context of the 'normal' ambiguity of their practice, the perceived points of conflict with the police appeared less clear. Staff felt that the general ethos of the police would not be compatible with their strongly felt welfarist orientation. But, as described above, the team accommodated a wide variety of approaches, working styles and attitudes towards offending behaviour. Indeed, the diverse and idiosyncratic nature of the range of practice was valued within the team. Why then should the incorporation of a further potentially different approach to work be seen as so problematic?

Some staff appeared to be concerned that the introduction of police staff would compromise the essential ambiguity felt crucial to the team. This was sometimes described in terms of a 'police approach' or 'way of working' which was thought to be incompatible with that of social work. The crux of this approach appeared to be a devaluing of ambiguity. The police were thought to value uniformity in their work, reproducing identical routines with little scope for attention to the individuality of the offender or the practitioner:

> They're used to a very specific structure, very specific routines [. . .] obviously it's a very different culture, they wear uniforms, very disciplined, very directed [. . .] police culture, because it's uniform, because it's group oriented, almost militaristic in some respects, in some of their work is that [. . .] they can't allow their officers to be too individual in their approach to their work. (Duncan, social worker)

Further, many social workers thought that police officers would not be able to cope with the flexibility and initiative necessary in working with young offenders.

> What do I do, I'm a police officer, I'm used to obeying orders and I haven't got any. I'm buggering off to the police station and seeing my mates. (Graham, team leader)

In other words, in the eyes of the social workers, police culture did not allow for the everyday management of ambiguity in their work. Consequently, police officers did not have the ability to cope with the conflicts and contradictions that were an essential part of youth justice work, resulting in an inflexibility of approach that was inappropriate for the work of the team.

This understanding of the police suggested a paradox in the culture of the team: while the diversity of practitioners' approaches to work with young offenders was prized within the team, they would not accommodate an ostensibly inflexible working style. But further, social workers' depiction of the inflexibility of police work is contradicted by much research which describes how discretion is essential to low-level policing (as encapsulated, for example, in Bittner's (1975) notion of the 'street corner politician'). By contrasting their own experiences with those of the police, social work staff eliminated those similarities of experience. In other words, articulating their own tolerance of ambiguity ironically made social work staff unable to perceive the elements of flexibility inherent in policing.

But, in addition, the claims of similarity and difference that the introduction of the police inspired had a further, crucial importance. By contrasting the work of the team with other criminal justice agents, such as the police, who appeared to represent a differing orientation in their work, practitioners eliminated and clarified the ambiguity of their experience to present an unproblematic picture of conflicting agendas. Complexities were reduced to opposition. In other words, the construction of a series of 'us and them' claims masked the inherent ambiguity of key elements of their professional identity. Inter-agency conflicts helped define the identity of the Youth Justice Team, and consequently the identity of those practitioners within it.

Ambiguity and the new youth justice

Many practitioners felt that the changes to the youth justice system signalled a shift in the climate of youth justice social work. Practitioners appeared to feel that their accounts of what they did as youth justice social workers were ceasing to satisfy. While it was recognised that ambiguity was a crucial part of the team's practice, some felt their work could no longer be justified in these terms. The refocusing of the youth justice system on a particular variety of knowledge based on risks, outcomes and evidence required a new form of transparency in their work. What did practitioners do with each young person? What impact did their interventions have? In this context, the inherent difficulty in demonstrating the technologies and impact of their work made the team's practice vulnerable to innovation.

The essential ambiguity of the team's practice made it at risk of encroachment from two directions: firstly, a shift in the culture of its work; and secondly, the absorption of other agencies into the team.

The new climate of practice

Practitioners feared that the transformation of the youth justice system had brought about a change in climate which directly targeted the discretion and flexibility prized in their work.

Standardising practice

Firstly, the interventionism heralded by the Act was perceived as newly prescriptive. A range of disposals would soon be available to the courts which allowed for formal intervention with those who were previously beyond the scope of the work of the team such as parents or children who had not been charged with an offence. Practitioners explained that they already worked informally with some of these groups: as one put it, it was an 'unwritten agreement' that parents would be involved in work with young people when it was felt appropriate and with parents' agreement. It was feared that by formalising this work, the new disposals would result in the imposition of rigid frameworks for practice and thus restrict practitioners' discretion. So, for example, staff thought that the introduction of Parenting Orders would require them to compel all parents subject to the orders to take part in parenting classes, regardless of whether they felt this was appropriate:

> Some of them [parents] aren't capable of going to classes. Their lives are that chaotic. You know, Tuesday nights you've got to come in for an hour's class, I don't think many would turn up. There are those on drugs out there, you know. (Tom, social worker)

Some felt that the new measures were indicative of a new climate in which the individualisation and discretion central to their practice was compromised. One practitioner illustrated his sense of this shift by describing a conference at which a Home Office representative spoke about the sanctions for breach of Parenting Orders:

> What'll happen if they don't comply, do we take them to court? That question was asked at the Home Office briefing we went to, what happens if they don't comply. Clear as a bell the answer was, 'they'll go to prison'. Now that shocked me. (Tom, social worker)

In other words, the flexibility at the core of social work practice would now be replaced by the clarity of standardised responses.

Monitoring and evaluation

Secondly, practitioners felt certain that the implementation of the new legislation would be accompanied by an increasing emphasis on assessment and evaluation. Staff would have to complete assessment forms (Asset) for each offender at the beginning and end of each intervention. Annual plans detailing targets and achievements were required by the Youth Justice Board. New, stringent National Standards currently being drafted would be accompanied by an escalation of assessment. Many staff thought that there was a new climate in which their practice would now be extensively monitored, and in turn this would shape their interventions. This was reinforced by the team's management:

> God are we going to be monitored, like never before. (Graham, team leader)

> We're going to be monitored to death. (Mark, YOT manager)

Yet the increasing emphasis on monitoring and assessment was thought to be inappropriate for the work of the team. The difficulty in articulating what they actually did, the intangible connection between practice and outcomes and the complexity of describing what constituted a 'success-ful' intervention made assessment of the work of the team extremely difficult. As one practitioner explained:

> It's [monitoring] sort of . . . it's about success with young people, about evaluating that success. That's very difficult to do in our work, evaluate success. [. . .] It's quite hard to quantify what you do. (Tom, social worker)

Moreover, were the essential elements of their practice in fact amenable to quantification (see also, for example, Munro 2004, Goldberg and Warburton 1979)? For example, the staff described the development of interpersonal relationships as the central task of work with young offenders, but how could this be described or measured? As meaningful measurement of their work was impossible, team members felt the only purpose of the new emphasis on monitoring could be cosmetic. The most the evaluation could show would be an ambivalent, qualified notion of 'success': as one practitioner put it, 'a success in Home Office terms'. The Youth Justice Board were thought to 'want results'. The new National Standards were concerned with the processes and mechanisms of the team's work, such as the frequency of contact with offenders and the speed with which reports were produced. As Munro (2004) argues, because of the difficulty of describing the core elements of social work practice and outcomes, data about such 'service outputs' are far easier and cheaper to collect than developing a reliable measure of the quality of practice. However, these lead to a focus on the management of supervision at the expense of user outcomes. Thus staff felt the standards to which they had to adhere had little to do with the content of their work.

We need to be seen to process young offenders quickly and efficiently. It doesn't matter one jot what we do. (Graham, team leader)

Instead, practitioners felt the increasingly stringent standards would detract from their core tasks. By demanding further controls over the management of their work rather than its content, the Standards represented 'a change of philosophy' in the work of the team:

> You can spend ten minutes and get nothing done, or you can go out, not see them once a week and try to understand the situation, but you've not kept to National Standards. Keeping to National Standards is what's going to be important. As long as you've dotted your i's crossed your t's and your files are kept up to date, as long as you feel that you can justify what you've done, it's very easy for social workers to do that, very easy to make your files look fantastic, very easy to write up and make it look like we've all done our work, while at the other end the young people may not be getting the service. (Gary, social worker)

Yet the change in climate which these innovations appeared to represent simultaneously made them impossible to resist. The shift in the terms in which their practice must now be articulated and accounted for made the work of the team impossible to defend. As one social worker acknowledged, the inability to quantify the work of the team or demonstrate its impact made it susceptible to criticism. It could appear to those outside the team that they didn't do anything at all:

> Mark [YOT manager] said, can people show me evidence of what they're actually doing, or is it just knocking on the door and having a cup of tea with them. [. . .] I do know where he's coming from, but he needs to hear that isn't the case. (Sally, social worker)

Defending functional territory

Further, the ambiguity of the practice of the Youth Justice Team made it difficult to defend against the encroachment of other agencies. What were the expertise or central tasks that were uniquely theirs – the 'functional territory' (Huntington 1981) of youth justice social work? For example, Tom described one supervision visit in the following way:

> We talk about his hairstyle, we spoke about all kinds of things, he's quite interested in trains, [social work student] took him out to Midlands Airport to look at trains, planes landing, to try and broaden his experience.

It is difficult to describe what differentiates Tom from other professionals or concerned individuals in his ability to perform these tasks. As Nellis (1995a: 36) comments, '. . . the knowledge, skills and values which, at a fairly abstract level, are indeed common to all forms of "social work" in Britain are also common to occupations that are explicitly not regarded as "social work", for example, youth work, counselling, psychology and psychiatry.' The inability to claim ownership of the central tasks of social work produces a further source of ambiguity: a lack of clarity in the boundaries of the profession. Because 'social work' could be and is done by other professionals, 'insiders, as well as outsiders, hold diffuse ideas about what social work is and about who is and is not a social worker' (Meyerson 1991: 136).

Importantly for the Youth Justice Team, the difficulty in delineating their unique expertise made them vulnerable to encroachment from other agencies. For example, Mike, the newly arrived police officer, thought he would be an appropriate YOT member because of his interest in community sport with young people. He described how, as a community police officer, he had run football teams with local young people:

> I wanted people to join my teams that I've run over the years because I respected their ability as a footballer – I didn't ask them to fill in a questionnaire about their lifestyle, criminality or anything else, I saw that they'd got something that I wanted to bring into my team, I approached them and said 'join my team, I like the way you play', and I think I treated them as a special person because I wanted them to get the best out of their sporting skill, certainly I heightened their self-esteem, and I always had a good rapport with the people I knew to be on the edge of criminality.

This account of an emphasis on the relationship with the young person with the purpose of developing their self-esteem has little to differentiate it from the way many social workers described their work. It was thus difficult for the social workers to defend the boundaries of the team by claiming ownership of the work they did.

In this way, the ambiguity that was essential to work of the Youth Justice Team also made it vulnerable to change. How could practitioners demonstrate the efficacy of their current practice? Instead, team members found themselves powerless to defend themselves against the innovations of the Crime and Disorder Act. As Tom explained:

> I think frankly we've always made a reasonable job of it anyway as a Youth Justice Team, so I think the fact is, we are sort of, being told we've failed because here's our government telling us 'you've got to do it this way', you know, and I think we did alright.

Notes

1 The implicit contrast here is with the differently gendered ethos of social work (this is discussed further in Chapter 4). There is thus an irony here: social workers are critical of a gendered machismo in the police, thus implicitly denying it in their own profession. Yet as discussed in Chapter 2, some practitioners experienced a similar form of machismo in the team. This indicates how perceptions across occupational boundaries eliminate the complexities of practitioners' own experiences. This is discussed further in the conclusion.

2 As a definition of the key outcome of the team's practice this is perhaps unexpected: the Audit Commission (1996) suggested that a focus on 'reducing offending' was precisely what was absent from many Youth Justice Teams prior to the Crime and Disorder Act 1998. It is likely this account of the team's role reflects the perception of a shift in emphasis towards reducing offending which the restructuring of the youth justice system was intended to set in train.

Chapter 4

An unrepresentative representative: being a police officer in a YOT

The absorption of a police officer into the Youth Justice Team in June 1999 caused considerable anxiety among many social work staff. As the first practitioner from a partner agency to join the team, Mike was a clear demonstration that the team's working practices were changing. But further, he was a representative of an agency thought to be working 'in opposition' to social work. Social workers assumed that the approach of a police officer to work with young offenders would conflict with social work goals and values, making co-working impossible. As explored in the previous chapter, these anxieties were founded on the problematic assumption that occupations have a clear and agreed understanding of the goals and values of their work, an assumption that is particularly problematic in relation to youth justice social work. But it also assumes that all practitioners from an occupational group are wholly and unambiguously attached to these values. In other words, staff expected the competing demands of different agencies would be played out among their representatives. Social workers felt that they could not work closely with someone who embodied such different occupational norms. Mike's position as a police officer on the team would compromise the cohesion of the team.

This assumption was implicitly questioned by some practitioners on the team. Although they appeared to identify the police with a clear set of unambiguous occupational norms, they also acknowledged that Mike might be differentially attached to these norms. Mike was different from other police officers. As one practitioner put it:

We're very lucky with the police officer we've got. He's thoughtful, more intelligent than most, backs it up with fact. (Gary, social worker)

And as the team leader put it, somewhat more ambivalently:

He's only used his stick [baton] twice. He may have kicked the shit out of them, but he's only used his stick twice [laughs].

In fact, Mike's experiences as the first police officer to join the team revealed the complexity of what it is to be an occupational member. The following pages explore problems of occupational identity and their implications for representing an agency in an inter-agency team. How did Mike understand what it was to be a police officer? What did it mean to represent the police on a YOT? And how did his understanding of his occupational identity shape his role in the team?

Being a police officer

Mike felt that he was not a typical police officer. Like many of the social workers, he thought police officers were often aggressive and violent. However, this was only true of a 'modern', younger generation of police officers who had an entirely different ethos from older officers like himself.

I've got nothing in common with young policemen. They're different animals, I'm afraid ... they're too violent. Young policemen are violent.

Mike thought there were two different cultures in the police, divided along generational lines and representing different 'eras' in policing. The aggression of younger officers was thought to be a product of a cultural difference between 'modern' policing and 'the old way of doing things'. He felt that officers were now exposed to more overtly adversarial encounters than he had experienced in his earlier career. However, the prominence of confrontation in officers' experiences had brought about a change in policing style, which was manifested both in a quicker tendency towards physical violence and in their manner of interaction:

The times we had to be violent were few and far between and I think it's thrust at young officers a lot more so they have to be a lot more wary and stand offish.[1]

Officers were not only aggressive towards the public they encountered but also towards their colleagues. Younger officers were described as ambitious and self-promoting: they have an 'in your face attitude', a 'go-getter attitude', 'thrust yourself forward . . . scramble up a lot quicker than your natural skills'.

Mike strongly identified himself with the 'old' ethos of police work. He presented his career path as both evidence of and explanation for his distance from younger officers. As he put it, he had been 'divorced from conventional police work'. After policing in the city for a couple of years he moved to work in special units for the majority of his career away from the locality, before returning to spend several years as a community police officer in a small local town. Moreover, although he had recently returned to community policing, this had been 'in a rural backdrop', away from the 'city policing' which he equated with the aggression of younger police.[2] There he had worked with other officers of the same generation as himself, who shared the same style of policing:

It was terrific, we'd all got our heads on the right way, we all thought the same, we policed approximately the same, although there were different skills within the group, we ticked over really well [. . .] But, I think by and large they were the same. They didn't get on with any ease with young officers.

In this way, he felt he had avoided acquiring the characteristics of 'modern' police officers.

With me having years away from conventional policing, I think I have missed the change, or my own change [. . .] when I was a young officer on the streets I wasn't violent. I could cause violence if needs be, towards people who wanted to be violent towards me, but by and large we weren't a violent sort of group.

It was clear that Mike felt that the 'older' group of officers to which he belonged were relatively powerless in the police organisation. As Martin (1992) shows, a subcultural or 'differentiation' perspective of organisa-tions often involves an engagement with the dynamics of power within that organisation. Where dichotomous or oppositional thinking defines subcultural boundaries, as in Mike's description of how younger officers were different from older officers like himself, one of the two subcultures is generally treated as having more power, status or value (1992: 84). Mike felt he was part of a subordinate subculture within the police. The older officers who shared his style of police work were in the minority: the rural police station in which he had felt comfortable had been disbanded. He now found himself in a police force with a dominant ethos to which he didn't subscribe. The disjunction between his attitude towards policing and that of the 'modern' police was encapsulated in the physical changes to the uniform. He resented carrying around the CS spray and truncheon, which he saw as physical evidence of a violent attitude of which he disapproved:[3]

> And they [young officers] look different, and I hate wearing CS sprays and a great big 2, 3 foot baton down the side. My truncheon was tucked in a side pocket, out of sight. It wasn't even used as an ornament, really. I can't get used to this aggressive mode of policing. You know, if I can't talk my way out of it, there's something wrong.

He felt out of place and distanced from his colleagues.

> I don't get on well with policemen, generally. [. . .] I never socialise with them.

In this way, Mike saw himself as unrepresentative of the dominant ethos in policing: an atypical police officer.[4]

Mike saw his difference from 'modern' police officers as an integral part of his move to the YOT. By joining the team, he was again taking an unconventional path in police work and distancing himself from a dominant occupational culture which he did not consider himself to share. The YOT offered an escape route from the displacement he was experiencing. But some ambivalence about his occupational identity may also have been necessary for him to have been able to consider taking a position on the YOT.

Moving to a YOT required Mike to take up a long-term (three years), full-time placement in a new organisation. It required a complete severance from the core roles and tasks of police work, emphasised by a physical separation from agency offices. Moreover, it required him to take on new duties, defined by the new structures in which he now worked. He would therefore necessarily become involved in new ways of thinking and working which distanced him further from the police service (Crawford 1994, 1997). As a consequence of these characteristics of inter-agency work, Crawford and Jones (1995) found that it is often denigrated among police staff as not being 'real police work' (1995: 29), especially in organisations where practitioners have to work outside their agency's traditional structures, roles and practices. A position in a YOT which involves an almost complete detachment from conventional police duties is thus likely to be perceived particularly pejoratively. But further, joining a YOT required the absorption into a kind of work which is generally denigrated in cultural terms. As Crawford (1997) argues, the perception of what constitutes 'real police work' is coloured by the highly gendered ethos of policing, and this is likely to have particular salience in the way the work of a YOT is perceived.

Joining a YOT involved becoming part of a predominantly social work team, working in social services offices and, potentially, carrying out social work duties such as case work. Such a close alliance with social services was likely to seem unappealing to many police staff. The dominant police culture of 'old fashioned machismo' (Reiner 2000: 97) and the promotion of those aspects of police work which emphasise action and excitement leads to the devaluing of work that does not have these characteristics (e.g. Foster et al. 2005). In particular, agencies that are perceived to take a less punitive approach to offenders are regarded pejoratively as having 'female' characteristics (Crawford 1997: 124). As an agency which espouses an emphatically 'welfarist' agenda and one perceived to have a high proportion of women staff, social work is especially likely to be invested with these gendered preconceptions. Crawford and Jones' finding that inter-agency work is perceived by many police officers as ' "social work" and "not real police work" and therefore "women's work" ' (1995: 29) is thus particularly likely to apply to the perception of the work of the YOT.

It is therefore likely that some sense of dislocation from the dominant ethos of the police was necessary for Mike to be able to consider taking up a post on a YOT. In particular, his detachment from what he saw as the police's 'masculine' ethos of aggression may have been a significant factor in enabling him to move to a differently gendered agency. But further, Mike felt it was his atypicality that made him an appropriate YOT member. Due to his detachment from the aggressive ambition of younger officers he was able to accommodate different working practices in a way which they could not:

> I feel that I blend in quite well with organisations, I'm not a prickly individual, I'm looking for the positive issues. I think many young officers coming into the job [as a YOT member] will be a bit too aggressive for the group . . . certainly their more in your face sort of attitude.

By distancing himself from the undesirable characteristics of younger officers, Mike was implicitly addressing the concerns of many of the social workers about a police officer joining the team. Their concerns were justified: many police officers had an approach to work which was wholly inappropriate for the type of work that the YOT demanded. However, within the boundaries of the occupation, there was a wide disparity in the way that officers identified with these norms. As an unrepresentative police officer, his team membership did not pose such problems.

Developing a police officer's role on the YOT

Mike's role was particularly at issue in the developing YOT. The only guidance offered by the Youth Justice Board at this stage, the Draft Guidance on Establishing Youth Offending Teams (Home Office et al. 1998), offered little direction. It suggested that a police role could involve liaising with wider crime reduction initiatives, organising and overseeing reparation work and overseeing curfew elements of bail conditions and court orders. But at the time of Mike's arrival, at this early stage in the development of the YOT, the Youth Justice Team had not yet begun to accommodate practitioners from different agencies and were not prepared to develop new practice of this sort. The emphasis was thus on Mike supporting the current work of the team. However, it was not clear what this might involve. It was generally assumed by all practitioners that staff from different agencies would provide specialist input to the existing work of the team. But while it seemed clear how practitioners from health, education or probation could contribute to case work, it was less obvious what specialist input a police officer could provide. There was thus more scope for flexibility in the development of Mike's role than in those of the other practitioners on the team. Consequently, there was also more scope for Mike to shape his role, thereby reflecting his expectations and understanding of his position on the team.

Putting aside 'real police work'

Soon after joining the YOT, Mike began to take part in the case work of practitioners on the team. As well as accompanying social workers on home visits, he started to provide sports activities for young people as part of their supervision. Social workers referred to him young people who showed an interest in sport. He took them running and boxing, accompanied them to football matches and ran 'outward bound' training courses, including lessons in first aid and navigation.

Mike seems to have regarded these activities as outside the remit of core police duties: they were not 'real police work'. In fact, it was this freedom from core police activities that initially attracted Mike to the YOT. He thought he would be able to develop his work in community sport in which he had previously been involved as a police officer, running a football team for young people:

> Well I've got a desire to continue working with youth, that . . . I've had for some time, I'm very keen on football, I'm very keen on sport, and I think there's a role to play in that area, for the introduction of sport to young people.

Equally, he felt it was this enthusiasm for 'non-police work' that made him attractive to the team. He described his appointment on the team as a reflection of the team's interest in his sporting skills over his professional expertise: at the interview 'I had my coaching head on that day, not my police head'.[5]

> I said originally, if they wanted a straight police officer, then maybe I'm not your man. But if they wanted a police officer with other interests, then I would be interested.

But Mike's interest in involving young people in sport differed from 'real police work' in a further way. He anticipated adopting an approach to working with young people which had less in common with the macho, action-oriented dominant ethos of policing than with the 'female' characteristics of social work. He described the core duties of the team in similar terms to many social workers, as outlined in the previous chapters. The primary aim of youth justice work was prevent reoffending. The mechanism by which this must be done was by changing the way young people thought about themselves: enhancing their confidence and sense of worth, or as Mike put it, encouraging them to feel 'proud':

> I would think a success in youth offending would be to take someone who has been involved in crime [. . .] to give them a pride in being part of a community, whereby criminal actions are low on their priority of involvement, apart from wanting to put other people straight in the way which they have been.

In Mike's view, sport was an ideal vehicle to bring about such changes. The skills young people learnt though sport would give them 'kudos within their peer group'. Indeed, some of the social workers on the team talked about the effects of Mike's training in sport in similar terms. For example, one practitioner described the effects of Mike's work in training one of her service users in boxing:

> The young man that I've got is now really really into training and self-discipline, motivation, it's really good to see, because by all accounts he's maybe a budding champion, which you know we could easily have lost this spark that he's got [. . .] it may not be much to some people but to this young person it is because he's doing something he's always always wanted to do, he's enjoying it, he's not on the streets creating havoc, he's very disciplined now, he's being trained not to use his fists in temper, but how to channel his energies into this hobby which is actually now more than a hobby, it's a career move. (Jenny, social worker)

But as well as the pride and skills that came with their achievement, Mike thought the activities would be a vehicle for him to develop a strong relationship with them. Mike described work with young people in strikingly similar terms to social workers. He explained that as a community police officer, he had run football teams with local young people, many of whom were offenders. He intended his training to encourage a 'rapport' with the boys and to develop their self-esteem – as he put it, 'treating them as a special person'. In this way, he thought the young people in his teams came to trust Mike and his colleagues, and they began to develop a civil and even social relationship with them: 'they started to come for a drink with us, converse'. Mike considered this evidence that they had decided to change their behaviour: he considered them to be 'good people', 'they certainly came on to the same area of thinking as I did'. He understood his work on the YOT to involve a similar emphasis on developing self-esteem and the relationship with the young person. YOT members needed to involve the young person in 'meaningful dialogue', so that they could 'engage properly with the client'. Communication with the young person was thus paramount, and this could only arise within a trusting and comfortable relationship. As he put it, 'people free up when they get relaxed'.

Although Mike considered this approach to young offenders to be an extension of his work in the local community as a police officer, he appeared to dissociate it from 'police work'. In fact, it seems that he felt his identity as a police officer would be detrimental to this kind of work. In particular, he was anxious to minimise the visibility of his identity by not wearing uniform:

I've no love of uniform, I can see it being quite damaging in some instances where we're trying to work with young people.

He thought young offenders would be 'frosty' if he was in uniform, and this would inhibit the 'freeing up' necessary for the development of a communicative relationship. This concern arises from a symbolic function inherent in police identity. As Reiner puts it, police officers 'represent authority, backed by the potential use of legitimate force . . . a symbol of an impersonal and universally accepted law' (Reiner 2000: 88). In other words, individual officers are invested with the weight of the law and the implicit threat of sanctions. Mike felt this intrinsic communication would prevent him being able to engage young people in 'meaningful dialogue'. In other words, the messages conveyed by Mike's identity as a police officer would prevent Mike from doing the work that he considered his very unrepresentativeness enabled him to do.

In this way, Mike felt it was his atypicality as a police officer that was both integral to his move to the YOT, made him an appropriate member and shaped his understanding of his work on the team. Indeed, he felt he should minimise his police identity by removing his uniform in order to be effective in his work.

An atypical police officer?

However, there was a fundamental dilemma in Mike's position as a police officer on the YOT. For while he felt it was his unrepresentativeness as a police officer that was integral to his move to the YOT and made him an appropriate member, his role on the team was to be a representative of the police.

This dilemma was reflected in Mike's ambivalence about wearing police uniform. While he felt the communicative element of his identity as a police officer was potentially detrimental to his work on the YOT, he felt this same communication of authority must also be an intrinsic part of his role on the team. For example, the presence of a police officer might make young offenders take seriously the work of the team. So, while he wanted to minimise his identity by not wearing his uniform, he also felt wearing police uniform and proclaiming his occupational identity was also a potential benefit to the team:

> However, I do see the benefits sometimes of putting a uniform on, possibly as strange as it may seem, I think it will have a good effect when we're bringing people into this building, where they're coming into *our* domain, and there happens to be a police officer. And it always is a sobering effect on many people when they walk into a police station, and be interviewed by a police officer, on our turf, and I think it could have a sobering effect here, if a police officer sat in some of the interviews.

This conflict about the minimising or declaring of his police identity reflects the ambivalent position in which Mike found himself. The work with young people and sport was understood by most team members, including Mike, as something that he could offer because of his personal skills and experience. It was these aspects of work that Mike felt would be jeopardised by the communicative elements of his police identity. But at the same time, he was aware that he represented the police as a whole – or, at least, aspects of police authority – and this indicated other functions of his role as a YOT member. The following pages explore what he understood these functions to be.

Representing the police: 'a hardening of the shell'

Mike understood his function as a police officer on a YOT as something separate from the duties or powers of the police service. Without being able to employ the core tasks of the police, what he embodied as a police officer was necessarily divorced from what he did. Instead, he understood the role of the police in terms of an approach to work. Mike described the key purpose of the introduction of police on Youth Offending Teams as bringing 'a hardening of the shell'. He explained:

> The police officer's general attitude is one of having a stricter guideline towards offenders.

What Mike understood by this 'stricter guideline' became apparent when he started co-working cases with social work staff.

A social worker, Sally, had gone to visit a young man who had recently been displaying increasingly violent and unpredictable behaviour. During this visit, he was hostile and aggressive towards Sally, and she became anxious about her safety. Graham, the team leader, decided that she should take Mike with her when she next visited the house.[6]

Mike's response to this incident was that the boy should be reported and possibly charged. Sally was horrified at this idea, and attributed it to conflicting aims between the two occupational groups:

> Mike comes in with the heavy-handed approach, whereas I'm thinking more about, well, this child needs help, he's a child still, he's only 17, he needs some help, [Mike]'s like you know he wants lifting, we'll take him down and we'll give him a good seeing to, or get him charged, or whatever, whereas I think social workers will tend to come from the point of view that well, this child needs help as well.

However, the differences in Mike's approach to this young man were more complex than this. Despite the implicit assumption that charging someone with an offence was incompatible with 'help', as Mike saw it, taking formal action against this boy's behaviour was an essential part of helping him.

> You don't help the person by not reporting it. There may be one of a number of issues as to why they were acting like that [. . .] but unless it gets reported and resolved, you can't take on the task of why they get involved in crime.

In other words, the apparent incompatibility between the responses of Mike and Sally didn't arise from an obvious difference in the purpose of the intervention. In working with young offenders Mike was not merely trying to 'lock them up' or 'nick them' as many of the social workers had assumed, but understood his work in the same terms as many social work staff, as 'help'. Instead, the difference between Mike and Sally's responses was grounded in a difference in assumptions about the nature of offending behaviour and what help would involve. While Sally saw the aggression of this boy as an indicator of underlying needs, Mike understood it as a way of 'testing' the professionals who were trying to work with him.

> The word gets round very quickly within this sort of area as what you can and what you can't get away with. And once they see a weak link, they will use that weak link every time.

This interaction was thus seen as a battle for control. The ability of the boy to threaten Sally was evidence that he 'controls too much'. The role of youth justice workers was therefore to teach young people that such behaviour was unacceptable.

> And if they control us, the people out there, their peers, haven't got a chance. We have to stand up to them. I think that's what the YOTs are all about. Standing up to the people who've come to the last chance hotel.

In this way, while there seemed to be differences in Mike's approach to work with young offenders, these appeared to be more complex than was generally understood in the team. Like social work staff, Mike understood youth justice work goals as oriented to 'helping' young people. But as discussed in Chapter 3, the notion of 'help' accommodates multiple meanings and is in part dependent on an understanding of the problems at hand. Mike seemed to understand offending behaviour and the appropriate responses to it rather differently to many social workers. These differences appeared to be intrinsically connected to his occupational background.

Firstly, Mike's conception of offenders as controlling and testing is likely to have arisen from a construction of offending behaviour developed through his training and experience as a police officer. As Mary Douglas argues, to keep their identifiable continuing form, institutions need to gain legitimacy by 'a distinctive grounding in nature and in reason' (1986: 112). They help construct reality for their members by providing 'a set of analogies with which to explore the world and with which to justify the naturalness and reasonableness of the instituted rules'. In this way, they shape the way their members 'think'. The differences in Mike's understanding of offending behaviour seem to reflect broad differences in his working assumptions, which were clear in comparison with the accounts of offending behaviour offered by social work staff. As outlined in Chapter 3, although these accounts were often contradictory and unclear, certain core elements were apparent which appeared to represent 'received ideas' (Rojek et al. 1988) in social work. Many social workers tended to locate the explanations for offending behaviour in young people's social and economic circumstances, and as a result young people were not seen as wholly responsible for their offending behaviour. Some social workers described their service-users as 'victims'. Consequently, if the practitioners' relationship broke down with the young person, it was seen as their responsibility to mend it. For example, Sally described a difficult session with a girl she was supervising:

> I'm tired, I've worked with [young person] for a long time and she's really difficult . . . I've stuck it out, it's been really difficult, but that's what you get paid to do, isn't it.

In contrast, Mike's account of the incident above placed the responsibility for the boy's threatening behaviour wholly on the offender. He felt it was a conscious attempt to control the interaction with Sally: the boy's motivations were manipulative. Consequently, the appropriate response was to reassert the practitioner's authority:

> That can't go on . . . and if it needs be that this person needs to be frogmarched to the nearest police station to be interviewed, that's the way it's got to happen.

In general, Mike's accounts of offending behaviour seemed to display a wariness absent from those of social work staff. Offenders, such as the young man involved in this incident were more likely to be seen as 'controlling', 'manipulative' and looking to exploit practitioners. This is likely to be a product of a suspiciousness which has been considered central to policing: something both deliberately encouraged by training and intrinsic to the particular conditions of police work (e.g. Skolnick 1966). As Reiner puts it, 'Police need to develop fine-grained cognitive maps of the social world, so that they can readily predict and handle the behaviour of a wide range of others, in frequently fraught encounters, without losing authority' (2000: 91). It is possible, then, that Mike's interpretation of the motivations behind this boy's disruptive behaviour and the appropriate response to it is an example of the way his training and experience as a police officer has influenced the way he constructs social reality. In this way, it is an essential part of his identity as a police officer.

Secondly, Mike felt that, as a police officer, he was more effective at 'standing up' to young offenders. In part, this was a function of the communicative element of police identity. Mike thought the authority that he represented made him a deterrent to offenders merely by his presence:

> And if someone's stepping out of line they're less likely to think they can get away with some of the things that go on if a police officer is present. And I would hope that would be the case.

But in addition, Mike felt he was able to be more effective in work with young people because he was liberated from their occupational history. Mike felt the norms and conventions which had emerged in social work constrained them to the point of impotence. For example, he described co-supervising two brothers with Tom, a social worker. Incredulous, he explained that Tom had made the supervision appointment for 1 pm 'because Tom said the boys don't get up until dinner time'. When they arrived at the boys house, their mother told them that the boys were still in bed.

> [Tom] said 'oh, OK then', and I said 'well, bloody tell them to get up' and went inside. Tom was hanging on my sleeve, saying, 'we'll come back later'.

Despite Tom's reluctance, Mike 'got them invited in':

> This is where the police training comes in, you don't just barge in but almost, 'you know, can I come in, duck, thanks'. She made us a cup of tea. Tom was saying, we don't come in unless we're invited. I said, 'she did invite us, she's made you a cup of tea'.

Mike knew that this way of 'getting invited' into a service-user's house was not acceptable to social workers. As he put it:

> Tom had beads of sweat coming down his face. I was shouting up the stairs, 'bloody get up'.

When the boys still refused to get out of bed, Mike threatened to go into their bedroom and pour a glass of water over them. Tom refused to let him: 'he was saying, "you can't do that, you can't say that".'

Mike attributed Tom's reluctance to enter the house and act once inside it to a culture of anxiety that had surrounded social work since the 'Pindown' inquiry in the late 1980s, which was strongly critical of the regime for restraining children in four Staffordshire children's homes during the mid to late 1980s (Levy and Kahan 1991). This had become a critical event for social workers in the team, something that they felt had put the perceived legitimacy of their practice in question.[7] Mike felt that social workers were 'frightened to death' of allegations of abuse in the aftermath of the inquiry. He felt this had effectively rendered them impotent in their work with young people.

> They wouldn't dream of going into a house uninvited, they certainly wouldn't dream of going into a bedroom.

Mike was equally aware that social workers wouldn't use the same 'friendly aggressive manner' that he did in his interactions with young people. Yet his experience in police work had taught him that this was the most effective way of communicating with them:

> You have to talk on their level, you know, I could say, 'young man, please would you get out of bed' and he'd be 'pig off'.

So, Mike thought Tom's discomfort over his actions and manner in this incident wasn't because his intervention was unacceptable in itself, it was that Tom feared the repercussions of this kind of behaviour. Mike thought social workers felt equally frustrated at their inability to act:

> The social workers want to punch through this coating of wax that has been put over them, because of Pindown.

He thought social workers were paralysed by fear of complaints, by the weight of paperwork that had become necessary to 'cover their backs'. As a police officer, Mike didn't share the history of Pindown or the resulting 'social worker bashing' (Carlen 1992) from the public and media. Consequently, he felt liberated from what he perceived as a stifling culture of anxiety. He felt he had more freedom to act and could potentially be more effective.

> I guarantee that if Bob [second police officer to join the team (in October 1999)] and I had been there he would have been out of bed in ten minutes and talking to us.

The 'hardening of the shell' that Mike understood to be the essential role of the police officers on Youth Offending Teams thus involved a more stringent attitude to young offenders who refused to comply with the requirements of the team's interventions. As he put it, young offenders were not being 'brought to book' for their behaviour:

> There's got to be a hardening towards what we actually do with them . . . we give them too many chances.

But as this implies, Mike also thought this 'stricter guideline' needed to be directed towards the practitioners on the team. Young people had been able to abuse their relationship with the Youth Justice Team because social workers allowed them to:

> Mike's said, oh you've been soft, it's gone on too long now, and that sort of thing. (Sally, social worker)

In other words, and reflecting the sentiments of the White Paper preceding the Crime and Disorder Act (Home Office 1997d), Mike felt social workers had been inactive, colluding and excusing. The introduction of the police officers with the formation of Youth Offending Teams was an indication that this way of working had to change. As Mike explained:

> I don't see that we should have left it that long for social services to allow people to get away with the sort of incidents that take place.

Consequently, the 'hardening of the shell' that Mike brought to the team was also a 'hardening' of the attitudes of the team members: he represented a change of ethos in youth justice work.

An unrepresentative representative of the police

In this way, Mike demonstrated two aspects of his understanding of his identity as a police officer on the YOT. On the one hand, he was unrepresentative of the dominant ethos of the police. It was this that accounted for his move to the YOT and which allowed him to undertake work with an approach similar to of the social services staff. On the other, he was a representative of an agency which subscribed to a 'harder' and 'stricter' approach to youth justice work. Both these positions were integral to Mike's understanding of his role on the team, and both were held simultaneously.

This dual position accounts for some apparent tensions in Mike's understanding of his role. Through his interventions with the YOT, Mike explained he hoped to give young people 'kudos within their peer group' and 'give them pride in being part of their community' by teaching them 'genuine life skills' and 'heighten[ing] their self-esteem'. Yet he also talked of the work of the team in more punitive terms: young people were 'being punished', 'rebuked' or 'reprimanded' by the intervention of the team, they were being asked to 'say they're sorry for the first time in their lives'. Mike's understanding of the importance of developing a good, 'meaningful' relationship with the young people he supervised meant that he felt that it was necessary to put in a good deal of time and patience in the supervision visits: he considered a 'sensible visit' to be two hours and took young people for walks, coffee, on training sessions and to football matches to make them feel relaxed. Yet his understanding of the responsibility of the young person for their behaviour means that he also criticised the team's practice of taking them on such visits: young people weren't 'put out':

> We do all the running, we do all the ferrying, we fetch them, we give them the bus fare, if they can't get the bus, we go and fetch them, if they haven't had their breakfast, we take them to McDonald's ... it's no way of learning, no way.

Complexity and clarification

Mike's understanding of his occupational identity as a police officer on a YOT was thus complex and contradictory. It was far removed from the unproblematic attachment to an occupational 'agenda' that some of the social workers described. Instead, the ambiguities of Mike's experiences and his fluctuating sense of disjunction from his home agency indicates the complexity of what it is to be an occupational member. It suggests that even if occupational members are able to describe the goals and values of their work – so, for example, if police officers understand that their work has a punitive orientation – members will vary in the ways in which they understand, identify or attach themselves to these.

However, these complexities did not seem to have been apparent to the other practitioners in the team in the first few months after Mike's arrival. Although Mike saw himself as an atypical officer, his new colleagues saw him primarily as a 'police officer', and thus someone they felt anxious about working with. They were therefore likely to invest in him their stereotypical preconceptions of police officers. While the complexities of occupational experiences appeared to be recognised within each agency (as described both here and in Chapter 3), across agency boundaries ambiguities were clarified and eliminated.

But in addition, the communication of Mike's occupational identity was complicated by his tendency to play on his colleagues' prejudices. He knew that social workers also thought that police culture tended to be characterised by a aggressive and macho ethos and guessed that it would be assumed that he shared these characteristics. Consequently, he decided to enjoy playing the part he felt was expected of him:

I think my verbally aggressive stance toward clients within the perimeters of the office is nothing more than playing devil's advocate a lot of the time. [I'd say to social workers] oh, give them a bunch of fives, that's what they need, and see what their reaction is [. . .] people that I'm working with do react to that, they don't know me from Adam, effectively yet, they don't know where I'm coming from, but I just do like to see the reaction of some of them, to what they're thinking, that is one of upset initially, 'you can't do that, you can't do that' you know.

This teasing was taken seriously by some social work staff. For example, soon after Mike's arrival on the team, the team leader commented:

Mike has said a few worrying things, like sex offenders should be shot. People have asked me, why don't I just tell him that he shouldn't say these things . . .

Mike's teasing illustrated some of the difficulties of his position as a police officer in the team. While his description of 'winding up' the social workers was ostensibly intended to illustrate his detachment from the aggression indicated by his language, his ability to take such a 'verbally aggressive stance' shows his detachment from the occupational norms of social work. It is unlikely that social work staff would have found it acceptable to talk about their service-users in this way, even in jest. It's likely that the shocked reaction of his colleagues that he is describing here didn't come from the belief that he was seriously advocating punching children, but that he was able to say such things at all. In other words, the striking thing about this language is that Mike feels able to use it.

But by teasing the social workers in this way, Mike risked reinforcing some practitioners' anxieties about a police officer joining the team. Like many of the social workers, he depicted an unproblematic conflict between the two occupational groups. In this way, the complexities of his attitudes and relationship with his identity as a police officer was obscured.

However, the clarification of practitioners' complex experience as members of an occupational group raised questions for the development of the team. In the case of the apparent polarisation of the positions of Mike and the social service staff, how would Mike be integrated into the team? How would his role develop? And would the apparent incompatibility of his approach threaten the cohesion of the team, as some social workers anticipated? As Sally, a social worker, put it:

I suppose we have sort of worried about that [effects on the cohesion of the team], especially with a police officer coming into the team, because of different ways of thinking, different rules, different values, and I'm sure it isn't going to be easy.

These issues will be explored in the following chapters.

Notes

1 This felt change in the experience of policing might reflect pressures produced by rising crime rates. Mike's perception of a change in ethos among younger officers might also reflect more general societal attitudes about the legitimacy of the police. As Reiner (2000) argues, a previous 'mythology' of the police as a 'species of social service delivering good works to a harmonious community of satisfied customers' (2000: 108) has been replaced over the second half of the twentieth century, and particularly in the last 30 years, by a politicised view in which the police are seen as increasingly unrepresentative and alienated from those groups they typically police (2000: 70).

2 A similar difference between urban and rural styles of policing has been noted in work by Shapland and Vagg (1988) and Cain (1973). In particular, Cain's study of 'county' and city police forces in the early 1960s attributes the 'stand offish' attitudes Mike describes to an urban style of policing. City policing was characterised by alienation from those communities policed, and an 'almost confrontation-style relationship' (1973: 232) between the police and the community. In contrast, rural police were more closely integrated into the communities they policed, tending towards a cooperative, informal style of policing characterised by 'empathetic understanding' (1973: 228). Such differences are likely to be explained by the different conditions of policing in rural and urban areas.

3 It seems many of the social workers also saw these weapons as evidence of a tendency towards violence among police officers. Mike's CS spray and baton needed to be kept in a locked room to comply with police regulations. The storage was discussed at length in two team meetings and in numerous informal conversations with the team leader. The extent of these discussions appeared to outweigh the actual practical difficulties with storing the equipment (it was eventually decided to store it in a locker in a gents toilet) and it appeared that the team's preoccupation with the equipment represented anxieties about the implications of the introduction of the police into the team.

4 It was notable that Bob, the second police officer on the team who joined in October, also described feelings of displacement in the police. He was critical of what he saw as a corrupt and lazy management. He worked with Mike as a community police officer in the local semi-rural town before joining the team, and was thus part of the group of older officers who, according to Mike,' 'all thought the same way'. Bob was married to a social worker, which the social workers on the team saw as significant in distancing him from 'typical' police officers.

5 Some of the social workers on the team may not have perceived such a clear distinction between Mike's interests in sport and his identity as a police officer.

Instead, it is possible that the encouragement of Mike's role in this kind of activity was also a reflection of key practitioners' assumptions about his identity as a police officer. The association of the police with sport may reflect the team's perception of the 'macho' nature of policing. No female offenders were referred to Mike, and the types of sports he became involved with were generally competitive or aggressive, such as football or boxing.

6 As Sally later said, this was like using Mike as a 'bodyguard'. It is likely he was fitted into this role partly because he was physically more able to protect himself and Sally from any potential attack. However, it is also possible that his identity as a police officer was thought to instil authority and an implicit threat of sanction, as described above. In addition, it may reflect social work staff's gendered assumptions of the role of the police officer.

7 The Pindown inquiry appeared to have particular resonance in the team and is referred to by practitioners in various contexts throughout this book. In part, this may be due to its geographical proximity: as a team in the Midlands, the site of criticism appeared literally as well as symbolically close to home.

Part 2

Change and Ambiguity

In September 1999, most of the remaining members of the Youth Offending Team joined the team. The education officer, probation officer, police officer and probation assistant were joined by an administration manager who headed a new administrative team of four people. Representatives from voluntary agencies who would be working in partnership with the YOT were introduced to the team. The only positions still to be filled were those of the management staff. Graham, who had been 'acting up' as team leader and operations manager was eventually appointed team leader the following month. The operations manager was appointed in November and took up post in early December. The team had now expanded to 29 people from its original 16.

The complete team met for the first time at a team meeting at the beginning of September. The meeting was led by Graham, the team leader, who emphasised that the team was now in a period of change:

> These are times of great change, with people coming, people going. But I feel there hasn't been space for emptiness to settle with people going, as new people are coming in.

The feeling of change was reinforced by Mark, the YOT manager, who held his first team meeting a few weeks later. A suitable building had at last been found for the team's relocation and the meeting was held at the new site. Although the offices were dirty and in need of considerable redevelopment, it demonstrated to the team that the move was underway and thus so was their transition to a YOT. Mark told the team that the YOT would now progress rapidly: 'I just want to get on with it now.'

However, while Graham and Mark stressed that the team was in a process of rapid change, it was also evident that it was unclear what these changes would involve. The roles of the new staff were uncertain. It was not clear how practitioners would function in a team. There were still two permanent management staff to be appointed. There would be an increase in workloads, which would increase further when the new orders came in. Graham emphasised to the team that he had no solutions to these concerns:

> I'm very aware that it's very new stuff to everybody, including me [. . .] We'll sort it out, one way or another, we'll work it out, out of adversity.

This part describes the way in which this period of change and uncertainty was experienced by the team. How did roles and practice develop in the team? What were the effects of this period of change for practitioners' sense of occupational identity and belonging? And how was their ambiguity and confusion managed?

Chapter 5

Joining an established team

The arrival of the rest of the staff from partner agencies in September 1999 brought about a dramatic and sudden transformation to the appearance of the team. The expansion in its size and the new multi-agency composition represented a clear break from its previously 'settled', social work membership. This was the transformation that many social workers had anticipated would mark the beginning of the new YOT: with the introduction of staff from partner agencies it would no longer be possible to think of the team as a social work organisation. However, when new staff arrived, it became apparent that the identity of the team was at issue. Rather than becoming part of a new, inter-agency organisation, practitioners felt they were joining an established, unchanging Youth Justice Team.

This chapter explores the problems of joining the team from a partner agency. It explores questions of power and exclusion, and the way these played out in the development of the roles of new staff. What is an inter-agency role? How were these defined in the Midlands team? Who defined them? And what were the consequences of the definition of their roles for new practitioners' experiences of team membership?

Joining an established team

The identity of the team had long been at issue. As described in Part 1, social work staff had known that the team was in a process of transition, yet the continuity with key elements of their working life had led them to feel that change was far off. When new staff came into post, the identity of team which they had joined remained ambiguous. Although their arrival marked such a clear departure from the social work team, there had still been no formal delineation of the end of the Youth Justice Team and the beginning of a new organisation. The team would not officially become a YOT for a further six months. Unlike practitioners from partner agencies, social work staff had not applied for new jobs on the YOT, but continued in their previous posts. Moreover, their work continued unchanged. There were no new orders yet available to the courts and no new multi-agency practice developed in the team. As Mike, a police officer, argued, such continuity deprived the team of an indication of the start of the YOT: new ways of working would provide 'a clear demarcation, this is a new way of dealing with the system'.

The identity of the team was further confused by problems with its premises. As described above, the team was currently based in a building owned by the Department of Social Services and occupied solely by social services teams. The offices were thus seen as the domain of a social services Youth Justice Team: as the new health officer put it, it was 'their building'. The planned relocation to new premises would declare the start of a new, multi-agency organisation. Colin, a social worker, explained:

> I think we do need these new premises where we can all go, we are not all then under the umbrella of social services which I think everybody to a certain degree thinks of it now.

Just as the new staff arrived, a suitable building was at last found – an old prefab building in a complex of working factories, intended for their sole use. The confirmation that new premises had been acquired made practitioners feel that at last the team was also able to progress:

> We will be a new team then. It won't be people joining our team, which it seems like at the moment. We'll be starting as a team, I think [. . .] we're all moving there together. (Tom, social worker)

However, the move to the new building was increasingly delayed. There were difficulties with fire regulations, insurance issues relating to the use of the building and negotiations over the decoration of the property. The date of the move became deferred from September to Christmas, and finally to the end of March the following year. The team became increasingly pessimistic about the move: the new office premises became known as the 'office promises'. Without the new offices, practitioners felt the transition into the YOT could not take place:

> To me personally, it feels though we're in limbo, it's always quite nice to welcome new colleagues on the team but I mean, the bone

of contention is we can't settle in this building which we'd all very much like to do. (Julie, social worker)

These important aspects of continuity with the Youth Justice Team confused the identity of the team. As Mark, the YOT manager put it, practitioners were denied a 'positive affirmation' of the transformation of the team in which they worked: there was no clear indication that it had become a new, multi-agency organisation. But further, the continuity deprived the team of an opportunity to renegotiate their practice and roles: to discuss how the team was going to function. Without a break in its routines, the team remained structured by the same social relationships, hierarchies and practices: the 'degree of organisation' that Elias and Scotson (1994) argue is a defining feature of 'established' groups. Consequently, many practitioners felt that rather than forming a new, multi-agency organisation, new staff were joining a cohesive, established social work team. For example, at the first team meeting with the new staff Graham, the team leader, announced 'this is a social work group of people with other people coming to join it'. Or as Tom, a social worker, put it, new practitioners were like 'a bolt-on team, they're bolted on to us':

It's probably because our work hasn't altered at all yet, they're just added on really, because our work hasn't changed at all, it'll change next year when the new orders come in obviously, so basically we're still carrying on the same work as we've always done, and we've got extra staff.

In other words, the boundaries of the team appeared to remain defined by the same claims about 'us and them' that had delineated the Youth Justice Team: practitioners from partner agencies were outsiders in a social work team. As Karen put it:

One of the challenges is to become part of the team, because, well I feel very much like the new girl you know. (Karen, health officer)

Being an outsider: exclusion and disjunction

The difference in the extent to which they felt integrated into the team had important consequences for the status of new practitioners. As Elias and Scotson (1994) argue, differences in cohesion and integration are significant aspects of power differentials. Some staff from partner agencies were concerned that they were not equal members of the team: as Mike described it, they did not have 'a feeling of being in the organisation'. For example, some practitioners felt their 'outsider' status was reflected in the physical arrangements in the offices. The large team room was unable to cope with the sudden influx of staff. There were not enough desks. The new staff brought with them files, books and boxes which the team room was unable to accommodate. The office appeared messy and chaotic: staff joked about sitting on each others laps. However, because they had long been resident in the offices, social work staff had the use of desks and filing cabinets and had organised the space and the facilities. Some new practitioners found themselves without the use basic facilities such as a desk or chair. As a result, they felt unwelcome and excluded: that they didn't have 'a place' in the team.

I was a bit worried when I first came because they didn't know I was coming, and I didn't have a desk, didn't have a chair, and I was quite a bit concerned because I felt oh, hang on a minute, I just thought, do they really want us here or not [. . .] I know it sounds stupid it's just being given a desk and a space is very important to me, that's where I'm going to be working from, so I've got . . . . I've got a place. (Louise, probation officer)

But practitioners' felt their outsider status was demonstrated most potently by confusion surrounding their roles. While social work practitioners were able to continue with their practices unchanged, new staff had no clear function in the team.

For many new staff, the work of the emergent Youth Offending Team involved a marked departure from important aspects of their previous working lives. The probation staff had not worked with young people before. Andy, a probation service assistant, described them as 'totally different clients, totally different' who would necessitate a fundamental change in working practice. Both Andy and Louise, the probation officer, envisaged that this difference in approach would involve a move away from their previous focus on offending behaviour. As Louise explained, work would no longer concentrate on the 'criminogenic needs' of the offender – those factors such as anti-social attitudes, drug dependency, low-level education skills, poor cognitive and interpersonal skills which 'contribute directly to offending behaviour' (Vennard and Hedderman 1998: 103) – but other aspects of young people's lives.

Underlying this shift in scope was a deeper difference in understanding of work with offenders: probation work encouraged a distinction between criminogenic and non-criminogenic needs (e.g. Chapman and Hough 1998), while youth justice social work did not. This difference in approach was all pervasive: it was even reflected in the terminology used in the team. Louise explained that probation staff are expected to refer to the people they supervise as 'offenders':

They are here because they have to be and they have to recognise they are here because of their offending.

In contrast, the preferred term among youth justice social workers was 'service-users':

It's not labelling someone as being an offender, because social services meets lots of needs that aren't just offending. It isn't just offending behaviour we're doing, is it. (Alan, social worker)

This difference in understanding of offending behaviour therefore created a dilemma for Andy and Louise. With such a different approach to work with young offenders, how could their professional experience be applied to their new roles? As Andy put it:

Probation is getting more and more to do with enforcement, and challenging offending behaviour, specifically looking at their offending behaviour [. . .] They [social workers] focus on other things. Offending behaviour is possibly not even on the list. (Andy, probation service assistant)

New practitioners faced other difficulties. Some had no previous experience of working with offending behaviour. For example, Karen, the health officer, explained that while some of her previous service users might have offended, the offending behaviour was not the focus of her practice:

I mean in my previous line you accepted that clients offended but it really wasn't that much of an interest to us, you know.

Some staff found the focus on offending a difficult adjustment to make:

Some of the offences, I know they're not just the majority, but some of them are extremely serious, you know, the acts of violence and aggression, is something that I'd not really thought about. (Karen, health officer)

And the nature of the work and the offending that goes on is completely different too, because my experience has not been to deal with that side, particularly with youngsters. I have an awful lot to learn [. . .] So I'm naive, really, to the capabilities of the 13 and 14 year olds, well any of them really. (Cath, education officer)

Karen also found that working with people on a compulsory basis involved a fundamental shift in the way she thought about her work. As she explained:

> It's a bit about me getting in my head that it's a different way of working. If somebody didn't turn up at [Drugs Agency], that's OK, it was up to them [. . .] it was really very much their choice whether they turned up. So there is a contrast completely to this.

In this way, practitioners from partner agencies felt their new positions required an entirely new approach to their work. They could not simply adapt their previous practice to the YOT. However, without the development of new practice in the team there was nothing to take the place of their old routines. They thus found themselves in a state of disjunction: disconnected both from their home agency and their new organisation. This position left many new staff feeling out of place and superfluous. The lack of a clear function in the team left them anxious and uncomfortable. Some were concerned that their previous skills and experience were now redundant and that they now found themselves essentially unqualified and inexperienced in a new organisation. As Karen said:

> And it is sitting back and thinking, no I'm not totally de-skilled, although all this is new and it's a barrage of information, my skills are still there, but at the moment, they're on the back burner, to a degree, while I'm taking in all this new information.

Practitioners' concerns about being excluded from the work of the team were exacerbated by their bewilderment at the language used in carrying it out. The technical vocabulary of the courts and terminology used in youth justice social work – 'on licence', 'area office' and so on – was further obscured by the prolific use of abbreviations such as PACE, TWOC, PSR. As Karen, the health officer, explained, this was incomprehensible to those who had just joined:

> It's almost like a different language to me you know, because they use a lot of abbreviations, don't they. So social work is a different language to me, it's a different language. The court language is completely different.

The prevalence of abbreviations in youth justice work contrasted with Karen's previous professional language:

> In nursing, years ago, [they] said no abbreviations. You can't write sort of abbreviations in notes, nurses used to write, or doctors would

write up, one tablet two ds, or one bd, and that all stopped, because it was seen as not safe to do that. Coming into somewhere that does abbreviations is very different to me.

Technical jargon was thought to be 'not safe' because it was excluding: the language spoken by practitioners was not shared by their clients, which could lead to potentially dangerous misunderstandings. Practitioners new to the YOT were similarly excluded by the use of jargon.[1] The impenetrability of the language used by social workers was thus an obstacle to the integration of new staff. Fluency in the language helped delineate the boundaries of the team, excluding those who could not yet understand it.

The feelings of exclusion experienced by new practitioners were not easily resolved. Contrary to the their expectations, there was no process of induction to explain what shape their roles might take or to train them in the current work of the team:

I thought I'd be shadowing, training quite quickly, but trying to bring me up to speed, an almost an intense period of induction to get me trained up to then move on, [. . .] work through it bit by bit, get trained up, feel confident in it, and start doing it. Whereas it's been very laid back. (Andy, probation service assistant)

In addition, most team meetings in this period were cancelled. Team meetings were the only formal forum in which the team could meet as a whole, and as such provided team members with an important source of information about their roles and status in relation to each other (see Chapter 7). The cancellation of team meetings thus deprived practitioners of the informal induction that these meetings allowed.

I don't feel introduced to people [. . .] as in we haven't collectively met since I've been here as a team, been introduced all together, where we're from, and then for them to know where I'm from as well, and then for us all to establish where our roles are in the team, and I think that's all part of the introduction. (Andy, probation service assistant)

In the absence of a formal induction, practitioners spent most of the their first months in the team shadowing social workers, attending court and PACE interviews and accompanying social work staff on supervision visits. But as they did not know whether this work would eventually form part of their roles on the team, some felt it merely reinforced their feelings of exclusion. As Cath, the education officer, put it:

If I don't know what I'm doing, I'm wasting this time. Today I went to court, is that a waste of time? I've been here over two months and I still don't know something like that. If I'm not going to court, then what am I meant to be doing?

Yet although having a function in the team appeared a crucial part of practitioners' feelings of team membership, questions of the roles of the new staff were not easily resolved. Instead, the development of their roles indicated the complexity of what it means to be a practitioner in an inter-agency team.

Developing an inter-agency role

A central feature of inter-agency working is some degree of fusing or melding of relations between collaborating agencies, where staff may become involved in new ways of working defined by the inter-agency structure (Crawford 1997). Similarly, it was clear from early official guidance that staff joining a YOT were encouraged to surpass their accustomed roles. While some degree of specialist input could be maintained, practitioners could take on work suited to the inter-agency team as well as those elements that flowed directly from their own professional background (Home Office et al. 1998). The central question for all YOTs was therefore the extent to which staff provided specialist expertise in the work of the team and how far they became 'merged' into what one practitioner termed 'a generic YOT worker', sharing common responsibilities.

However, both these aspects of inter-agency roles were far from straightforward. How are the specialisms of different agencies defined? How far should staff set aside their accustomed professional identity in place of that of the inter-agency organisation? How far was this tolerable, or indeed possible? And, in an organisation that had yet to take shape, what was a 'generic YOT worker' and how was it understood? As the following pages describe, the way in which these issues unfolded was intrinsically connected to the power differentials between the 'outsiders' from partner agencies and the established team.

Defining specialist expertise

It was generally assumed in the team that a core role of practitioners from partner agencies would be to provide specialist expertise to supplement cases held by social workers. As Graham, the team leader, put it, 'we can have a central work approach, but others can help on specific issues'. For example, social work staff would refer young people with particular education needs to Cath, the education officer, who would be able to provide skilled interventions and access to resources. Many social work staff found this an extremely practical and important contribution to the work of the team. For example, one said:

> Sometimes we can make half a dozen phone calls trying to get to a particular person [. . .] now I feel as though we've got direct access into that service whereas before I don't think we had [. . .] we've got link people in the building and they will have links into different resources, different disciplines, specialisms, and I think the knock-on effect is that hopefully it will all gel together, so that we have a comprehensive package for young people. (Julie, social worker)

However, some new staff had a different understanding of the specialist skills they might provide. For example, while Cath anticipated that part of her work would involve assisting social workers, she had also anticipated providing different kinds of educational support and was frustrated that she did not have the opportunity to put these into practice:

> There's a desperate need for prevention in schools across the city, and that's what I want to be doing [. . .] [I thought that] I'd be doing group work within schools [. . .] I would like to be able to offer schools more, I'd like to have a role, perhaps piloting a preventative project in schools [. . .] I just think I'd like to be able to do something preventative, you know, do a ten week programme and if it works take it somewhere else.

This kind of preventative work would have fulfilled the requirements for measures for early intervention emphasised in the reconfiguration of youth justice interventions following the Crime and Disorder Act (see Chapter 1) and could thus reasonably be seen as part of the work of the team. But the premise that Cath would supplement the existing work of the social work staff precluded the creation of the opportunities for such initiatives.

The ability to define what constituted the specialist input of practitioners from partner agencies reflected the power differentials within the team (see also Crawford and Jones 1995). As the established group, social work staff were in a more powerful position to influence the definition of the roles of new staff. Not only were practitioners from partner agencies newcomers to a cohesive team, but they were strangers to each other. As a result, they lacked organisation and cohesion as a group. They were thus unable to 'close their own ranks and fight back' (Elias and Scotson 1994: xxii).

It became apparent that many of the social work staff assumed they had considerable control over the allocation of tasks to other practitioners in the team. For example, one social worker described how social work staff had involved new team members in their casework, and added:

> I think we need to be a bit more imaginative about how we use Mike [police officer] and Karen [health officer]. (Sally, social worker)

The assumption that practitioners would supplement the existing work of the team excluded any other interpretation of their roles. As one social worker acknowledged:

> I'm quite aware I'm talking from my perspective all the time, you see, about how they can help me do my job, not the other way round. (Tom, social worker)

Not only was the assumption that new practitioners would supplement the current work of the team frustrating for some new staff who felt constrained in their role, it resulted in a wide discrepancy in the workloads of new staff. Louise, the probation officer, took on the administration and supervision of every probation order: her caseload rapidly grew to an unmanageable size. Almost every case known to the team had some health or education needs and Karen and Cath became concerned that the dominant understanding of their roles would lead to an unfeasible workload: as Karen said, 'one health worker couldn't do everything on health, it would just be too big a task'.

In contrast, it was less clear how the Andy, the (unqualified) probation assistant or Mike and Bob, the two police officers, could contribute to the existing work of the team. The skills and qualifications they brought did not easily fit into the team's current practice. Andy had previously worked in a residential hostel and so had no experience of field social work nor the qualifications to supervise probation orders. And as discussed in Chapter 4, core police duties were thought by many social workers to be incompatible with the work of the team. Social work staff were therefore at a loss about how to involve them in their cases. As a result, these practitioners' workload was relatively low. Other team members were unable to account for their input in the team's practice. Denise, the administration manager, said:

> There's an uneven case load. We get nothing [paperwork] from the police. Not a thing. Odd. I don't know what they're doing.

The disparity in workloads was a cause of considerable resentment and frustration. Cath felt she was 'working my socks off. I'm working with about 30 people'. Louise began formal grievance procedures against the YOT management for not appearing to address the problem of her workload.

Developing common practice

Practitioners were told that as well as providing specialist expertise, there would be some development of common practice among team members. At his first meeting with the new team, Mark, the YOT manager, informed them that while he wanted members to retain their identities as practitioners from their own agencies, he also wanted them to become 'merged' in the YOT.

Although it was not yet clear what such 'merging' would involve, Mark emphasised that it would not require new practitioners to 'become social workers': simply to adopt the practice of the social work staff. However, as no new practice had yet been developed, the only 'merging' of practice in the team at this stage involved new staff taking on some social work in precisely this way: writing PSRs, supervising court orders and being involved in assessments and reviews. All new practitioners were allocated their own caseload. This understanding of 'common practice' caused a series of problems for the team.

Firstly, it raised some practical questions. Were staff from different agencies qualified to take on 'social work' tasks? Only Louise, the probation officer, had appropriate qualifications and experience. Although other staff had extensive experience in their home agency, their level of qualification in the new YOT was at issue. As one practitioner explained:

Parity-wise, Mike [police officer] has done 25 years in crime prevention, he's vastly experienced, he's on a different pay scale as well, he's paid a lot more than social workers [are] paid, but what kind of level he comes in at, I don't know. (Tom, social worker)

Further, their inexperience made new staff extremely anxious. They felt unqualified and unprepared to undertake the social work tasks with which they were being entrusted. As Cath explained, their lack of experience had serious implications:

That's another thing as well. I've just done a PSR on my own [. . .] see, I don't think I should be doing that at all [. . .]. I've done no risk work, nobody's ever gone through how to assess risk, I've done no offence analysis work, but suddenly I'm looking at offence analysis and risk assessment [. . .] I'm not saying I'm not capable of doing it because I fully believe I am but I don't think it's right that I should be doing it. Certainly not without more training. [. . .] I think it's a very grave thing. I think it's an extremely important, it's somebody's justice, it's somebody's liberty, and I think, justice I take so seriously.

This made for an anxious and unhappy working life:

I feel totally out of my depth, and unsupported on a few of my cases, who've got real, social work needs . . . I'm just sort of trying my best. (Cath, education officer)

If a session went badly you can feel like a piece of shit, is it me . . . (Karen, health officer)

But in addition, the adoption of 'social work' duties such as supervision and writing PSRs was experienced as eroding the different occupational identities of new staff. In particular, Karen, the health officer, and Cath, the education officer, expressed concerns about the extent to which they were taking on such 'social work' duties. They felt they were spending more time in these tasks than in specialist interventions that they could provide as a practitioner from their home agency. But, moreover, by participating in tasks that were seen to be the domain of social work staff, Karen and Cath felt they were replacing their own specialist skills with that of another agency. These concerns were exemplified by the task of writing PSRs (pre sentence reports). PSRs were seen as a tool exclusive to social work practice: they were previously written by social workers alone, and involved an expertise that was part of the social work training. As Karen explained:

I've done a PSR. I don't want to do another one. Well, it detracts from what I'm here for, doesn't it? If I'd wanted to be a social worker on the YOT, I would have trained as one, wouldn't I? (Karen, health officer)

Cath and Karen felt they were 'becoming social workers'. As Cath put it:

We need to get the balance right, between us being a social worker, and being an education officer.

The ability to use the expertise or 'functional territory' (Huntington 1981) of their home agency thus appeared to be a crucial component of professional identity. In other words, the ability to be able to lay claim to a particular expertise was not in itself sufficient for practitioners' sense of occupational identity. It was necessary to be able to put these tasks into practice. The replacement of their own central tasks with those of another agency was tantamount to assimilation into a different profession. Yet this was not what they thought YOT membership should involve:

> I didn't want to be a social worker. Do you know what I mean? I could have gone and done the DipSW [social work qualification] just as easily as everybody else could have done, I didn't want to do it, I wanted to work with young people, and I knew I definitely didn't want to be a social worker and I definitely didn't want to be a teacher, so I found what I wanted to do through education work, and that's what I feel passionate about. (Cath, education officer)

In this way, some degree of distinct identity in their practice was thought to be an essential part of being a YOT member. The apparent dissolving of this identity into another agency's practice was an obstruction to team membership. Karen's resistance to being absorbed into the social work practice of the team led her to distance herself and her work from the team. For example, when working with young people with drug-related needs she would only take with her the health-related forms and case notes, leaving the rest of the social work file in the office so that she could 'keep the work separate'. She agreed to collect a folder of information about health issues for the team but kept it in her own files because if she left 'there is no argument about who it belongs to, I can take it with me'. In February, she began looking for alternative positions in the Department of Health.

'Becoming social workers'

Karen and Cath's concerns about their diminishing identity in the YOT revealed something further about their occupational identity. Their concerns about 'becoming social workers' through taking on core social work tasks implied that they considered their professional practice and body of knowledge to be the only significant differentiation between their occupational background and that of the social work staff: in other words, they were not distinguished from the social workers by clearly perceived differences in culture or ethos. This was problematic in maintaining a distinct identity in the YOT: without employing their 'functional territory', what was left to distinguish them as a practitioner from their home agency?

In contrast, Mike and Bob, the two police officers in the YOT, were thought to have an occupational ethos that was strongly distinct from the social work staff. As described in earlier chapters, many Youth Justice Team members thought that the police had a distinct culture and set of values, and were in conflict with the work of the team: police officers' understanding of the aims of youth justice interventions and attitudes to young offenders were in opposition to those of social workers. As one social worker described it, 'it's a them and us situation'. Yet this understanding of the distinct occupational culture of the police raised further problems for the status of Mike and Bob's membership of the team. The common practice developed in the team involved taking on social work tasks, but was it appropriate for Mike and Bob to take on work of this kind?

These questions again crystallised over the question of writing PSRs, a task that had seemingly taken on particular significance in the development of the team. Writing these reports was considered a crucial strand of social workers' practice: the wording of PSRs was thought to be of central importance in helping determine the outcome of a sentence and therefore an opportunity for social work staff to put in practice the 'welfarist' orientation of their work. But while Karen and Cath had been encouraged to write PSRs, their concerns that the police had a conflicting approach to youth justice work made some social workers feel that it was inappropriate for police officers to write these reports:

> When you look at things we're very much social workers, he's [Mike's] very much a police officer, and I don't know how that would affect writing a PSR where we tend to, you know, if you've got something coming along and you say oh, I don't want to up the tariff and be put on a supervision order because if they carry on then what's left then, we try, unless there's welfare issues, we try not to give supervision orders, you know, depending on the case anyway. (Sally, social worker)

In this way, practitioners' understanding of their colleagues' occupational identity appeared to be of crucial importance in determining the status of their membership. Because of their occupational background, Mike and Bob were prevented from taking part in functions of the team in which other practitioners (including new staff such as Karen and Cath) were able to participate. They were apparently restricted from these tasks not because of questions of skill (Karen and Cath had no previous experience in writing PSRs) but because of a more ambiguous notion of occupational values.

However, in the first months of the inter-agency team, practitioners' understanding of Mike and Bob's occupational identity was revealed to be more complex. It quickly became evident that Mike and Bob had very different styles in their work with young offenders. As Sally, a social worker, put it, Bob was 'different in his approach, just in the way he is with the kids'. She explained that she and Mike shared the supervision of a boy who was on a bail support package and needing frequent contact. When Mike visited the boy, Sally felt he was 'very negative', 'saying he [the boy] doesn't want to change'. She explained that one day Mike went to collect the boy from his home. His sister said he wasn't in but Mike knew he was in bed.

> He said, 'that's the last fucking time I'm knocking on his door', and I said 'well we've got to work with the kids.'

The boy said he wouldn't work with Mike. Sally asked him if they weren't getting on because Mike was a police officer, but the boy said he thought it was 'a clash of personalities'. Because of these difficulties, Bob was asked to take over supervision and 'he [the boy] thought he was great'. In other words, although Bob was a police officer, he was seen to have an approach that was more sympathetic to the social workers' style of working with young people. Several social workers mentioned that Bob was married to a social worker, and this seemed to be understood as further evidence of his sympathy with a 'social work' approach to young offenders. In contrast, Mike's acknowledged tendency to take on a 'verbally aggressive stance' (see Chapter 4) reinforced some social workers' conception of the differences in his working assumptions to theirs.

The difference in the working styles of the two practitioners had implications for the development of their roles in the team. Because Bob's manner in his work was thought to be similar to that of the social work staff, he appeared to be readily involved in the work of the team despite his background as a police officer: he was frequently asked to provide assistance in casework. However, he was still a police officer, so his occupational background restricted what his involvement in cases could be. In the absence of any obvious specialist interests (unlike Mike, Bob had no involvement in sport or other activities), how could he contribute to the work of the team? Although social work staff had problems finding an appropriate role for Bob, their eagerness to involve him in casework meant that much of his time was taken up with providing transport for the young people supervised by the team. One social worker described his work as 'babysitting', another said she was worried that he was 'put on' – 'people have him running here, there and everywhere'. Bob described his role as 'the best paid taxi job I've ever had'.

In contrast, the team appeared to struggle to find a role for Mike. Although Mike had initially become involved in training young people in sport (see Chapter 4), fewer young people were referred to him as the team developed. After some months he was asked by Mark, the YOT manager, to organise what Mike termed a 'reparation roadshow'. He was asked to contact all local organisations that might be interested in becoming involved in running projects and training for young people as part of the forthcoming reparation orders (these included local sports organisations, the territorial army, voluntary groups, and so on). These organisations would then be invited to a presentation at the YOT in which their potential role would be explained. Mike was pleased to be given a project to take on, and spent much of his first months on the YOT contacting these organisations. Yet Mark did not follow up Mike's work and showed no further interest in organising the event itself. Graham, the team leader, felt this was because Mark thought the team was not yet in a position to give a coherent presentation: 'He said he didn't want things going off half cock'. But Mike felt this was indicative of a lack of role for him in the team. He felt 'fobbed off'. As one practitioner put it:

> I think Mike feels that these are things which are designed to get rid of him almost, keep him at bay. (Duncan, social worker)

In other words, Mike felt he was not accepted as a member of the team. He responded by withdrawing from the team: he spent several months off sick and took more time off to pursue personal sporting interests followed by further months on sick leave. This was commonly understood by the team as a reaction to an apparent lack of interest in his role and in particular the response to his work on the 'reparation roadshow'. One social worker described the deterioration in his mood:

> He was very very enthusiastic when he came, he made loads of links with the community, then it just went. I think Mark [YOT manager] snubbed him. (Jenny, social worker)

Yet his withdrawal from the team further compromised his team membership: his continued absence became a cause of resentment among the overworked staff. As one practitioner said:

> It's just taking the piss, in't it. It [his absence] has big implications for everyone else in the team, he's co-working our cases. I don't know what he's doing on the team, anyway. (Sally, social worker)

Becoming a YOT

The integration of new practitioners in the team therefore raised a series of problems about professional identity and team membership in inter-agency teams. What was the appropriate balance of professional expertise and generic practice in practitioners' roles? How were these defined? Who defined them? Both these elements of inter-agency roles, and the balance between them, risked practitioners' membership of the team. The difficulty in absorbing the police officers into the work of the team led them to feel marginalised. Yet the feeling that they were 'becoming social workers' made Karen and Cath unhappy and dissatisfied with their work.

Both aspects of the roles of staff from partner agencies reflected broader problems of the power differentials inherent in being 'outsiders' in an established organisation. Without a fundamental reorganisation of the structures of the team, practitioners from partner agencies felt their status as team members was compromised. As Mike explained, new staff felt they did not have ownership of their work:

> I think we've got to start day one with a new group of people in the way in which we work. [. . .] It may well be the case that it works much on the same lines as the youth justice [team], but it'll give everybody who's now party to it a feeling of being in the organisation. I think that's very important.

Some practitioners argued for them to feel equal members of the team, it was particularly important that the work of the social work staff should also be seen to change. All practitioners should now become 'YOT members':

> I want to go to Jeff [operations manager] and say 'you know you were saying to me we're not probation we're YOTs, well we're not social services as well we're YOTs'. Social workers should be doing YOT work like we are. We've all been seconded to the YOT. We should draw together all the best parts of the team. (Louise, probation officer)

However, some practitioners from partner agencies felt the problems they were experiencing were largely due to a resistance to change on the part of the social work staff:

> The hardest thing is the youth justice team changing. [. . .] They're set in their ways. But they're not in social services youth justice, they're seconded to a YOT now. They should have told the youth justice team you'll be going over to the YOT team, here's a job spec. (Louise, probation officer)

In other words, the ambiguous identity of the team gave force to this perceived resistance. Why should the established practice in the team change when it retained its identity as a social services team?

However, the following pages explore a different view of the pace of change in the team, and the further challenges these raised for the practitioners within it.

Note

1 This then raises the question of whether the abbreviations used by the YOT might also exclude their service-users. If practitioners without social work training don't understand the terminology used in the youth justice system, are young people similarly excluded?

Chapter 6

Change, resistance and fragmentation

As described in the previous chapter, practitioners from partner agencies were concerned that they had joined an established team which was not adjusting to accommodate them. Rather than developing into a YOT, the team remained an established social services organisation in which new staff felt marginalised and excluded. However, while newly arrived practitioners felt frustrated at the apparent lack of progress in the team's development to a new, inter-agency organisation, considerable changes were in fact under way.

This chapter examines the experience of organisational change. It explores the diverse ways in which it was experienced, the strategies used to resist innovation and the profound impact it had on members' sense of occupational identity and belonging. In particular, it shows how the processes of change – above all, the development of multi-agency practice – called into question the notion of established boundaries between social work staff and practitioners from other agencies.

A changing team

As outlined in Chapter 5, staff from partner agencies felt the team needed an explicit break from the conventions of the Youth Justice Team so that new roles, structures and practices could be put in place. As long as this did not take place, the team could not develop. However, while there had not been an explicit reorganisation of the Youth Justice Team, the introduction of practitioners from partner agencies itself set in train fundamental changes to its structures and practices.

Becoming detached

Firstly, it was becoming clear that the arrival of new practitioners had fundamentally changed the team's relationship with partner agencies. The staffing, management and funding of the team were now no longer provided solely by the Department of Social Services. The social services were thus no longer the 'home' agency of the team: instead, they had become what Mark, the YOT manager, called 'a stand-alone' organisation.

This financial and administrative detachment was mirrored in the team's accommodation in Midlands House. With the introduction of practitioners from partner agencies, the team's position in a social services-owned building became increasingly untenable. As a multi-agency organisation, their entitlement to the resources in the building was in question. Consequently, the social services administrative team for Midlands House began withdrawing services from the YOT. The reception desk would no longer handle the phone calls for the team; the YOT had to start to contribute money for the stationery supply; the team had to provide their own tea and biscuits for meetings; they even had to have a separate 'signing out' sheet from that used by all other Midlands House employees for entering and leaving the building. Many staff thought these measures were of symbolic rather than practical value, intended to demonstrate that the YOT was no longer seen as part of Social Services:

> I think it was just about ostracising really, let's see what things we do for the YOT and let's stop them. We're perceived as not being part of the building, not part of social services, so we can't have certain services. (Denise, admin officer)

Practitioners spoke of feeling increasingly unwelcome and isolated from the other social services teams. As Denise explained:

> You feel as though you're putting on people because you're asking them, really, you feel as though you're not welcome in the building.

In this way, the ostracism of the team from the other units in Midlands House reflected a perceived ostracism from the Department of Social Services. The change in the boundaries between the team and the DSS was reflected in the physical boundaries of the team's offices.

Previously, the apparent detachment of the Youth Justice Team from other social services units had been an important part of the team's identity. As described in Chapter 2, the specialist work of the team as well as the gender and class of its members was seen to distinguish and thus separate the team from other social work teams. This perceived detachment was a source of pride: it helped describe the boundaries of team membership and thus strengthen the team's identity. However, the identity of the team was now in a state of flux and uncertainty. The team were being severed from their previous home agency without a clear sense of what they were becoming. Rather than strengthening their identity, the separation from their home agency now highlighted its uncertainty. Again, this was reflected in the physical boundaries of the team: while the team knew they were no longer part of Midlands House, they had no new offices to which they could move and develop their new identity. They appeared to be rootless.

Changing practice

Secondly, it was becoming clear that despite the apparent continuity with the conventions of the Youth Justice Team, the introduction of practitioners from partner agencies was inevitably bringing about a restructuring of the practices within the team.

In his first meeting with the newly arrived inter-agency team, Mark, the YOT manager, told staff that a re-evaluation of the practice of the team was an inevitable part of their new stand-alone status. As an independent organisation, the YOT now had sole responsibility for its budget. As all decisions involving money had larger budgeting implications, every expense should now be questioned. The team should look critically at every way of working, to see if it works and how it could be made more efficient. Every process and routine needed to be re-evaluated, including administrative procedures: 'Do we need to type three copies of a letter?' The purchase of every piece of office equipment should be seriously considered – even the stationery used: he didn't want to spend money on 'things like pens, but on kids'. The financial detachment of the YOT from the Social Services therefore demanded a fundamental shift in thinking about financial decisions, and this would inevitably necessitate changes to the way the team currently worked.

However, despite Mark's declaration that changes to the work of the team were under way, there was no comprehensive re-evaluation of their routines or practice. Instead, changes were generated in a more subtle and pervasive way from practitioners themselves.

As new staff became introduced to the routines of the team, they questioned the way the team currently worked. Some of the current practice seemed confusing and ineffective. Why did practitioners visit young people in their homes rather than tell them to come to the offices? What was the reasoning behind the system of allocating caseloads? Why did there not appear to be a formal system of supervision? In this way, the problems experienced by new practitioners exposed anomalies and inefficiencies within the team's practice. For example, if new staff should not write pre-sentence reports because they did not have social work qualifications or training, why were these currently written by other social work staff who also did not have the appropriate training? As Cath, the education officer, said:

> To be honest, it's only the probation staff who have done that sort of training, PSR writing, I don't think anybody here has done PSR-writing training [. . .] but that's wrong again, isn't it.

In this way, the concerns about the level of training of new staff brought into focus issues of qualification that related to the whole team, including social work staff. Currently, there was little differentiation in responsibility between unqualified and qualified social work staff, and all practitioners performed almost the same tasks. As Cath explained:

> I mean, this is what's crazy, it's crazy, Jenny [social worker] case-manages two of my cases, she's an unqualified social worker, so what sense is that making then?

Mark, the YOT manager, thought this was purely a convention that had evolved in the old team and understood it as working to the detriment of those workers who were unqualified. Why should they bear the burden of responsibility for which they were unpaid?

> You've got qualified and unqualified and everybody's doing the same thing, so why bother being qualified? There must be some distinction in terms of levels of responsibility, we've family support workers that didn't even have a job description that reflected any way the work they were doing whatsoever, and they are paid way below everyone else. (Mark, YOT manager)

Instead, Mark proposed that all supervision, court duty and PSRs should be carried out by qualified practitioners alone. Graham, the team leader, thought that in practice this would mean that unqualified practitioners could still do the work, but would be supervised by a qualified 'named person' to carry through an order and go to court. Reports written by unqualified staff would need to be countersigned by qualified practitioners.

However, while Mark felt that this was an uncontentious and fair proposal, many team members were furious at his suggestions. Unqualified staff felt deskilled and undermined. One social worker argued that she didn't want to become 'a dogsbody' for other members of staff. As one unqualified practitioner put it:

I'm getting the union in on it. Because they'll either have to up my grade or I'll have to do nothing. Because there'll be no supervision, no court and I aren't working for someone else to put my name on it. That's bull. I'm sitting here and I'll have done 15 years for nowt. (Alan, social worker)

Some staff from partner agencies felt the opposition of some social workers to the examination of the team's routines was indicative of a resistance to change. Social work staff were 'set in their ways'. Mark, the YOT manager, felt social work staff needed to 'ditch some baggage that they've been dragging around with them':

People ... particularly, again, social service staff, look at the government re-organisation, they talk about [adopts world-weary tone] 'oh, in 1995 . . .' it's like the Berlin wall was put up, you know? And there's all stuff, just historical stuff that we need people to air and then dump [. . .] it's just stuff that's hung on for years [. . .] things like, 'oh no, we don't work on the evenings, we don't on Saturdays', you know? 'Oh we're the ex-court team', you know, get real.

However, the defence of the current conventions in the team appeared to be founded on more than a stubborn resistance to change. Instead, the challenges to the routines within the team represented a significant shift in social work staff's perception of the identity of the team and their self-perception as practitioners within it.

Practice, tradition and identity

Firstly, challenges to the practice within the team were an indication of a move away from the occupational traditions of youth justice social work. Practice that had been developed within the team was now being contested: the questioning of the routines of the team was itself a sign of change. Or as Louise, the probation officer, put it somewhat disparagingly, members of the Youth Justice Team were not used to questioning the practices within the team: 'they're doing it because they've always done it'.

But such challenges to the practice within the team had further implications for the occupational identity of its members. It revealed the way in which the mundane daily routines of the team were inextricably connected to practitioners' sense of occupational identity.

Some practitioners explained that the conventions and routines in the team were shaped by and reflected their occupational values. For example, preferences about the site where young people were supervised were thought to reflect fundamental differences in working assumptions. Louise, the probation officer, thought supervision should take place in the team's offices, as this indicated a concentration on their offending behaviour which as a probation officer was her primary concern:

> There's got to be facilities for us to have people to come into the office [. . .] because I need that individual person, to actually look and recognise what he might have done, what he might been able to have changed to not get into that, what might he be able to do, how his thinking might need to change.

In contrast, she thought the social workers' use of the young person's home as a place of supervision indicated a wider scope of interest:

> I mean because the social workers have always worked the other way [in homes], and the social work part has been very strong and not been focused on the offending, they're used to doing that and I don't think that they're about to change.

Some social work staff were strongly opposed to Louise's suggestion that young people should be supervised in the office. As Tom explained, it revealed underlying beliefs about an approach to work with young offenders that he believed conflicted with those held by many social work staff:

> I think probation workers work in different ways, certainly, than we do. Because they're used to working with adults. We're used to working with children. Probation officers say come to the office, 2 o'clock on Friday next week, I know what would happen if I said 2 o'clock next week, nobody would turn up. It'd be forgotten. [. . .] We give them [young people] a lot of chances, we visit them in their homes, we give them a chance.

In other words, Tom thought social work staff had a different view of young people's capacity to take responsibility for their supervision. By supervising them in the office, social workers attempted to give the young person every opportunity to comply with their orders. In contrast, probation were thought to treat young offenders as what Tom described as 'mini-adults', valuing rigidity and compliance over flexibility and scope for failure.

In this way, practitioners' defence of this routine aspect of their practice reflected a defence of underlying deep-seated aims and values in their work. The possibility of change allowed for the introduction of competing traditions, embedded with alternative conceptions of the underlying aims and values of work with young offenders.

However, while practitioners were able to articulate ways in which they felt their routines were shaped by their occupational values, the connections between values, practice and identity appeared to be more deeply embedded than this. The routines in the team were the particular way youth justice social workers were accustomed to working. Thus by performing these routines, practitioners were reinforcing their identity as youth justice social workers and the values they felt this identity represented. In other words, the practice of the team didn't just flow from their values, but constituted their values as well.

The way in which the professional values and identity were embedded in the practice of the team was indicated by social workers' reactions to criticism of the way they did their paperwork. Many practitioners from partner agencies were surprised at the amount of time currently spent writing reports of the visits carried out and work undertaken with young people. Karen, the health officer, thought that 'recording probably takes as long as the travelling'. They felt this was inefficient, and would be unsupportable when the workload of the team increased. As Mike, a police officer, explained:

> I think we ought to try up to that stage to get rid of a lot of the paperwork we now carry, in the way in which it was dealt with as a youth justice [team] [. . .] We haven't got the staff or the resources to run 50 per cent more work in the manner in which it is being run now [. . .] I see no requirement why we should have a six-inch thick file on an individual and that it should be several of those on each person's desk.

The emphasis on extensive report writing was attributed by some team members to the anxiety surrounding social work practice after the 'Pindown' enquiry in the late 1980s, outlined in Chapter 4. As Jenny, a social worker, explained:

> Like he [Mike] mentioned why all of this writing, I said well, our history says we've got to cover our backs, and that's horrible, and it's pathetic, but you've got to keep on covering your back with all this writing everything down, whereas a policeman wouldn't.[1]

In other words, the current form of report writing was a norm that had arisen from a significant event in the history of youth justice social work, and as such was closely associated with the occupational history of the profession. However, it seems likely that this is a rationalisation of a more integral association of the conventions of paperwork with practitioners' occupational identity: that their identity as youth justice social workers was bound up in material details such as this way of filling in forms. The conventions of paperwork both reflected and constituted an important aspect of what it meant to be a youth justice social worker. Thus, after the official launch of the YOT the following April when the team was seen to have been severed from its occupational history (see Chapter 8) and new routines and practice – including new paperwork – were in place, the conventions of paperwork were no longer defended in these terms. In fact the practitioners defending it became its critics in the same terms as the criticism from staff from partner agencies: the paperwork was a burden on their workload and detracted from their core tasks. As Jenny put it:

> I was never interested in being a form filler. If I was I would have worked in the tax office.

This implies that it was not the conventions of paperwork itself that were being defended but the identity and values they were seen to constitute: when these were seen to be changing, the paperwork became less emotionally powerful.

In this way, the resistance of some social work practitioners to the innovations introduced by staff from partner agencies and encouraged by the YOT manager were not merely a sign of conservatism, as Mark claimed, but a focus for anxieties about the changing identity of the team and of the meaning of team membership.

These issues emerged in particularly potent form with the introduction of groupwork, the first piece of new, multi-agency practice developed in the emerging team.

Introducing groupwork: ambiguity and innovation

The introduction of training for working with young offenders in groups was the first new working practice established after the formation of the YOT. The team was preparing to run three groups for violent offenders, sex offenders and persistent young offenders. In preparation for the launch of the groups, a drama consultant from a well-established community theatre group was employed to train practitioners. Justin was introduced to the team at the team meeting in the new office premises in September. Practitioners were told they were all required to take part in the training. They were encouraged to choose which of the three groups of offenders they would like to work with, and were allocated blocks of training days which took place during the following months. The groups would start in the new year and would take place twice a week, over a period of ten weeks.

The initiative for groupwork originated from Mark, the YOT manager. He explained that groupwork was a response to an anticipated increase in young people who came in contact with the YOT:

> I think first of all there's going to be an increase in numbers, and so you have to have some practical response to numbers.

As Justin put it, groupwork was a 'better use of resources': meeting eight young people for an hour individually was less efficient than meeting eight young people together for two and a half hours. Groupwork was also intended as a more effective way of working with young people. The use of drama in the groups was intended to engage young people in the interventions by using a method which encouraged them to participate:

> I think there's also something about the group dynamics that are very powerful, you have to get kids to interact in groups, it isn't like a school class where they sit there and listen [. . .] we call it the interactive programmes, because it's to directly engage kids and to make them interact, so groupwork is a good way to do that. (Mark, YOT manager)

Justin explained that his brief was to provide a programme that was 'interactive and engaging and challenging, and groupwork is all of those things when it's done well'.

However, groupwork may have held a rather different appeal in the developing YOT. In fact, its benefits as an intervention were somewhat less certain than Justin and Mark presented: the intensive training and commitment it demanded put in doubt its efficiency as a means of dealing with an increasing workload. In addition, the three groups established by the team represented the most 'serious' offences and thus could only involve a small proportion of service-users. Further, the efficacy of groupwork was not as clearly established as Justin and Mark had claimed. As Brown and Caddick put it, 'It cannot be said that the appeal of groupwork rests on clear and systematically established evidence that its use with offenders is effective in meeting their needs, or the interests of the agencies which provide the facility' (1993: 3). While research has shown that the kind of interactive activity such as role-play that Justin describes can be effective form of intervention with offenders (e.g. Vennard and Hedderman 1998) it has also been shown that it is this type of work rather than the forum in which it is carried out (such as groups) that determines its efficacy (e.g. Vennard and Hedderman 1998; Goldblatt 1998) In other words, while groupwork can offer an arena for this kind of activity, there is little evidence to show that the group method itself necessitates this kind of engagement. Instead, groupwork describes a broad range of activities (Senior 1991; Brown 1992). Brown defines groupwork in the following way:

> Groupwork provides a context in which *individuals help each other*; it is a method of *helping groups* as well as helping individuals; and it can enable individuals and groups to *influence* and *change* personal, group, organisational and community problems. (1992: 8, author's italics)

The definition of 'help', 'influence' and 'change' are equally as broad and ambiguous as the purported aims of casework (see Chapter 3). As a method of intervention then, its efficacy is equally hard to demonstrate as that of social work with individual offenders. As Brown puts it: 'The research-based case for groupwork is no more proven, but certainly no less so, than for casework' (Brown 1992: 4).

Instead, the attraction of the introduction of groupwork into the team may have been in its innovation. Groupwork marked a clear departure from the recent practice of the Youth Justice Team. As Mark argued, the formation of the YOT provided an opportunity to try out new programmes:

> I think it's also, to try and explore different ways of working, and what we've done with sex offenders, I mean there's very little group work with sex offenders done nationally, so it's just quite a new approach, and it's a time to expand on it, I think [. . .] There is that opportunity, isn't there, just to try new things and to test them out. (Mark, YOT manager)

In other words, the lack of clear direction over the establishment of new practice and roles in the team provided space for experimentation. Thus, while the uncertainty they were experiencing was a source of anxiety for many practitioners, it was also a source of creativity. As Martin and Meyerson (1988) explain, 'When expectations, preferences and evaluation criteria are unclear, there is no apparent right or wrong outcome. Because there is no risk of being "wrong"' (1988: 119). Consequently, a working environment in which ambiguity is pervasive 'brings a sense of safety, and with that safety autonomy for acting, playing and experimenting' (1988: 120). And further, the groups were a conspicuous and splashy programme of work. As Brown (1992) argues, 'Groupwork is more visible to others than one-to-one work, and tends to attract proportionately more attention in the agency' (1992: 18). In this way, groupwork allowed Mark both to demonstrate a change in the work and thus the identity of the team, and to raise the profile of the emergent YOT.

Groupwork and professional expertise

The benefits of groupwork as a form of intervention were called into question by some of the long-serving social workers in the team. There was strong and vocal opposition to the introduction of groups from Tom, Duncan, Alan and Gary, who argued that groupwork had already been tried and failed. As Tom put it, 'We did all this 20 years ago, it's what we got criticised for'.[2] At best, they argued, groupwork was ineffective: previous experience of it entailed 'driving around in a bus' (carrying groups of young people). At worst, it was counter-productive. Tom argued that young people learn skills from other offenders: 'they learn how to be a better twoccer'.[3] Groupwork would create opportunities for networking among young offenders:

> I look at groupwork and I think there are more cross-overs where you get young people knowing each other across the city, you get small groups of people all with criminal histories all knowing each other, it has to be handled very well. (Duncan, social worker)

In other words, these practitioners felt their previous experience in youth justice work had shown that groupwork with young offenders was misguided: its difficulties outweighed the value of working with offenders in groups. Consequently, they thought the introduction of groupwork was an ill-informed decision.

> As I'm saying, I'm seeing all the negatives, I can't see that many positives [...] if we then get a dictate from higher office saying because of finances or because we think it's a good idea you're going to be doing groupwork, if that isn't done correctly it could be doing more harm than good. It throws up more questions than answers, and more concerns as well. (Tom, social worker)

For these social workers, therefore, groupwork was unproven and its reintroduction could not be defended. However, the establishment of groups appeared to have particular resonance for these practitioners. Its introduction appeared to dismiss their knowledge as experienced professionals. Despite their knowledge and experience of the failings of groupwork practice, they were being co-opted into a programme that they believed to be retrogressive and counterproductive. Mark's insistence on establishing the three groups and ensuring the cooperation of all team members thus appeared to discount these practitioners' professional expertise. As Parker (2000) argues, the notion of professional identity is a particularly powerful form of occupational identity. Delineations between those with professional expertise and those without imply the claim that 'only the professional really understands the central purpose of the organization' (2000: 200). In this way, professional identity and its claims of sole expertise can thus become a powerful resource to resist or sponsor change. Similarly, some social work staff felt this negation of their expertise in establishing the groups was indicative of the development of the YOT as a whole. The team was being managed by people with no appreciation or understanding of youth justice social work. As Tom put it, the groups were 'imposed, without any talk about will this work or not, it's all this will work, you will do it':

> I find it so frustrating that people are trying to devise things that haven't got a clue what social work's about. People who are organising this [the YOT] have no conception of what social work's about. (Tom, social worker)

These practitioners' anger at the apparent denial of their professional knowledge was manifested in resentment towards the groups and the drama consultant employed to run them. In contrast to the expertise of the social work staff, Justin was portrayed among these practitioners as a foppish drama-school type with no experience of social work, and who didn't understand the needs of young offenders or practitioners. He became known as 'Huge Grant': the training was described disparagingly as 'this thespian course'.

Resisting change

Yet despite these strongly felt criticisms of groupwork, practitioners claims of professional expertise had little effect in resisting the implementation of the groups. There were two key obstacles to this resistance.

Firstly, their claim that groupwork was 'imposed' on them by managers with little understanding of youth justice work could be rejected. Mark, the YOT manager, was an ex-social worker with extensive experience in youth justice social work. As May (1994, 2001) argues, such 'professionals turned managers' are able to challenge supposedly 'outdated beliefs in the old' by references to their own experiences as professionals (2001: 178). In other words, Mark was able to counter these practitioners' claims of expertise with his own.

But secondly, the inherent ambiguity in social work practice made it hard to defend against innovation in the methods used. As outlined in Chapter 3, social work casework is characterised by 'loose technologies' (Meyerson 1991: 136) and an elusive relationship between these technologies and demonstrable outcomes. This inability to quantify the effects of the interventions of the team was thought to be an inevitable characteristic of youth justice social work: the work of the team 'sort of clicks in'. However, as some practitioners acknowledged, the difficulties in demonstrating the impact of their work made it susceptible to criticism. How could they show that their work had any effect at all? Consequently, the work of the team was vulnerable to change. The difficulty in defining the effect of the team's current methods of supervision made them prone to criticism that they had no effect:

I'm not convinced that the one-to-one work actually impacts on people's behaviour, mainly because people haven't got sufficient time to make it have that impact. (Mark, YOT manager)

Similarly, the indeterminacy inherent in casework and the consequent problem of articulating what it actually involved led to criticism that practitioners' practice was directionless and confused. Justin explained his experience of beginning work in the team:

I couldn't work out what a youth justice officer did, and I was trying to work it out, and all I could see was that they were ferrying kids around in cars, taking them to court, taking them home, taking them back, doing this, doing that, write the occasional report, so I said when you get a supervision order what do you actually do with them, and that's when he [Graham]'s shown me [programme of supervision designed for adult offenders], and he said occasionally people will go to that and they may use exercises, and a lot of exercises in it are written exercises, which arguably isn't brilliant for adult offenders let alone young offenders, very wordy, and even me and I'm very familiar with looking at programmes, I looked at it and I thought Christ, if I was a member of staff here and I'd looked at that I'd be overwhelmed. (Justin, drama consultant)

Groupwork was proposed as a solution to these apparent problems. Even though the definition and impact of groupwork is arguably as hard to prescribe and demonstrate as casework, it was presented as a structured, defined programme of work with a clear training plan. Its outcomes appeared to be clearer: the aims were to 'engage' young people in 'interactive' sessions. How, then, could its implementation be resisted?

Sabotage

As the essential ambiguity of their practice prevented practitioners from demonstrating the success of their current modes of working, they attempted to defend their practice against unwelcome innovations by other means.

Some social workers did not participate in the training sessions. Some didn't turn up, others drifted in and out of the sessions. Some practitioners argued that they had too many work commitments to attend the training sessions: training was an extra burden on practitioners at a time when the team was understaffed. As Alan, a social worker, put it:

> The amount of staff time has caused untold harm to the team [. . .] We're trying to please everybody, with a caseload and training, how can you do it all?

By the end of December, no referrals had been made to the sex offender or violent offender groups that were due to start the following month. The persistent offenders group started with a small number of young people, but only ran for three sessions because, as Justin said, 'the kids didn't turn up'.

Some of the problems in running the groups were seen by some practitioners as inevitable. Groups had their own dynamic which was unpredictable and, if unsuccessful, insurmountable.

> Groups aren't static things, some groups may fail anyway. It's not a failure of groupwork, per se. (Jeff, operations manager)

Non-compliance was an unavoidable problem: participation in the groups was voluntary rather than a requirement of court orders, so young people were not compelled to attend. As Louise, the probation officer put it, the participants 'haven't agreed to it, so we're starting off with a struggle'. Referrals were also an inevitable problem: there were only small numbers of young people eligible for the groups and of those only some would be suitable for referral:

> If they're going to enjoy it, or feed off it, they aren't going to go [. . .] It's not a catch all, not a cure all, it's a specific way of working with specific people. (Graham, team leader)

However, Justin and Mark did not feel these reasons were adequate explanation for the low rates of referral and the subsequent disbanding of the groups. As Mark explained:

But the kids are there, and we've all sorts of reasons as to why they shouldn't be in groups, few of them stand up to any scrutiny.

Instead, the failure of the groups was a result of the opposition of some social work staff to the groups. The lack of referrals was indicative of a 'substantial resistance' among social work staff: practitioners were choosing not to refer to the groups. This was a form of 'sabotage'.

Not referring is the best way of sabotaging a programme. Referrals is the number one killer. Because people don't bother. (Justin, Drama Consultant)

Groupwork and team membership

However, these practitioners' resistance to groupwork was thought by some team members to have further significance. As the first major programme of new, multi-agency practice, the groups were seen as a site of resistance towards the developing team itself.

In contrast to some of the long-serving social workers, some practitioners were extremely enthusiastic about the groups. Sally, a social worker, Cath, the education officer, and Bob, a police officer, requested to be involved in the violent offenders group. Louise, the probation officer, was involved in the sex offenders group. Andy, the probation assistant, planned to participate in the group for persistent offenders. Cath in particular became a strong proponent of the potential of the groups. She described her excitement at the first sessions that took place:

You could so see it working, just in that, it was brilliant, cos you could see that this could really work, and I think all the group-workers, even groupworkers who were a bit sceptical before, we were all, can't wait to get on with it, we really think it can work.

For these staff, their colleagues' resistance to the introduction of groupwork was frustrating. Rather than giving credence to practitioners' concerns about the efficacy of the method of groupwork itself, their antagonism towards the groups was again thought to be founded in an anxiety about change itself. Groupwork was a clear deviation from the practice of the previous Youth Justice Team. Mark thought it was this that was the source of resistance:

I mean it's quite a substantial change in thinking. It may not sound that much but, for people here, yes, it is [. . .] just the move even into groupwork, working in groups. I mean there's been substantial resistance.

Groupwork was perceived as an attack on the previous modes of working in the social work team, and this prevented the social work staff from being receptive to innovation:

> It's mostly social services staff, because it's their work that's, if you like, under scrutiny really, because what we're saying is well, you're to do these things different to what you did before, whereas people coming in from other agencies haven't actually got those pre-conceived ideas, so they're all up for working in groups and different things where social services staff are struggling. (Mark, YOT manager)

Yet as the first new practice since the team's transition into a multi-agency organisation, groupwork had a different importance for practitioners from partner agencies. It provided a new focus for their work in the team. For some practitioners, this was the first opportunity they had had to develop practice with offenders. As Cath explained:

> It's the only offending behaviour work training that I've had, and I've loved it, I've learnt so much.

But moreover, it allowed team members to find a role within the YOT. Andy, the probation assistant, explained how he planned to develop his position on the team:

> And the groupwork, hopefully, there's a meeting next week, with Justin and I'll be part of that [. . .] I want to do work on the violent offenders group or something like that. [. . .] I think that's a good start, almost.

Groupwork gave Andy a role with a clear purpose and tasks where previously he had none. In other words, groupwork demonstrated the evolution of new, multi-agency practice. Practitioners from partner agencies were able to take part in the development of the groups from their inception. They were equal collaborators in a practice to which they had equal ownership and understanding. For the first time, practitioners could, as Louise put it, 'have a place': they were able to develop a new role in a new organisation.

In this way, groupwork training became a focus for attitudes towards the formation of the new team. Training had importance not just as a preparation for groupwork, but as one social worker put it, as a 'team-building exercise'. The reluctance of some social work staff to participate in the training was seen by some as indicative of a resistance to the development of the new team. Tensions grew between practitioners in the team and exploded in one heated team meeting. Cath, the education officer, argued that the 'half-hearted' involvement in the training was disruptive. It was 'distracting with people coming and going'. Directing her comments to long-serving social workers who had been criticising the training, she added:

> Can I just say that I am so enthusiastic and so looking forward to doing these groups and some support over something that would be really really hard work would be really appreciated. So fuck off.

Duncan replied angrily that 'it was the nature of social work training that people come and go'. In other words, Cath's comments revealed that she understood little about the professional expertise of youth justice social work: by her frustration at the social workers' actions she had proved herself an 'outsider' in the team. Graham, the team leader, thought the attitudes towards groupwork was indicative of refusal to cooperate in a team: 'I'm seeing this as deciding we're not going to work together':

> This is where the team starts to malfunction, because we don't have a consistency of approach. We're all under immense pressure. [. . .] If you want this team to work as a YOT, you'll have to understand that this is very very busy. It's time to decide if you want to play on this team or not. People who are new to the way we work and are influencing the way we work, and that's healthy. But we have to pull it together as a team. (Graham, team leader)

Developing practice: the aims and values of youth justice work

The arguments surrounding the development of the groups had further implications for the experience of team membership within the developing YOT. For the first time, the team were developing new practice and administrative procedures and routines to support it. Yet as discussed above, such routines both reflected and constituted deep-seated values about the purpose of youth justice interventions. In this way, the establishment of new practice and procedures involved an engagement with key issues that underpin youth justice social work. New routines had to be developed to support the groups, but what was the underlying ethos that would shape them?

For example, it soon appeared that the provisions for transporting young people to the groups were inadequate. The initial practice of the team was for the groupwork leaders to collect young people from their homes and take them to the site of the workshops. However, in the context of the pressure of work that the team were experiencing, some team members felt this was inefficient. But underlying this question was the more complex issue of responsibility and the purpose of the intervention. Should young people be responsible for getting to the groups, or was this the responsibility of the team? As Cath argued, this was 'a question of ethos'. She felt the crucial point was that the groups took place, and since the launch of the groups had not been easy – 'for the pilots we have had that many barriers' – the team should now do everything possible to make them work. However, Alan, a social worker, felt strongly that young people should make their own way to the groups: 'I disagree. If they have to come to the group because of an order, they should do it.' Louise, the probation officer, argued that it was an important part of the work of the team to encourage young people to learn to take responsibility for their own actions:

> So it's about it's working with them I feel, that to learn about that independency, to help them shift to take responsibility, I see the role as helping them to actually help themselves, to enable them to do that. (Louise, probation officer)

At the crux of this discussion was the question of how far the young person should take responsibility for compliance with an order. While the long-established routines in the team had prevented a reassessment of these questions, the development of new practice brought them to the fore.

Questions about the ethos and purpose underpinning the work of the team emerged in a particularly potent form over the question of breaching young people for not attending the groups. Attendance at the groups was not a requirement of court orders so in theory was voluntary. But breaching for non-compliance in essence made attendance at groups compulsory. As Cath explained, this was a source of strong disagreement among practitioners:

> In group we had big debates about, people didn't want to refer to group, including group leaders, because we were being quite strict on breaching, so if they didn't come, they would be breached, and what groupworkers wanted to do is say well we won't breach them we'll just go back to court and ask for a supervision order.

This dilemma divided team members. Should young people be compelled to attend and sanctioned if they didn't? Or were they allowed the freedom to refuse to participate? The question of voluntary versus compulsory attendance is a key issue in writings about groupwork (e.g. Brown and Caddick 1993; Brown 1992; Canton et al. 1991). Some practitioners think compulsion is incompatible with the principles of groupwork practice – for example, Canton et al. (1991) say that groups should provide 'a setting without threat or discomfort and this may well be incompatible with compulsory attendance'. (1991: 209). Yet as groupwork is often part of the requirements of a court order this is problematic. Brown and Caddick conclude that 'We have no easy solution to this dilemma, except to observe that, if a group is to have any impact on offending behaviour, what really matters is that the offender is motivated to participate actively . . . it is not enough simply to be present.'

The question of compulsory versus voluntary attendance was therefore a central issue in the adoption of groupwork. The dilemma appeared to exacerbate practitioners' confusion over the ethos and aims of the work of the team. What was the purpose of their work? Was it effective? What should young people's role be in the process? As Cath explained:

> People breach more easily on a supervision order, they didn't want to breach for a group because they felt that they perhaps weren't coping with the group, if a young person didn't like the group, and didn't want to come because they didn't like it, they felt that they should return it to court, get a supervision order and not breach them, but other people thought, well they're at the group instead of going to prison, so they have to darn well come. [. . .] Other people feel that young people get away with a lot, and they don't take supervision orders seriously, because you're allowed to, because they're not hard, to comply with a supervision order is not a big deal, I don't think it is, whereas going to a group I think is hard work, all quite challenging.

In this way, the development of new practice in the team brought to the surface underlying questions about the aims and purpose of youth justice interventions. Practitioners were now engaged in explicit debates about these issues. But as Cath implies, the inherent ambiguities involved in these questions also exposed the diversity of approach among practitioners in the team. How was this experienced by team members?

Ambiguity, diversity and fragmentation

As described in Chapter 2, the dominant presentation of the Youth Justice Team as united by shared aims and values had obscured the complexity of practitioners' understanding of and approach to their work. By contrasting the work of the team with that of other criminal justice agents, practitioners eliminated and clarified the ambiguity of their experience. The possibility of conflict, diversity and confusion among the team was excluded. However, the development of a piece of multi-agency practice made these 'us and them' claims impossible. Consequently, the ambiguity inherent in social work practice was brought into focus. As Cath explained, there was wide disagreement among all practitioners about the stance on breaching:

> Everybody within our group, and we're multi-agency group-workers, we all disagreed on what we should do. [. . .] There's a lot of different philosophies out there about what the team is, punitive approaches, and welfare approaches [. . .] I think it's individual, social workers disagree, you know, not arguing about it but just disagreeing.

It was now not possible to see the team as divided in their response to such questions according to agency boundaries. There were disagreements among practitioners from the same occupational background. But moreover, practitioners' own views on these issues were exposed as uncertain and shifting. As Cath explained, the issue of breaching revealed her own confusion about the balance between a 'welfare' and 'punitive' approach to the interventions:

> I didn't originally but now I do, I think, you know, that's what they've been told they have to do by the court, they should come and if they don't come then we have to breach because we need to . . . I mean I'm very welfare based, but I do think that anyway, that's sort of what I've come to think over the six months I've been here, but then . . . I *thought* I was very welfare, I've come here, and I am within the work that I do I'm very welfare, but I think they have to comply. I know that if it was one of my young people on the group and I had to breach them I would hate it, but I think we have to do it.

In this way, the team was no longer felt to be defined by clear boundaries within which practitioners had a clear and agreed set of beliefs. Instead, it now appeared to be rife with shifting and uncertain responses to particular issues. This indicated a shift in the 'home perspective' (Martin 1992, and see above) of team members. The dominant presentation of the team as a united, cohesive group had been subsumed into that of a fragmented mesh of fluctuating alliances. This had much in common with a way of thinking about culture that Martin and Meyerson (Martin 1992; Martin and Meyerson 1988; Meyerson and Martin 1987) term a 'fragmentation' perspective, where 'issues temporarily generate concern, but that concern does not coalesce into shared opinions, either in the form of agreement or disagreement' (1992: 118). Practitioners found they had particular affinities with other team members over specific issues at specific moments. As Martin describes, 'the salience of particular issues for given individuals fluctuates, realigning the salience of subcultural identities and creating transient issue-specific coalitions' (Martin 1992: 157).

In this way, although ambiguities had always been inherent in the work of the team, the departure from the conventions of the previous Youth Justice Team and the debates that it provoked brought into focus these ambiguities and the uncertainty of the responses it generated in its practitioners. Yet this shift in the way the work of the team was perceived was a further source of anxiety. The previous team-wide consistency and consensus appeared to have dissolved: practitioners talked of how the team had become 'fractious' and 'bad-tempered'. They would 'end up in chaos'. But in addition, the now apparent ambiguities in the YOT had implications for practitioners' experience of team membership. As Louise, the probation officer, put it:

I think everybody feels they're working in isolation. It's got worse, its fragmented more over the last few weeks. (Louise, probation officer)

In other words, the ambiguities felt by practitioners were experienced as a loss of 'team'. Without apparent stability and clarity, what did team membership mean? As Andy explained:

So if you say am I joining a team, in some ways it feels like I'm coming to a place where there's people working, but I don't think it feels like a team at the moment. (Andy, probation service assistant)

Notes

1 Mike's questioning of the amount of report writing undertaken by the team may also be a consequence of his own occupational history. As Manning (1980) and Chatterton (1989) argue, paperwork is given low status among police officers. As Manning puts it: 'Paper is the defining characteristic of formal operations, but is rejected as irrelevant [by the lower ranks]. In this way paper becomes the negative or contrasting conception, against which real police work is measured' (1980: 108).
2 As Brown (1992) argues, the use of groupwork emerged as a mainstream method of British social work in the late 1970s. The emergence of Intermediate Treatment in juvenile justice, the strong anti-custody ethos that characterised juvenile justice at this time, and the funding from the DHSS for development

of programme alternatives to custody (e.g. Pitts 1999; Haines and Drakeford 1998) encouraged an increasing use of groupwork with young offenders (e.g. Denman 1982). However, while groupwork became increasingly widespread in work with adult offenders and is now used throughout all settings of the probation service (Caddick 1991), its use in work with young offenders is less well documented. These practitioners imply that its popularity may have declined with the decline of IT. In this way, the use of groupwork may have seemed a return to a previous era in youth justice work that had since been strongly criticised with the 'repoliticisation' of youth justice (Pitts 1999).

3 Car thief (TWOC is a common abbreviation for Taken Without Owner's Consent).

Chapter 7

Managing ambiguity and change

In the months after the arrival of staff from partner agencies in September 1999, the confusion and uncertainty in practitioners' working lives became increasingly apparent. Practitioners' roles and future workload was unclear, their identity and sense of team membership uncertain. This overwhelming sense of ambiguity was unfolding in the context of increasingly fractious team relations. In this climate, the management of the team took on a new importance.

Many practitioners felt that some direction had to be imposed on the team. The current atmosphere in the team was unsustainable:

> It's all very up in the air. By this time we should be sorting out who is going to be doing what. We'll end up in chaos. We need a few clear guidelines. (Louise, probation officer)

Or as Duncan, a social worker, put it, 'vision and clarity is what we want.'

Many staff thought such vision and clarity could only be supplied by the managers of the team. It was their responsibility to provide the guidance that was desperately needed:

> I mean I've come from a setting where it's very clear what your role is and what you should be doing and what you aren't doing, and [. . .] I just want someone else to tell me that that's what I'm meant to do. (Andy, probation service assistant)

This chapter explores questions of management, power and powerlessness. How did practitioners experience the management of the team? What were the difficulties in managing a developing team in the context of pervasive uncertainty and instability? What were the creative strategies used to manage these difficulties? In particular, it explores the challenges in managing the team in the context of the new relationship between the central and local governance of youth crime created under the Crime and Disorder Act.

Looking for guidance

As the management of the team became increasingly salient, practitioners became increasingly aware of its deficiencies. Many practitioners thought this was largely a problem of personnel. While they felt the team needed guidance, they did not feel there was anyone available to provide it. Even though three managerial posts had been created, no one appeared to have the authority to make the decisions needed.

In part, this was because the management team were not yet in place. The team had created three posts: a YOT manager, operations manager, and team leader. Yet when staff from partner agencies arrived in September, only one of the three posts had been filled. The team were repeatedly unable to appoint an operations manager and interviews for the team leader post were yet to be held. In the meantime, Graham was doing both jobs in a temporary capacity. Consequently, Mark, the YOT manager, was the only permanent member of the managerial team. However, although he had been in post for 18 months, he rarely made contact with the team. He explained that his role was not concerned with the daily functioning of the team:

> First of all, my role is not operational. So that's the first thing. So I'm a step removed . . . I'm not involved in the day-to-day management. (Mark, YOT manager)

As a result, he did not attend team meetings or supervise practitioners. He seldom visited the offices at Midlands House and there was almost no communication between Mark and team members.

Some practitioners recognised that Mark's apparent lack of involvement with the team was an indication that decisions about the practice of the team were not his concern: he was 'too high up'. However, as the management of the team took on increasing importance, Mark's absence became increasingly resented. He was felt to be out of touch and uninterested in the team. As one social worker said, 'I'm not sure whether Mark works for us or not.' But most importantly, Mark's detachment from the team was thought to be depriving staff of access to much needed information and guidance. As one practitioner put it:

And all that happens at the moment is that Mark is apparently planning, making massive plans, in his ivory tower somewhere, and none of it is percolating down to us. (Duncan, social worker)

Practitioners' frustration exploded shortly after Mark formally introduced himself at a team meeting soon after the arrival of the new staff in September. As described in Chapter 6, Mark told staff that changes would be made in the new team. New pressures of budgeting resulting from the team's new stand-alone status meant that each team member now had to think carefully about every financial decision they made. As he explained, he didn't want to spend money on 'things like pens, but on kids'. After the meeting, practitioners reacted furiously to Mark's comments. The force of their anger was directed at his remarks about stationery. In the context of increasing antipathy towards his apparent neglect of the team, Mark was thought to have been deliberately antagonistic: 'the pen comment' was seen as 'aggressive', 'unhelpful', 'it gets people's backs up'. In response, some practitioners went round the office collecting every pen they could find and putting their name on it. Some began labelling their hole punches and mouse-mats. One filled his pockets with biros.

Because of Mark's absence, Graham's position became particularly important. He was the only member of management staff available to practitioners. He felt he provided crucial continuity for practitioners in the transition of the team, and could thus act as 'an anchor' throughout the forthcoming changes. Although he had earlier been unsuccessful in his application for the operations manager position, he felt confident that he would be appointed to the new team leader role. However, in October it suddenly appeared that the creation of the post was in question. Midlands Department of Social Services thought a three-tier management structure was superfluous and the team leader position expendable. The new uncertainty surrounding Graham's position had a marked effect on the atmosphere in the team. As Graham put it, there was a 'mood of despondency' among practitioners. As well as creating further instability, the temporary nature of his position meant that Graham could not provide the direction staff needed. As one practitioner explained:

You can't really expect [Graham] to stand aside for a week or two and work out procedures which will be countermanded in two or three weeks' time when someone else comes in. (Duncan, social worker)

In this context, the impending appointment of the operations manager took on increasing importance. It was assumed that the new manager would take on responsibility for developing the roles, practice and structures in the team. If other management staff could not make authoritative decisions about these it must not be their job to do so: a representative of a voluntary agency said 'no one really wants to tell people what you're doing as they don't feel it's their role'. As Jenny, a social worker, put it, 'until the operations manager [arrives], we're all muddling through.'

Legitimacy, authority and resistance

By the beginning of November, both management positions were filled. The team leader post was finally sanctioned and Graham appointed. After a third round of interviews, Jeff was eventually appointed operations manager and took up post at the beginning of December, three months later than initially planned.

However, Jeff's appointment did not resolve practitioners' anxieties. Firstly, he had not previously worked in youth justice and for some staff this was a serious concern: how could he be a credible manager when, as one social worker put it, 'he knows FA about youth justice'. It was assumed he was a bureaucrat with little interest in the professional arena in which he was placed. But moreover, Jeff's occupational background further placed his credibility in question. Most social workers in the team had assumed the management positions would be filled by staff from the social services. But Jeff was an ex-police superintendent.

The appointment of a police officer to a senior managerial position was a shock to some social work staff. Practitioners joked about there being a 'police takeover'; Jeff became known as 'the police officer'; when it was announced further administrative staff would be appointed a social worker said 'have we not got any police applying? We could hold it open for them.' In part, this reflected concerns about the assumed difference in occupational ethos between the police and social work and its consequences for the team. The apparently macho, inflexible and aggressive approach to work in the police service would be reflected in Jeff's style of management:

> The police manage in a totally different way. It's a male hierarchy, isn't it. In the police, if the man at the top says 'jump', others say 'how high'. (Graham, team leader)

It was assumed that such a rigid structure would be accompanied by other signs of hierarchy that were felt to be alien to the social work team, such as deference to senior staff. Graham thought it was a 'big cultural change' for Jeff 'not to be called Sir, not to have people present things to him, "cup of coffee Sir?"'

In this way, many practitioners assumed that Jeff would exercise authority according to a set of values which they felt were incompatible with their own. These concerns had implications for the legitimacy of his position, and consequently the extent to which he would be able to provide the strong managerial direction that practitioners felt they needed.

Legitimacy comprises the moral aspects of power relationships and is crucial for generating normative commitments towards compliance (Beetham 1991; Sparks and Bottoms 1995). Yet the exercise of power will only be seen as legitimate by those subject to it if it is believed that the rules of power are morally justifiable: that they can be justified in terms of 'shared beliefs' (Beetham 1991: 17). The assumption that Jeff ascribed to values that conflicted with the prevailing approach of the team thus placed the legitimate basis of his authority in doubt. The perceived 'legitimacy deficit' (Beetham 1991) in Jeff's position thus had implications for his exercise of power: some practitioners implied that they would not comply. As one social worker commented 'if he tries to run it as a police superintendent, then he's in for a bit of a shock'.

In the first months of Jeff's appointment, there were frequent attempts to undermine and dismiss his actions in the team. Practitioners attempted to demonstrate publicly that he had little understanding of their work or the values they thought underlying it. For example, at one team meeting, Jeff attempted to address the increasingly pressing issue of disparity in workloads among team members. He asked social workers how they might quantify their workload so that it might be monitored and imbalances redressed. Yet Jeff's repeated attempts to involve practitioners in this process were met with an apparent reluctance to help or engage:

Jeff: What would you consider a high level workload?
Sally: It's hard to say, it depends on each case.
Jeff: Can you quantify it?
Julia: At the beginning of the order it's far more work than at the end of a two-year order.
Jeff: I accept that, but how can I pick that up?
Jenny: Some have complex issues, it can take all week – you're always playing catch up. Five or six [cases] can be a full workload.
Jeff: Can you weight them or categorise them?
Alan: [sharply] I think it's familiarity, Jeff, you know within your own team what you've got.

Jeff's attempts to impose order on the workloads of the team were countered by social workers with evidence of how their professional experience negated his knowledge. Attempts to quantify the amount of work involved in each case were not just impossible but inappropriate: one practitioner responded to Jeff's suggestion that each case folder should be marked with stars according to the intensity of work involved in the supervision that 'every child is a five star case as far as I'm concerned'. As discussed in Chapter 6, claims to professional expertise can be used to dismiss the views and experience of others: they imply that 'only the professional really understands the central purpose of the organization' (Parker 2000: 200). Jeff's attempts to categorise the work of the team could be dismissed as the mark of someone who did not fully understand the purpose or needs of youth justice work, whereas the social work staff had the 'familiarity' to enable them to 'know within your own team what you've got'.

However, these practitioners' attempts to construct boundaries between Jeff as a 'police officer' and their 'own team' revealed a further problem with his appointment. The appointment of a police officer to a senior management position clearly demonstrated that these occupational boundaries had now dissolved. Jeff was not only a member of their 'own team', but in a position of power over these staff. His seniority meant that Jeff could not be marginalised, unlike other police staff in the team. But in addition, the appointment of a senior manager with a different occupational expertise had further significance. Jeff represented what May (2001) describes as a 'blurring of knowledge boundaries' between the two occupational worlds, by which different forms of occupational expertise and their underlying assumptions and values are embodied within an organisation, 'thereby blurring the ability to create boundaries between different forms of knowledges and hence effective resistance to transformations' (2001: 178). In other words, Jeff's appointment was a marked demonstration both of a change to the identity of the team – that the perceived dominance of the social work staff and the associated approach to youth justice work was now in question – and of the impossibility of preventing these changes. It is possible that these practitioners' hostility towards his appointment also reflected antipathy towards these developments.

Management, power and powerlessness

In this way, practitioners' feelings that there was a lack of 'management' in the team reflected a perception that there was no one available to them who had the authority to give the guidance they sought, or whom they invested with the authority to do so. They did not have access to a manager who both understood the problems facing the team and was senior enough to resolve them. However, their concerns were also shared by the management staff themselves.

While staff demanded strong managerial guidance, management staff faced a series of problems which resulted in a perceived inability to take responsibility for directing the team. In part, these appeared to be a consequence of the new relationships between local and central governance of crime created through the establishment of the YOT. The following pages explore the challenges these created for management staff and their implications for the development of the team.

Developing a management team

As outlined in Chapter 1, while YOTs were charged with a series of centrally defined obligations, they were given considerable autonomy in the way that these were carried out. So, like the other posts in the team, the number of posts and the structure of the management team was not prescribed by the Youth Justice Board but was to be locally determined.[1] The precise nature of the roles of the management staff therefore had to be negotiated by those in post. Thus the three-tier management structure of the Midlands YOT was a local innovation. As such it indicated some of the difficulties in developing a new and individual solution to the management of the team.

It became evident that the roles of staff in the management structure and the distribution of responsibilities among the posts were not clear. As outlined above, Mark, the YOT manager, described his role as purely strategic: he did not see the 'operational' tasks of the team as his concern. Mark's conception of the 'hands off' nature of his role and his subsequent detachment from the team made other management staff responsible for decisions about practitioners' roles and practice. However, the relationship of these two posts were particularly problematic.

Mark described the team leader as 'the back-up to the operations manager and to assist in supervision': someone who could step in when the operations manager was occupied elsewhere:

> Because we have a team the size of 20 people [. . .] a lot of the work needs an instant response to meet the time-scales of the national standards, and somebody's got to make those decisions, so you can't get into a situation where you're thinking about well, who am I going to act up now, it would just be ludicrous, so that's why we created the team leader position.

However, the apparent closeness of the two posts in the management hierarchy was confusing. How would the duties be distributed between the two posts? How were the lines of authority arranged between them? For these reasons there had been opposition at Chief Executive level to the creation of both of these posts: as Graham described it, 'You've got

one at the top, one leading the team, why do you need somebody else?'
He felt the difficulty in appointing an operations manager reflected the
lack of clarity in the positioning of the post: it wasn't 'a high-level
management position, it's somewhere in between'. But moreover, as
these two posts dealt with the daily management of the team, such
confusion had direct implications for practitioners. How were the two
managers going to work together? Who was able to make decisions
about the roles and practice of the team?

This confusion over the responsibility for the daily management of the
team was exacerbated by the circumstances within the YOT. Despite his
junior position, Mark's detachment from the YOT left Graham responsible
for the entire operation of the team, as he put it, 'doing the strategic stuff
as well as encouraging a developing team'. Jeff's inexperience in youth
justice work meant that Graham had to train him in the job. As Graham
put it, 'I mean he's a very intelligent man, but he didn't know anything':

> Here's Mr [Jeff's surname] 'right, why do you do this, why, what's
> the history, why can't I do that, can I do that?' and me, almost
> having to explain everything as we go along.

In these months then, the seniority of the two positions appeared to be
reversed: Graham was in a position of greater experience and expertise.

In this way, Graham found himself in a position of responsibility
beyond the role for which he had been appointed. Although he was the
most junior of the three managers, he now found himself in a position
where he felt himself solely accountable for the way the team functioned.
As he explained:

> I said to him [Mark], if you get it wrong, you're out of a job. He said,
> 'no, if I get it wrong, you're out of a job, because you're going to be
> delivering'.

As a result of this arrangement, Graham's position in the team appeared
to fluctuate between widely different levels of authority. While he was
coping with being in a position of responsibility beyond his appointed
role, Graham was intermittently made aware of his junior status. For
example, he described how shortly after his appointment in 1998, Mark
gave a talk to the chief executives of 'Midlands' City Council about the
role of the YOT. Mark didn't involve Graham in the talk, and didn't even
introduce him to the Chief Executives: 'I wasn't introduced. It was just
"I want you there"'. Graham's only involvement in the meeting was
when Mark asked him to 'put pamphlets on chairs' before the meeting
began: a task that Graham felt demonstrated his subordinate position in
the management hierarchy.

But in addition, Graham's position in relation to the practitioners in the team was also precarious. His insecurity became evident when the position of team leader appeared to be in doubt. Graham knew that if he wasn't appointed, he would return as a senior practitioner on the YOT: as he put it, 'the rug could be pulled out from under me' and he would be back working on the same level as his colleagues. As a result, he was concerned to 'avoid animosity' in his dealings with the team. Yet although he was eventually appointed to the post, the repositioning of the team leader role within the management hierarchy made these concerns remain salient. With Jeff adopting the responsibilities that had until recently been his, what would Graham's status be within the team? Would there be much to distinguish him from other senior practitioners?

Therefore the power relations within the team were uncertain and fluctuating. Who was able to take responsibility for making decisions about the team's roles and practice?

Autonomy, ambiguity and isolation

A second problem in the management of the YOT concerned the strategic decisions at senior level. As described earlier in this chapter, practitioners thought that the anxieties and confusion they were experiencing could be resolved if only Mark would turn his attention to them. Mark's detachment from the team and poor communication along the management structure prevented crucial information and guidance from reaching practitioners. However, rather than withholding the information from the team, it appeared instead that the ambiguity experienced by practitioners was mirrored and amplified at the level of senior management.

As Mark explained, taking up a new position in an entirely new structure meant that he had to create the YOT from scratch, with no guidance or support. As a 'stand-alone' service, the YOT was not supported by the financial and administrative networks that surround long established local authority departments. Further, there was no constitution established for ways that partner agency executives would work with each other. The relationships with partner agencies, the channels of communication, the allocation of funds and resources all had to be negotiated. As the manager of the YOT, he didn't have 'a right to anything':

> There's no structure within which to work, and there's no processes already established for you to use, and you don't have a right to anything. Whereas if, say, if I was Assistant Director of Social Services you have access to a particular range of resources and

processes and you work within a structure that's quite predetermined. So the first thing really was that. Trying to find a way to work.

Similarly, every working practice within the team had to be created from scratch. There were no established procedures for the working practices within the team on which Mark could draw. Routines and structures previously used by partner agencies were inappropriate for the multi-agency composition of the team. The Youth Justice Board had not developed any protocols. Consequently, every aspect of practitioners' work had to be developed within the YOT itself:

> It's every, every single thing has to be written. And it's got to be written by someone here, there isn't some huge back-up to the organisation, 'oh yes, we want a supervision plan, oh yes, I'll get it over here', and then one appears, you know? *We* have to do it.

In this way, Mark was faced with an immense and overwhelming task. As he put it:

> I just think, there's so much to do, it's just incredible [laughs], we're supposed to have all these things up and running, at the same time we're supposed to bring a new team of people together. [. . .] I think the Board has seriously underestimated the task. Certainly I did.

At the same time, establishing the YOT as a 'stand-alone' structure rather than a part of a larger department meant that he had no formal channels of support. He described the bewildering isolation he experienced when he took up the role of YOT manager:

> You come into a new city [laughs], you've no contacts, you know, you can't even find your way around, you don't actually belong anywhere, you're not part of social services, you're not part of anything, you're a sort of satellite on your own.

Moreover, Mark felt that this isolation could not be resolved. Instead, it was an integral part of the ethos of Youth Offending Teams. As he saw it, YOTs were intended to be 'visually different' from the previous Youth Justice Teams. They were intended to demonstrate a departure from previous youth justice work by a visible detachment from all the partner agencies:

> One of the big things was really that Youth Offending Teams should not just be a re-badging of the Youth Justice Teams, under that

Youth Justice Teams were social services, and that there was a move to try and change that culture.

As the channels of interaction between agencies had not yet been formalised, Mark felt it was important that the relationships he established communicated the new status of the YOT: it needed to look as though it was 'a separation from *all* the big organisations'. In particular, this meant detaching himself from the social services. He was concerned he might be seen as partisan: he was 'technically' employed by the social services[2] and his background was in youth justice social work. As he explained, 'I think I have to be very careful not to be seen as part of social services'.

> In terms of coming in you have to be careful where you positioned yourself. So, [laughs], on the one hand you want to be friends with everyone but belonging to nobody, you know?

The networks of support available to senior mangers in the partner agencies were no longer available and had not been replaced by alternative networks. Mark was thus personally and professionally isolated from his peers – and this isolation was an inevitable and integral part of his position.

In addition, Mark's relationship with the Youth Justice Board was a further source of ambiguity. The emphasis on local autonomy in the Crime and Disorder Act 1998 meant that the Youth Justice Board was detached from the 'ground-level' decisions necessary in establishing the YOT. In practice, however, Mark perceived this detachment as evidence of the Youth Justice Board's lack of interest in the practical difficulties he faced:

> I think there are issues about the communication between the Board and Youth Offending Team managers, and I think it's changed substantially from the early days when it was 'oh we're all in this together', and 'we're there to support you', and 'we're here to actually implement stuff so we have to work closely together' and it seems as if it's got more into, more ... what's the word, 'oh well here it is, off you go and do it' [...] it's coping with the speed, and the degree of change, with, if you like, minimal support to the service overall, you know, this notion that you set up youth offending teams, now go off and do it.

But at the same time, Mark was required to fulfil the directives of the Youth Justice Board when these were issued. Consequently, the decisions he made at a local level were prone to change in a manner over which he felt he had no control:

I mean it's up to me to try and work out what to . . . sort of set the framework within which we're going to operate, doing the protocols, that sets out who's going to be responsible for doing what and how it's going to operate, then I communicate that to the management team here, and we work out how we're going to implement that. And that's the theory of it. But the practice is that I will say something one week, and then the guidance will be changed the next week, so I have to say, well, hold on here, it's something different now.

The ambiguity Mark described appears a consequence of the 'complex and shifting' (Crawford 1994: 497) relationships between the state and civil society and the new administrative arrangements for local governance that are emerging in contemporary crime control (see Chapter 1) whereby 'local structures with elements of relative autonomy march in tandem with a centralization of broader statements of policy and the allocation of public funds' (1994: 503). Mark's position demonstrated how this could be experienced by those actors charged with negotiating this new relationship with the state: he was simultaneously overwhelmed with the responsibility of autonomy and constrained by the dictates of the state via the Youth Justice Board.

In this way, Mark appeared to feel overwhelmed, unsupported and powerless. In the face of the isolation and ambiguity he was experiencing, how could he provide the clarity and direction demanded of him by the team and other colleagues? He recognised that his position made him vulnerable to criticism, but was powerless to address it. For instance, he described how a member of the probation service complained about a lack of supervision procedures in the team:

One of their senior people criticised us, saying 'well, my people just aren't being supervised in the way that they should, what is your supervision system and what's your workload allocation system?', I said 'well, we're working on it', I said 'you've had 30 years to develop your supervision and your workload allocation and we're putting all this together in under 12 months, it'll be there as soon we can, I have to write it', I have to write the supervision [laughs] and the workload allocation . . .

But in addition, the state of flux and confusion experienced by Mark and the rest of the team also appeared to be reflected at government level. Guidance issued by the Youth Justice Board was, at this stage, infrequent, often sketchy, and prone to change:[3]

Everything is in such a state of change, that the guidance and everything else keeps changing, right up to the last minute [. . .] So, I mean, all the time you get those sort of conflicts and tensions, and it's just that I think it's the degree of change and the speed of change, that everything keeps tripping over itself.

The confusion in the Midlands YOT thus appeared to pervade all levels of the youth justice system. The practitioners in the YOT, the senior management and the Youth Justice Board were all in the process of creating a service from scratch, with few resources on which they could draw. There was therefore no immediate source of clarity available to the team, and no easy resolution to the ambiguity they were experiencing. How then could the management staff provide the direction and clarity that practitioners demanded when none appeared to exist?

Managing ambiguity: paralysis and creativity

In this way, the managers of the YOT each appeared to feel they were unable to resolve the problems experienced by the team. They were faced with the bewildering task of managing a working environment pervaded with confusion and insecurity. This confronted them with a further, apparently insurmountable problem: how could they resolve the demands of an increasingly anxious team? As Martin and Meyerson (1988) argue, such ambiguity can lead to 'behavioural paralysis': actors simply do not know what to do. 'When a situation is ambiguous, it is difficult to know if action is called for, which actions would be appropriate, and what their consequences might be. The frequent result is inaction' (1988: 112). As a result, the management staff felt powerless. The authority to make the decisions needed appeared to lie elsewhere. Faced with wavering and uncertain positions of authority, Graham, Jeff and Mark all felt they were unable to act.

However, while the ambiguity faced by the management staff may have been experienced as disabling, it was also a source of excitement and innovation. For example, the lack of guidance and structure in setting up the YOT clearly made Mark feel overwhelmed, but it also allowed him freedom to shape the team as he wanted. He was able to create new and flashy programmes, like the groupwork schemes (see Chapter 6). Graham commented that he thought Mark was aiming to create a 'show YOT': one which would draw attention to his work. Similarly, although Graham's fluctuating status within the team was unsettling and frustrating, it also provided a flexibility in his role which allowed him to take on more responsibility than he would otherwise be entitled to. This was indicated by his later reluctance to devolve some of these responsibilities to Jeff:

> Eventually, you know, there came a point where he was saying, 'alright, you're the team leader, I'm the operations manager, why aren't you giving me operational stuff to do, why are you doing it all?' I said because I have to, and I have had to [. . .] in the 18 months before you came I was doing all of this, and now there's an additional person which is you saying, why aren't you giving me the work to do, why are you taking it upon yourself. (Graham, team leader)

In this way, ambiguity was a source of power as well as paralysis. But in addition, it provided management staff with a way of creatively managing the apparently irresolvable problems they faced.

Crawford and Jones (1995) argue that the demands of working in environments in which conflict is pervasive often leads to the use of 'creative' practice as a form of conflict management. Such practices generally involve ' "getting through the day's business" and meeting managerially defined objectives, rather than pursuing any moral or political mission' (1995: 23). In other words, actors 'manage creatively' conflicts without necessarily resolving them. This kind of conflict management may take informal or private forms, and may not be addressed openly or even acknowledged (Kolb and Puttnam 1992).

While the uncertainties confronting management staff were uncomfortable, at the same time they appeared to provide valuable scope for creative practice. So for example, the ambiguities in the roles of the management staff provided scope for eluding conflict. Mark's construction of his role as 'strategic' and thus divorced from 'operational' matters appeared to be one form of conflict management. His clear division between the 'strategy' and 'operation' of the team appeared somewhat artificial: decisions at both these levels were closely interconnected. For instance, decisions about staffing or the development of protocols or practice for the new orders appeared to require close attention to the daily operation of the team. It seemed possible that Mark's freedom to define his own position as 'a step-removed' from the YOT allowed him to avoid having to deal on a daily basis with an increasingly fractious and anxious team. Similarly, Graham's ambiguous status within the team allowed him to slip between positions, enabling him to avoid censure for his actions. For example, in one team meeting in November, Graham confronted staff about their opposition to groupwork training. He began in a strongly directive manner. Groupwork training was compulsory: if practitioners objected their alternative was to leave:

> If you're not prepared to play the game then there are options available to you. Training is not optional. [. . .] It's time to decide if you want to play on this team or not.

Some practitioners objected to the perceived aggression of these options and argued they were too busy to take part. Graham replied:

> I do understand the pressures. I've not long come out of practice myself. I haven't forgotten. But one of the messages clearly from above is that if you don't like it, your options are there.

The suggestion that practitioners complied or left now appeared to originate from Mark: Graham was under orders as well, a practitioner like them. Some social workers responded that the suggestion from 'Mark' was 'unhelpful' and 'threatening', 'gets people's backs up', 'I don't think its conducive to team building'. Graham then replied 'neither do I. So we have to be strong as a team.' In this way, he had distanced himself from his own comments, and had seemed to side with practitioners against the apparent threats from senior management. In other words, while this slippage between positions reflected the fluctuating, transient nature of Graham's actual status within the team, it also enabled him to make authoritative, unpopular statements while shielding himself from their repercussions.

Further, while the management team felt powerless to make decisions because of the uncertainty and confusion of their working environment, the avoidance of decision-making was itself an exercise of power (e.g. Lukes 1974; Crawford and Jones 1995). The avoidance of overt conflict by postponing decision-making left the dominant power relations in the team unchallenged and unchanged. Indeed, as Kolb and Puttnam (1992) argue, 'avoidance and tolerance may keep disputes below the surface and make it more difficult than with public conflicts to change existing structures and systems' (1992: 21).

Questions of power and conflict avoidance crystallised over the management of the regular, fortnightly team meetings.

Managing team meetings

Team meetings had been held throughout the duration of the previous Youth Justice Team, but had not been seen as a significant part of team life:

> The culture on the team was that we're mavericks and we do our own thing, don't go to meetings. The culture's never been challenged before. (Duncan, social worker)

However, in the current climate of anxiety team meetings took on a new importance. They were the only point at which the team met formally as a whole. As such, they were the only forum available to the team in which issues could be raised and discussed in an open and accountable manner.

Writing on inter-agency collaboration emphasises the importance of formal meetings (e.g. Crawford and Jones 1995; Crawford 1997; Pearson et al. 1992). Although addressing conflicts informally may appear to present a 'more workable basis' for negotiation (Pearson et al. 1992: 65), and may have an important role in allowing public expressions of conflict to run smoothly (Bartunek et al. 1992), such informality also has implications for accountability and confidentiality. As Crawford and Jones write: 'Informal contexts leave differential power relations unchecked, hide decision-making processes from any review and remove them from any democratic input or control' (1995: 26). Instead, conflict should be 'overtly confronted in public through constructive negotiation' (1995: 31). This requires addressing conflict in a formal setting, set apart from ordinary routines and regulated by safeguards. Such formal procedures make conflict visible, allowing for its constructive management (1995: 28).

Team meetings fulfilled these criteria. They were held at regular times, during which all work would stop. Meetings would be marked by changes to the physical layout of the room, sometimes a change of location, which would help to set the meeting apart from the rest of the working day. They would usually follow an agenda and minutes would be taken, providing a record of the meeting and so acting as a safeguard for accountability. In this way, they became seen as an important problem-solving forum by all team members:

> This is a social work group of people with other people coming to join it, with different ways of behaving [. . .] We're not going to move forward if we don't talk about what we expect. (Graham, team meeting, September)

> We are a team, we need to iron out any difficulties. We can only do it formally within a team meeting. [. . .] We need people to attend, or we'll have the team built on the views of those who attend. (Graham, team meeting, November)

> At least [a team meeting] lets everyone air their views. At the moment I think it's needed because of the problems that are happening. (Louise, probation officer, team meeting, November)

Some practitioners said they needed more meetings: there were calls for them to take place weekly. In November, Graham told the team that attendance at meetings was now compulsory: the only appointments practitioners should make on team meeting times were unavoidable duties such as court duty and attending PACE interviews.

However, the espoused value of the importance of team meetings conflicted with the informal practices in the team. Meetings were repeatedly cancelled. The cancellations began just at the time when practitioners from partner agencies began to join the team and the development of the YOT was seen to be underway. From mid-August until mid-November 1999 only two meetings were held, and even these were different in character from previous meetings. Instead of acting as forums for discussion and negotiation, they took the form of an 'address' to the team by the two managers in post. In both, there was little opportunity for discussion, and when discussion arose it was not encouraged. All other meetings in this period were cancelled.

The reasons given for the cancellation of team meetings seemed unconvincing. Sometimes Graham said he was unavailable to hold the meetings: he had to go on a home visit, visit a young person in the secure estate, or was unwell. He cancelled one meeting because several practitioners were on leave. One was cancelled because 'I asked if anyone had any issues to discuss, and they said they didn't'. While some of these incidents may have been unavoidable, they appeared to conflict with the espoused importance of the meetings.

Instead, it appeared that the cancellation of the meetings was a means of managing ambiguity. As manager of the team, Graham's role in team meetings was both central and risky. Firstly, meetings demanded decision-making. They could only function as a site of problem-solving if staff felt there was the possibility of action. For example, after one cancellation Graham suggested that practitioners hold a meeting without him. Yet because staff felt no decisions could be made at the meeting, it took on the characteristics of 'informal' or 'non-rational' conflict handling (e.g. Bartunek et al. 1992; Kolb and Puttnam 1992): practitioners complained and gossiped. Graham's role in the meetings was therefore crucial: only he was able to make authoritative decisions about the problems discussed. Yet in the light of his own sense of powerlessness, team meetings risked exposing both the problems experienced by the team and Graham's inability to address them. This kind of exposure in the context of a team meeting had particular potency. As Schwartzman (1989) argues, meetings provide an important commentary on the relative status of individuals within an organisation. They provide an organisation with a forum for making itself visible and apparent to its members – they are thus 'the organization or community *writ small*' (1989: 39). Meetings therefore provide individuals with a place to witness what their relationships are to each other. 'We say that an individual is or is not a powerful person, but often we only 'know' this based on how we read and interpret events in a meeting' (1989: 312). In this way, team meetings risked exposing and further compromising Graham's already wavering and uncertain authority.

Secondly, rather than resolving issues, team meetings had the potential to unsettle any order that existed in the team. By providing a forum for staff to highlight the problems and anxieties they were experiencing, meetings could result in further conflict and insecurity. They thus appeared both unpleasant and counterproductive. Graham recognised team meetings had become a source of anxiety both for himself and the team. When one practitioner questioned the cancellation of a previous week's meeting, he said:

> I was all set up for having a meeting last week. I was so pissed off at frankly having to make everyone so upset by having to deliver the news from the Youth Justice Board and raising everyone's anxiety.

Some practitioners also recognised that meetings were becoming unbearable. Some team members thought that meetings were being cancelled because 'it was too bad-tempered last week, that's the underlying reason', 'there's no good news is there, only bad news'. Some argued that the meetings were not helping the team: they were 'time consuming', raising the same issues 'over and over again', 'we might as well just wait and see'.

In this way, the formality that gave team meetings their importance as a site of accountable discussion and decision-making also made them intolerable for Graham. The cancellation of the meetings appeared to be a form of conflict avoidance (Black 1990; Kolb and Puttnam 1992): a 'creative practice' (Crawford and Jones 1995) to manage the ambiguity in the team.[4]

However, the cancellation of team meetings had the effect of making team members even more insecure. The removal of the team's only channel of communication with each other and with senior levels of management left practitioners feeling uninvolved and powerless over the developments within the team. For example, one social worker responded to the cancellation of another team meeting in the following way:

> All these new people, we don't know who they are. And then a note comes along from the boss, 'oh by the way, you've now got an operations manager'. We never see him [Mark, YOT manager]. It's impersonal, in't it. (Jenny, social worker)

But in addition, practitioners were deprived of an important public demonstration and negotiation of their positions within the team. Schwartzman argues that this function of meetings as a 'sense-making form' (1989: 9) is particularly important in contexts in which structural and cultural ambiguity is pervasive, where the status of individuals is frequently in flux, and where there are very few ways outside meetings for individuals to negotiate and determine their status and social ranking. In a team in which the roles and status of staff were problematic and uncertain, a forum for such negotiation was of particular importance. The cancellation of team meetings thus left staff without a means to position themselves against their colleagues: to see how they 'fit' into the team. Some practitioners described this problem in terms of not knowing who their colleagues 'were': as Louise said: 'I haven't been to a meeting where I've met everybody'. But as Andy, a probation practitioner, pointed out, there were of course opportunities for informal introductions to team members. The process of a collective 'introduction' in the formal context of a meeting had a greater significance:

> I don't feel introduced to people. I've gone and spoken individually to people and I know where they're from and a little bit about them, but introduced as in we haven't collectively met since I've been here as a team, been introduced all together, where we're from, and then for them to know where I'm from as well, and then for us all to establish where our roles are in the team, and I think that's all part of the introduction. (Andy, probation service assistant)

In other words, the 'introduction' provided by team meetings gave practitioners some explanation of how they would fit into the team. Consequently, with the nature of the YOT uncertain and the removal of the only available sense-making forum, how could practitioners interpret themselves at work in the YOT? As Andy put it:

> I don't think it feels like a team at the moment, and that's because I don't feel introduced to people. (Andy, probation service assistant)

In this way, many team members thought the cancellation of the meetings deprived them of a crucial source of clarity and communication. Moreover, the manner of their cancellation appeared to exacerbate the anxiety and confusion practitioners were experiencing. Meetings were usually cancelled at short notice, if any, and with little communication to the rest of the team. Practitioners would often discover the meeting had been cancelled only when it did not take place. This added to the feeling of confusion among team members: as one put it:

> All the fiasco over these team meetings not happening . . . last week [a cancelled meeting] caused such a lot of messing about, it was really confusing. (Cath, education officer)

By the cancellation of the fourth consecutive team meeting, practitioners' frustration was evident. Staff had assembled for the meeting to be told that it was cancelled. Graham was unable to attend and had asked them to make a list of points that could be discussed at the next meeting. At this point, one long-serving social worker walked out of the office in frustration, saying 'Tell him the lack of direction because I haven't got a clue where I'm going.'

After pressure from practitioners, team meetings were reinstated at the end of November. From December they were co-chaired by Jeff who was now in post. Yet although meetings now took place, other strategies were used which appeared to counter their inherent formality. For example, while meetings had been previously been recorded by a member of the team and minutes circulated after each meeting, minute-taking was now sporadic, and when it occurred, frequently inaccurate. As a result, the 'procedures and safeguards' crucial in formal negotiations (Crawford and Jones 1995) were not available. As one practitioner put it:

> The team meetings aren't minuted, they haven't been since before Christmas. So everything said in the team meetings, they're [management] not accountable for. Because they say different things in different meetings, they're not accountable for anything they say. (Cath, education officer)

As a further strategy to deflect attention away from decision-making, Graham and Jeff would ask staff to 'make a list' of problems they were experiencing or would like to discuss. For example, at the end of a fractious team meeting at which practitioners had detailed their concerns, Jeff said 'Give me a list of those issues you are unsure [of] or want to discuss . . . we need a question list.' Frustrated by this strategy, four team members including Cath, the education officer, did make a list of perceived problems and proposed solutions. These included issues that practitioners felt were urgent, in particular devising a policy regarding the transportation of young people to groupwork. Cath had recently been threatened with assault by one of the young women in her drama group who she then had to drive home alone. As she argued, the lack of a policy regarding such incidents could have serious implications for the management staff as well as practitioners:

> There's no violence to employees procedure, I had no induction to come here, no training. If anything had happened, they wouldn't have had a leg to stand on.

The list of proposals was circulated round practitioners for comments, and then passed to Graham and Jeff. However, this did not elicit a response: 'It was just put back on my desk with no comments on it.' It appears, then, that rather than fulfilling a function necessary for the resolution of the issues facing practitioners, list-making was a means for the YOT managers to defer making decisions about the issues raised.

Deferring decisions, postponing change

As a result of this creative management of the meetings, decisions on issues appeared to be endlessly deferred. For example, Cath, the education officer, described how it had been decided 'on numerous occasions' that the number of practitioners on court duty should be increased to two instead of one, yet this change had still not taken place. As she asked in one team meeting:

> That's an example of things not happening. We've discussed that now, we agreed we need to do it, do we need to wait for the Youth Justice Board to tell us to do it, or can we go ahead and organise it?

Consequently, many staff felt that the management staff were failing to make any decisions at all. As Cath put it: 'I haven't seen a decision made since I've been here.' They interpreted this as management staff refusing to taking responsibility for the running of the team. Cath said the apparent 'stupidity and incompetence' of the management staff made her tired and disillusioned:

> The reason I came here was I thought it was so exciting, so many opportunities to put it right. And nothing.

Some practitioners openly discussed looking for alternative jobs and this itself became a topic of discussion among other staff members. It was seen as proof of a failing team with failing management. As Cath put it, 'there've been no decisions, apart from everybody deciding to fuck off'.

However, the assumption that practitioners were helpless in the face of the inability of management staff to take responsibility for decision-making in the team is questionable. Firstly, it depicts the management staff as having complete control over team members, who are unable to act without the direction of their managers. Secondly, it assumes that action can only arise from a decision, whereas, as Brunsson (2000) argues, 'Making a decision is merely a step towards taking action. The decision is not the end product' (2000: 18). In fact, in his meeting with the team in September Mark had explicitly informed the team that all team members needed to share responsibility for the running of the YOT. Every decision they made – whether about buying pens, writing letters or working cases – was of crucial importance. As he later explained:

I think in terms of the culture it's about trying to make people feel 'well this is all ours and unless we really do the stuff then it's not going to work, and there's no one else to blame'. I mean I think that's a big shift. And it does matter. This whole thing will work or not work depending on all of us here, and that's different in itself.

Or as he told the team in September, 'if you aren't happy with the YOT it's because you're not doing it right. There's no other answer.' In this way, practitioners were perhaps not as powerless as they described. This was acknowledged by one social worker at a team meeting:

We should be making decisions and being assertive, some of it is being dictated to us, sure, but some of that is in our control. (Anthony, social worker)

It seems, then, that by prioritising the responsibility of management decision-making as a means of initiating action, practitioners were bypassing their own ability to accelerate the changes taking place in the team. In this way, they were contributing to the organisational paralysis they were experiencing. This was implied by one comment at a team meeting:

Vision and clarity is what we want. There's lots of obfuscation here. That's what we're good at. (Duncan, social worker)

It is possible then that practitioners' role in perpetuating the state of inaction in the team was a form of resistance to change. Although team members undoubtedly found the state of ambiguity and confusion they were experiencing unpleasant and a source of profound anxiety, their inaction was a tool by which change could be further postponed.

A disintegrating team?

By January 2000, many practitioners felt their anxiety had reached an intolerable level. The strain of coping with the uncertainty that pervaded every aspect of their working lives was becoming manifested in declining team relations. As Tom, a social worker explained, 'you can see it in the team meetings now, can't you. Everybody's quite fractious now.' In addition, many practitioners now felt their workload was unmanageable. The team had lost four social work posts over the previous year and the caseload from these posts had been spread over the remaining team members. Then, in January, the team were informed that the Department of Social Services were not going to be filling the posts. The DSS were making swingeing cuts across all departments and these posts were to be the YOT's contribution.

Some practitioners felt that the level of work was now unsustainable. As Tom put it, 'People are not coping.' This was thought to be demonstrated in a decline in the quality of practitioners' work. Tom explained: 'People are making mistakes. Only small mistakes, so far.' He described how one practitioner forgot to produce a PSR for the courts. This was a serious mistake and one that shocked the team: 'It's probably the first time ever we've missed a report.' The mistake was not exposed because there happened to be a delay in the court proceedings. But otherwise, the credibility of the team would have been in jeopardy: 'We would have been embarrassed in court, otherwise, we would.' Such mistakes seem intrinsically connected to the pressures felt by staff. Weick (1991) argues that stress affects the way teams perform. It can be beneficial to the performance of a team only if the team functions in a team-like way – if practitioners coalesce into a 'distinctive entity exhibiting distinctive functional relationships'. Yet it is destructive if members 'merely act in the presence of another and respond and fall apart, more like individuals than like groups' (1991: 125). The mistakes Tom described were results of a breakdown in communication among team members: in other words, in Weick's terms, the YOT appeared to be functioning like a group of individuals rather than a team. The loss of 'team' feeling and fragmentation described by practitioners thus seemed to be reflected in its performance.

Then, at the beginning of the new year, Duncan, a social worker, died suddenly of a heart attack. He had been a key member of the team and his death had a great impact. It was widely seen as a result of stress. As Alan, a social worker, said:

> [The increase in workload] has very serious implications for members of staff and conditions. We are starting to see the detrimental effects.

Duncan's death was seen by some practitioners as a tragic culmination of the unwelcome changes that they were undergoing. His colleagues thought his death was precipitated by being forced into groupwork by an unresponsive management.

> It was the stress of the job, and trying to push him into doing something he didn't want to do, he had a block of five days' training, Duncan said he had too much work, he said I can't do both, he was told he had to go in no uncertain terms. It was the pressure of management, which they took no responsibility for. (Tom, social worker)

Duncan's death thus appeared to mark the culmination of practitioners' anxiety about the changes to their occupational identity and working lives. The team now appeared to be in a state of crisis.

Notes

1 The only post delineated in the Draft Guidance (Home Office et al. 1998) was that of the YOT manager, but even these specifications were vague, allowing for a wide scope for interpretation of the role: the YOT manager 'will play an important leadership and resource management role and will need to be able to address strategic issues and forge an effective multi-agency team at operational level' (1998: para. 43). There were no further recommendations about the number of posts created or the responsibilities of the management team.

2 YOTs are not constituted employers and thus cannot employ personnel directly. Mark was 'technically' employed by the Department of Social Services, who also paid the largest proportion of his salary (40 per cent – the rest was shared by the other partner agencies). But as Mark explained, that relationship 'is solely if you like for employment purposes': he was not part of their divisional or departmental management team.

3 For example, the Youth Justice Board's guidance for the administration of orders that became available to the courts on 1 June 2000 (Action Plan Orders, Parental Responsibility Orders, Final Warnings) arrived at the YOT offices on 19 May. The team thus had eleven days to read the guidance and prepare for the administration of these orders. But as Mark explained, the guidance was not operational, and this also fell to the team to resolve:

> The stuff that's in the guidance [for Final Warnings] clashes with the police offence resolution policy, in the gravity factors and some of the offences are not included, so those are things that I don't see as up to us, to have to sort out locally [laughs] [. . .] we're not being given . . . we shouldn't have to work out the guidance [laughs] and how that's going to operate.

4 At the same time, there appeared to be a suspension of other formal opportunities for accountable decision-making. In particular, supervision meetings were suspended. These were meetings in which practitioners would discuss their practice with their supervising managers and air concerns. The issues raised were documented and a plan of action agreed. New staff complained that they had not had any supervision meetings with the management staff since their arrival in the team. It appears that the suspension of these was a further form of ambiguity management.

Part 3

A Youth Offending Team

In the last weeks of March 2000, many practitioners described a feeling of mounting panic. They felt unprepared for the official launch of the YOT on 1 April, and had little confidence in the ability of the team to cope. As one practitioner explained:

> A lot of people are under [a] misapprehension of what they're supposed to be doing. I'm unsure of my role [. . .] Workload is up, training is taking place . . . I don't think we're going to be big enough. From what I've read from the Youth Justice Board handout, we're not going to be big enough, unless we work 16 hours a day. The majority [of young people] are now coming out with supervision [orders], we've got 14 cases in the crown court, [working with] 16, 17s is a different world altogether [. . .] there are serious repercussions on staff's ability to cope with what's asked of us. (Alan, social worker)

The final part of the study explores the launch of the Youth Offending Team in April 2000 and the first few months of its new, official identity. How had the team changed from its incarnation as a Youth Justice Team a year ago? How was this perceived by its members? And what did it mean to be a member of a YOT?

Chapter 8

A youth offending team

In the last weeks of March, the team learnt that they were finally able to move into their new offices: the fire regulations had been approved, the redecoration completed and the telephones installed. The team began to pack up their offices in Midlands House, and on 27 March 2000, four days before the official launch of the YOT, moved into the new building.

The move was followed by a dramatic change to the mood of the team. The anxious tension that had surrounded the team suddenly seemed to have diffused. Practitioners commented that the team was now 'calmer', 'settled', 'quiet'. As Graham, the team leader, put it:

> [The stress] was building up, and up and up and up and up, and it's a very difficult thing to disperse. [...] And then of course we arrive here [new offices] on Monday morning, and all of that perceived stress and real stress and tension just go.

Becoming 'settled'

The apparent change to the mood of the team seemed to have been brought about by a rapid series of resolutions to some of the more tangible problems team members had been experiencing. Firstly, the relocation seemed to mark the end of a period of instability. As Cath, the education officer, put it, the team was finally 'settled'. The team had been waiting to move into the new building for six months. The threat of imminent disruption had been unsettling and distracting:

> There was also the fact that we were moving, so the unrest, not knowing what that was going to be like, that we were all going to

be split up, just little things like that. And relationships within the office, sitting with different people, you know, even things as simple as that. (Barbara, social worker)

Staff could now settle into a stable working environment. As Cath put it, 'I feel more organised, so I just feel a lot happier.'

Secondly, the move to the new building appeared to resolve practitioners' anxieties about a lack of an authoritative managerial presence in the team. The large building had space for an office for Mark, the YOT manager, and he moved into the new offices with the team.

A new building: a new management

Mark's presence promised a new style of management in the team: it now seemed that there would be a constant, active source of authority in the YOT. This was demonstrated on the day after the move, when Mark called the team together to give them what Graham termed a 'pep talk'. In the meeting he made explicit team members' concerns about the lack of accountable channels of communication between practitioners and management staff. Formal, structured supervision with a named supervising officer would be reinstated. Team meetings would now be compulsory, and absence would have to be accounted for. Mark would meet each practitioner individually to find out how their roles were developing and what their concerns were. In this way, Mark both acknowledged and declared an end to the avoidance of decision-making that practitioners felt had characterised the previous months in the team. As Cath explained, such acknowledgement alone gave her a new confidence in the management of the team:

> Just the fact that they've been said and acknowledged that there's a need for those things, cos I feel confident that if they don't happen its a good reason they're not happening, that there's other things going on, but that they will happen, the fact that the intention's there and people are actually thinking the same as me, makes me feel better and trusting and, prepared to wait, whereas before, I felt it was just incompetence and stupidity [laughs], and so therefore I had no understanding of it, it just made me angry and impatient. (Cath, education officer)

In other words, the transparency of Mark's statements of intention and his promise of clarity in his management style gave practitioners confidence. There now seemed to be a source of visible, legitimate authority in the YOT, which signalled the end of the perceived neglect of the team. As Cath put it:

> With Mark being in the building as well, that gives me a lot more confidence in the management structure, that Mark's going to be here, I just feel I can trust him a bit more. I just think he gets things done and he will get things done. (Cath, education officer)

In addition, Mark's presence in the team appeared to act as a catalyst for the repositioning of the management staff within the management hierarchy. Mark's closer supervision of Graham and Jeff and Jeff's increasing confidence in his own position appeared to bring about a stronger differentiation of their roles. Jeff took on a more senior role, making decisions about the practice of the team and becoming closely involved with the supervision of team members. Graham's role was now primarily concerned with daily supervision of individual practitioners: he was no longer involved in strategic or operational decisions. In this way, there now appeared to be more stability in the previously fluctuating power relations among the management staff. This was not an entirely happy development. As described in the previous chapter, the previous ambiguity in their roles had provided the freedom for management staff to take on new tasks and responsibilities, while simultaneously shielding them from some of the repercussions. The clarification of the roles of the management staff took this freedom away. Graham seemed unhappy at relinquishing the responsibility that he had adopted over the previous year and felt that his experience and expertise was being undermined:

> The strangest thing is, Mark's talking about developing the team and roles within the team, I know what needs to be done, because I've done it, but now it's got to be diplomatically shared. I know what works, I know how to get the work done, I know how to motivate people, these people on the team. 'Cos I know them individually, personally. (Graham, team leader)

Also at this time, Mark instructed Graham to take on a caseload for the first time since acting in a management position. This was ostensibly an attempt to address the lack of resources and surplus of work experienced by the team, but Graham felt it reinforced his apparent demotion and was intended to signal his junior status.[1] In this way, Graham's previous concerns that 'the rug could be pulled out from under me' and he would find himself returning to work alongside practitioners whom he had recently been managing appeared to have come to fruition. This was clearly an unhappy move for Graham and he discussed leaving the team. As he explained, 'I have to rethink my role now. So it has been a time of change for me.'

But moreover, the relocation seemed to bring about an end to the instability and ambiguity surrounding the identity of the team. It was seen to mark the end of the team's transition from a Youth Justice Team into a multi-agency YOT.

A new building: a new team

As staff had predicted, the physical relocation to the new building made evident the organisational relocation of the team. The move demonstrated and reinforced the team's detachment from the Department of Social Services. It severed the remaining connections between the team and the other social services units in Midlands House. As Graham explained, the team previously had 'daily links' with the senior management of the social services units and the fostering and adoption services in the building. The team were now isolated: 'We have to go out of our way to go to meetings.' The physical distance of the YOT from the other services formalised the communication between the teams. Practitioners in the YOT now had to 'refer in' to other units, for example if they suspected a case of abuse, instead of informally discussing the case with the teams in the building. Personal relationships with colleagues also became more formal. Graham described a change in his relationship with a senior manager of the children and families units whom he had invited to visit the YOT offices:

> I said 'oh you must come over', and he said, 'phone my secretary and make and appointment'. And I said, 'fuck off, just come over'. 'No no, make an appointment'. [. . .] And he's somebody I had to deal with a lot.

The physical detachment of the team therefore necessitated a reorganisation of the structures of work and communication that had attached the team to the Department of Social Services: aspects of the 'degree of organisation' (Elias and Scotson 1994: xviii) that had previously structured the team. The break from the structures and practices of the social services now appeared to enable the team to be seen as a new, multi-agency organisation in which all practitioners could have equal status as team members. This was implicitly acknowledged in the first team meeting in the new premises, when Barbara, a social worker, made a plea for the team to ensure they were not 'cut off' from the social services. But, as she added, 'that's how all the other agencies felt when they came to join'. In other words, social workers now had the same status and relationship with their home agencies as staff from partner agencies.

In addition, the association of the move with a perceived start to the new team was strengthened by the timing of the relocation: a few days later, on 1 April, the team was officially launched as a YOT.

A new building: a new identity

The clarification of the identity of the team brought with it a clarification of the identity of its members. As Graham explained, it was no longer possible for social workers to see themselves as members of a social services organisation:

> People came here with [a] social work identity, and they'll now be leaving that behind. Which has been an issue for everybody else who's joined the team, who do they belong to, what are they part of, that then becomes a reality for people who are social services. (Graham, team leader)

The move out of Midlands House brought about a new sense of finality to the social work staff's changing identity. Graham likened the move to 'leaving home':

> So I went in on the Thursday afternoon, before the move on Friday, everything was in boxes, packed up, echoing rooms, all the stuff that you go through when you're moving house, people popping in to say goodbye, like neighbours do, it was most bizarre. [It was] as if you've ended something. And it's that similar feeling that you get, you've gone, left. Your career in social services is finished.[2]

In his meeting with the team following the move, Mark made this finality explicit. As he later explained, he felt that there was a lack of commitment to the YOT among some social work staff, who felt 'we don't have to make our minds up yet' about their position on the team. He told the social work staff that he wanted a 'positive statement' from them that they wanted to be in the YOT: 'They can either decide they want to be with the YOT or I'll send them back to social services for redeployment.' In other words, social work staff now had a choice: to return to their home agency or sever their links with it.

Some social workers said they found Mark's comments 'threatening'. Yet there was little sign of outrage or protest in response. This lack of collective outrage was particularly notable in comparison with the reaction to Mark's comments six months previously, when he had suggested team members buy their own pens (see Chapters 6 and 7): a comment deemed to be so provocative that it was still being discussed at this time. In contrast, this meeting attracted little comment. In part, this may have been an indication of a feeling of resignation: the change to their professional identity now appeared conclusive, so there was little point in protest. But in addition, some staff felt Mark had inadvertently helped alleviate the anxious tension that had characterised the previous months. As one practitioner explained, Mark had addressed the confusion and anxiety that social workers had experienced over the identity of the team and their position in it:

> They [social workers] felt there was no formalising of their roles. There was no support from the social services, they didn't know what was going on. [. . .] The past hasn't been properly finished. They've had difficulty moving on. They haven't had a proper cut-off point or start point. (Denise, admin manager)

Mark's talk provided such a 'cut-off and start point'. Practitioners now had an explicit statement about the identity of their team from its senior manager, and were asked to make the commitment to be part of it. As Graham put it, 'so that's resolved it'.

In this way, the new calm among the team was thought by many practitioners to be a reflection of an end to a period of ambiguity and anxiety. Some practitioners now felt that the team was at last able to develop as a YOT. As Graham explained: 'The team feels like a team: the more it's isolated the more it will gel together.' The move out of Midlands House 'had a real feeling of closure, now there's a feeling of opening'.

This 'feeling of closure' appears to have prompted reflection about the transformation to the team. The following pages explore how practitioners understood what it meant to be a member of a YOT, and how their experience of team membership had changed.

The changing nature of team membership

The most immediately noticeable difference to the team was a sudden change in the atmosphere in the team's offices. The offices in Midlands House had been noisy. There had been a constant stream of jokes flying around the large team room. This banter had now virtually disappeared: staff worked silently at their desks.

Some practitioners thought this new, quiet atmosphere was a consequence of their new premises. Instead of the chaotic, cramped conditions of the offices in Midlands House, the new building was spacious. Staff were no longer grouped together in one team room, but were divided into two large rooms at opposite ends of the building. To reach one from the other they had to pass through a lobby and entrance area, through two sets of security doors. Practitioners' desks were positioned in the corners of the team rooms which appeared to discourage interaction. Previously, staff had thought the single team room in their old premises in Midlands House had facilitated the easy sociability which was prized in the team. Similarly, their new physical separation was thought to have destroyed it. As Graham explained:

> It's not far from this end of the building from your mates at the other end, but it is, in terms of seeing people, it's a long way. You've got two security doors to go through, you have to do two security codes to talk to somebody. (Graham, team leader)

Team members were now 'isolated' from their colleagues:

> I would think if it was me up in the other end [of the building] I would feel very isolated, because everything seems to be going on down this end, with the kitchen, the toilets, admin, the photocopier, the shredder, it's all down here. (Barbara, social worker)

Some thought the social atmosphere in the team had also been disrupted by a vast increase in workload, in particular in their paperwork, which was associated with the new team. New administrative requirements had been introduced with the launch of the YOT: revised National Standards increased the required frequency of contact which in turn increased the amount of reporting; Asset assessment forms now had to be completed for each young person at the start and end of their orders, which required staff to give a numerical rating to the 'risk conditions' young people faced and their assessment of change in behaviour. As this required a very different way of thinking about young people and their circumstances (see Chapter 3), staff thought they would take considerable time to administer. Some felt swamped with paperwork. As one practitioner explained:

> Before, there'd be supervision and that's it, you'd do it, whereas now, there's more paperwork, more meetings, it seems to create so much work. (Sally, social worker)

This pressure was thought to prevent social interaction. Brian, a social worker who had been seconded to the secure estate, said that he noticed a marked difference in the team when he returned for meetings. The atmosphere was 'bloody miserable – I haven't heard a joke all day':

> They haven't got time for anything. [. . .] And you come back here, and there's nobody to talk to because they've all got their heads down doing paperwork. They don't seem to have time. (Brian, social worker)

Or as Sally, a social worker, put it:

There's some banter here, but it'll never be the same, because of the sheer workload. [. . .] At Midlands House we sat in the office, pratting about.

Detachment and team membership

The new silence in the team had further significance: it was thought to be a reflection of a fundamental change to the nature of team membership. The social atmosphere and banter that had previously pervaded the Youth Justice Team had been thought to be an integral part of the experience of team membership. It had been produced by the familiarity of team members with each other and was thus evidence of a 'camaraderie' that united team members (see Chapter 2). The loss of this social atmosphere was thought to reflect a loss of a feeling of closeness. Some staff described a feeling of detachment from their colleagues. For some, this was an indication that the team had fragmented:

> What team? We've disintegrated. Because everyone's working so hard, we don't see or speak to each other. When you see people you want to grab hold of them and spend time with them. (Jenny, social worker)

However, other staff felt that a lessening of the camaraderie in the team was instead crucial for the team to cohere. Graham, the team leader, felt that part of the overwhelming anxiety described by team members in the previous months was a product of a mounting panic. While the team were undoubtedly facing an increase in workload, their anxieties were disproportionate to the pressures they actually faced: as he put it, team members were experiencing both 'actual stress and perceived stress'. The prominent social environment in the team had encouraged the development of a 'hysterical' mood, which was exacerbated by the close physical proximity of team members in the offices:

> There was this kind of escalation, this kind of build-up, and because everybody was so close together there was no escape from how people were feeling.

The dispersal of the social closeness with the separation of team members in the new offices had also dispersed this feeling of collective anxiety. Practitioners could now begin to take a calmer, 'collected' approach to their work. In this way, after the previous months of apparent paralysis, practitioners now felt they were able to function. Some practitioners felt this productivity was essential for them to conceive of the YOT as a team. As Barbara, a social worker, explained:

> I'm a lot happier now we've moved [. . .] because I can get on with
> my work better, cos the rooms are quieter, I can get on with things,
> I feel that we're a Youth Offending Team now.

It seems therefore that, despite the losses associated with it, the dispersal
of the overwhelming feeling of a close 'team' and its replacement by a
more detached sense of co-working to have brought with it a sense of
relief. This implies that while the closeness and camaraderie had been
presented as universally prized in the youth justice team, it may also
have been experienced as stifling. Paradoxically then, some practitioners
felt the team had been too cohesive to allow the YOT to develop. As
Graham put it, the shared emotional atmosphere of the 'group' had now
been replaced by a calmer, productive atmosphere.

> Certainly people's attitudes are much calmer because there's not a
> group, the group's gone, you've got a set of offices with people in.
> So there isn't that collective, panicking, hysterical, too much stress,
> too much work, not enough time to do it.

The move towards a more loosely defined structure seems to have
allowed these alternative experiences of team life to be acknowledged.
In other words, rather than demonstrating a collapse of the team, the
feeling of detachment that practitioners described was now part of the
experience of team membership.

The changing boundaries of team membership

However, the shared social atmosphere in the Youth Justice Team had
been thought to have further significance than an emotional closeness: it
also represented a team-wide consensus, which reflected a shared and
cohesive culture. Social work staff felt they had a similar approach to and
understanding of the aims of their work. Although many of these
important aspects of team life were in fact characterised by the essential
ambiguities of social work practice, its members were able to construct
clear boundaries to the team by making claims about unity and division
in their membership, practice and values: the team could be seen to be
constructed by clearly demarcated '"us" and "them"' claims (Parker
2000, and see above). The new sense of detachment of the YOT now
seemed to reflect a change in practitioners' perceptions of the team as a
'settled' organisation. Instead of being demarcated by clearly defined,
stable boundaries, these key aspects of team life now seemed to be
characterised by a state of constant change and overt ambiguity. This
was brought into focus by the introduction of Detention and Training

Orders (DTOs) on 1 April 2000: the first of the new disposals under the Crime and Disorder Act 1998 to represent a significant change to the practice of the team.[3]

A permanent state of change: the introduction of DTOs

The radical restructuring of the youth justice system which practitioners were experiencing had extended to its custodial institutions. A review prior to the Crime and Disorder Act 'found little positive to say' about the arrangements for providing secure accommodation (Home Office 1998a): standards were inconsistent and often poor (see also Moore 2000), and did not address the offending behaviour or needs of young people within them. Further, there was 'no definable juvenile secure estate': children were held in a range of institutions with little coherence or planning. In sum, the current arrangements for custodial provision were 'chaotic and dysfunctional' (Home Office 1997d: 6.2). As a result, a series of reforms amounting to 'dramatic changes' (Hazel et al. 2002) were introduced to attempt to bring about greater coherence in regimes and placements, and to introduce new common standards. The range of custodial institutions (Young Offenders Institutions, secure training centres, youth treatment centres, local authority secure accommodation or any other secure accommodation) now collectively became termed the 'juvenile secure estate', and were brought together for the commissioning and purchasing of placements in custody. In April 2000 the Youth Justice Board was given the statutory duty to purchase places for, and place, children and young people remanded or sentenced to custody. It also became responsible for planning and prescribing the nature of the regimes. At the heart of the new approach to the 'secure estate' was the introduction of Detention and Training Orders (DTOs), which would now comprise the vast majority of custodial sentences given to young people under 18.[4]

The introduction of the DTO was intended to bring about a marked change in the nature of custody for young people. Custodial sentences would now become more 'constructive' and 'flexible' (Home Office 1998a). Orders are for four to 24 months. Half of this time is spent in a secure institution and half in the community under the supervision of the YOT. The same YOT worker is to supervise both halves of the order. This was intended to have two advantages. First, it would provide continuity in the work with the young person on their release from custody which was essential for preventing reoffending. As the Youth Justice Board put it, 'The transition from custody to community has to be seamless if the aim of preventing offending on discharge is to be achieved' (Youth Justice Board 2000: 1). Second, the orders would themselves provide a more 'constructive' use of custody (Home Office

1997d, 1998). Custodial sentences would now detail a programme of work intended to 'address offending behaviour and the factors associated with it' (Home Office et al. 2000: 2.21), aimed at preventing reoffending. In the first days of admission into custody a 'training plan' would be agreed between the young person ('trainee'), his or her parents or primary carer, and the supervising YOT member in consultation with the custodial staff. These might include measures such as a commitment to anger management courses, therapy for drug abuse, educational commitments and vocational training.

DTOs therefore necessitated a shift in the relationship between the YOT and the secure estate. YOT staff would have an increased level of intervention with the young people in secure institutions, and liaise more closely with custodial staff during both parts of the court order. As the Youth Justice Board announced:

> The new Detention and Training Order [. . .] will change the way people work in secure facilities. They will see more of the staff from YOTs, who will have overall responsibility for the delivery of individual sentence plans. The staff inside secure facilities should be encouraged to work with young offenders outside those facilities and for the first time follow them to the community part of the sentence. (Youth Justice Board 2000: 1)

As the following pages describe, the nature of these orders brought into focus the ambiguity that now appeared to characterise not only the composition and practice of the team, but also the values previously thought to define it.

The changing boundaries of team membership

After a period of stability in its membership, the composition of the team again appeared to be in flux. The increased involvement with young people in custody made significant demands on the YOT resources and extra staff were seconded to cope with these. Firstly, Brian, a long-serving social worker on the YOT, was seconded to a new role of Community Support Worker, working between three local YOIs to set up bail support packages, run training programmes and act as a 'mentor' to young people and help resettle them in the community on release. As he explained, the secondment of a youth justice social worker to the juvenile secure estate was a significant development in the team: 'There's never been a social worker in prison, I'm the first one.' He was followed by the arrival of three social work staff who were to be based in YOIs to focus on through-care arrangements such as inductions, welfare and child protection issues. There was talk of further posts to help alleviate the pressures on the team. New practitioners were appointed: two social workers, a careers officer and a third police officer with responsibility for prevention schemes in schools and youth centres. Staff now appeared to view the membership of the team as continually increasing. As Graham described it, the team was an 'ever expanding empire'.

But further, it had now become increasingly difficult to delineate the boundaries of the team. The creation of numerous partnerships with the expansion of the YOT brought about a new form of partial or peripheral team membership. For instance, the three social workers appointed to work in the juvenile secure estate were employed and managed by their respective YOIs where they were also based. However, their posts were coordinated by the Midlands YOT and they attended team meetings, came in and out of the offices freely and some had their own desk in the offices. Their status as team members thus appeared unclear.

In this way, the nature of team membership appeared to have changed. It was no longer possible to describe the team by the 'us and them' divisions that had defined the membership of the Youth Justice Team. Practitioners no longer had a clear conception of the team's membership: as one put it, 'it's such a fucking big team and people haven't met before'. Instead, the YOT's boundaries were now in a constant state of flux, allowing practitioners from different agencies to move in and out of the YOT easily.

But further, this new flexibility indicated a further change in the nature of team membership. The permeability of the boundaries of the team not only allowed staff from partner agencies to enter the YOT, but also allowed YOT staff to expand into the traditional territories of other agencies. There appeared to be a shift in the way the team was perceived: it was no longer merely vulnerable to encroachment by other agencies, but was itself able to extend into new terrain. This became particularly evident in the shifting relationship between the team and the juvenile secure estate.

It appeared that many YOT members viewed custodial staff with suspicion. The prison service had not been made statutory partners by the Crime and Disorder Act 1998 and were therefore seen as an agency quite separate to the YOT and, according to some YOT members, in conflict with it. Secure estate staff could not possibly share the anti-custodial ethos that was thought to be fundamental to the work of the team. As Tom, a social worker, put it, 'I think there's a great majority, people seeing their role as locking up children.' Another social worker added, 'you can't work with people like that'. The punitive ethos of the secure estate was thought to be reflected in the views of their staff: custodial staff were seen as 'Neanderthal', 'racist', 'thick'. After a training day to facilitate working relationships between the YOT and prison staff, staff reported that the antagonism was mutual.

One of the exercises that we were asked to do was look at the stereotype of social workers and the stereotype of prison officers and so we got all the usual, oh ripping kids away from mothers, and wearing sandals and tweed jackets and very very negative, very negative. (Barbara, social worker)

Cath, the education officer, described how one prison officer 'actually called me a do-gooder, in front of everyone'.

Practitioners' perceptions of the mutual hostility and incompatibility between the two agencies had strong similarities to the way that social work staff had described their anxieties about police officers joining the team almost a year previously (see Chapter 3). However, this similarity revealed the way that practitioners' understanding of partnerships had now changed. Instead of being concerned about an encroachment on the ethos and responsibilities of the team, some team members seemed to view this close partnership as an opportunity to expand the YOT's influence in the juvenile secure estate.

YOT staff could now physically encroach on the traditional space of other agencies. Brian and the new social work staff were now able to work in areas of the prison which had previously been restricted:

Brian will have a key to both institutions so he won't be offering what we usually do, we book a visit, and go and see the young person in the visitors centre, and Brian can actually go into the prison and see them in the cells or while they're having their dinner, somewhere within prison [. . .] actually go down to the education, and see what they're doing there. (Graham, team leader).

In this way, the team would be able to expand their reach into areas which were previously denied to them. This would provide for more effective interventions:

What you get in a visitors centre is young people saying, 'I'm alright, nothing wrong here', and that's part of the culture. And that's the perturbing bit, because you can see how distraught young people are when they're first locked up, and maybe after a week or two they're absorbed into the culture, they learn not to let their feelings show, they learn not to tell anybody how bad it is, how violent it can be, how frightening, and they say 'I'm OK'. So, that'll change. Brian and whoever else is in there will be able to see them in the prison [. . .] go on to some of the work placement, paving courses and bricklaying courses, can go and see how they actually interact on that, whereas from the out, they just tell they're doing bricklaying. So I'm hopeful that that will work. (Graham, team leader).

But, moreover, staff anticipated that embedding social work staff into the secure estate would inevitably bring about a change of culture:

> [Having social work staff in the secure estate] will be different because there's a whole different ethos, and different way of working with the young person and with the institutional representatives as well, the screws, the prison staff, so that will change. (Graham, team leader).

The new close working relationship between the YOT and the secure estate therefore indicated a change in the way the staff perceived the power and status of the YOT. Instead of being vulnerable to encroachment, it was the YOT that could now penetrate more deeply into other agencies and even influence the ethos of their work. In this way, the new state of flux in the membership of the team no longer seemed to be a source of overwhelming anxiety. Instead, it appeared to be accompanied by a new confidence in the possibilities of expansion.

The changing boundaries of practice

Secondly, the introduction of major new court orders made it evident that the practice of the team would now be in a constant state of change. The introduction of DTOs were to be followed by a large range of new community orders under the Crime and Disorder Act. Action plan orders, parenting orders, reparation orders, curfew orders and final warnings would become available on 1 June. It was inevitable that this would represent significant changes to the practice of the team. Staff were aware that their work would continue to change after that date: the imminent introduction of Intensive Surveillance and Supervision Programmes (ISSPs) and referral orders would require the development of new practice. As Graham put it, the constant introduction of new practice 'feels like a conveyor belt'.

Some staff reported feeling unprepared for the changes ahead. At this early stage of the new youth justice system, there was very little guidance about how to run the new measures. Barbara, a social worker, supervised a girl who received the first DTO in the team. She explained that the only assistance she had in the administration of the order was the lengthy circular distributed to YOTs by the Home Office (Home Office et al. 2000). It was left to individual practitioners to make sense of the guidance and determine how to proceed:

> I went through it, and just made my own notes, handwritten notes, crib sheets, you know, an idiot's guide, really, so that, I know what I need to do, when I need to do it.

Barbara's confusion was shared by the custodial staff:

> The prison staff that I've spoken to they've felt that they haven't
> been given enough training and information about what they've got
> to do.

The YOT staff therefore had no external sources of support or guidance
in the administration of the new orders. Instead, practitioners had to
manage their own uncertainty about how to deal with the new
provisions in the context of widespread confusion in the secure estate.

As Mark explained, learning to cope with the ambiguity of constant
change was going to be a permanent feature of life in the YOT:

> The first of June's going to come and go, you know, I think what
> we're trying to do is manage the speed of change, and at the end of
> the day, it's not just about meeting some requirements, it's about
> trying to move towards a way of working that's going to be
> effective, so in some points we will take longer to get it right, and
> even if that draws criticism at the start, I think well, live with it.
> (Mark, YOT manager)

The acceptance that practitioners' working lives would now involve
managing the uncertainty and confusion that accompanied change
involved a significant re-conception of what it meant to be part of a YOT.
Such confusion had previously been seen as pathological. As described
earlier, practitioners had been anxious that they were unprepared for the
launch of the YOT on 1 April: the upheaval and ambiguity that
practitioners had been experiencing in the previous months had been
seen as a sign of not 'being ready' for the looming deadlines. Managing
these deadlines was now a constant feature of YOT life. As one
practitioner put it:

> I've had a lot of fears as to, are we going to be ready on time, will I
> have the knowledge, that I need to have, will I have all the
> information that I need for the deadlines. So, April 1st has come and
> gone, and that wasn't so bad, I think that was mainly to do with the
> fact that a lot of the orders have been put back to 1st June, so that's
> the next stumbling block really. (Barbara, social worker)

The experience of being a YOT member therefore incorporated the
anxiety and confusion that was an inevitable part of constantly changing
practice.

The changing boundaries of values?

In addition, the introduction of DTOs appeared to allow the possibility of change in the values that had previously been thought to be fundamental to the social work team.

As outlined in Chapter 3, an 'anti-custody orthodoxy' (Haines and Drakeford 1998) was a defining philosophy for youth justice social workers. Social work with young offenders was sometimes described in terms of 'keeping kids out of lock up', and staff felt this defined the orientation of their work in relation to other, more punitive criminal justice agencies. Some staff explained that custody was not a viable disposal for any young person. One practitioner explained that this stance was a defining feature of their roles as youth justice social workers:

> Part of our policy is not to recommend custody, part of our role is to recommend alternatives to custody. (Tom, social worker)

Some staff accepted that in some circumstances, custody had to be used as a last resort for some young people. Yet, as Mark, the YOT manager, suggested, to make this explicit would be intolerable:

> You would never, ever recommend custody in pre-sentence reports. You would imply it [laughs], it would be dressed up in words that said that, but you would never actually say, you know, I feel I would have to recommend a period in custody.

However, the introduction of Detention and Training Orders appeared to represent a challenge to this anti-custodial ethos. As outlined above, DTOs were intended to denote a new way of thinking about custody. They would involve a programme of 'positive work' (Home Office 1998a: para. 76) and a 'constructive engagement with the offender' (Home Office 1998a: para. 74). In this way, DTOs would bring about a change in the way custody was managed: it would be a 'constructive' experience for young people. What, then, were the implications for practitioners' beliefs about the use of custody for young people?

At this early stage of the implementation of the orders, there was much scepticism among YOT members about the claims for the positive effects of a custodial regime. As Mark said, 'I'm not convinced about that one yet'. The official claims about DTOs were certainly contentious. Some commentators were sceptical about the extent to which the orders represented a significant departure from and improvement on the previous regimes. Pitts argued that to claim so 'strains credulity' (1999: 70): the DTO instead 'merely offers "business as usual"'. But, moreover, the concept of 'constructive custody' is highly problematic. As Goldson puts it, as a method of dealing with youth crime, incarceration is 'spectacularly ineffective': 'Children invariably leave prison not only more damaged but also more angry, more alienated, more expert in the ways of crime and more likely to commit more serious offences – in fact more of everything that the children themselves and the community need much less of' (Goldson 2002: 159–60; see also, for example, Moore 2000). Studies have described the 'corrosive and brutalising inhumanity' (Goldson 2000: 258) of custodial institutions, with a culture of widespread bullying, assault, intimidation, deeply embedded racism and high risks of self-harm and suicide to which young people are particularly vulnerable (e.g. Commission for Racial Equality 2003; Goldson 2002; Liebling 1992). There is thus a fundamental mismatch between the notion of a programme of positive work and the 'the anti-rehabilitative or anti-therapeutic effects' (Pitts 1999: 154) of the custodial environment. In addition, some feared that the framing of DTOs as a constructive measure would make them seem an attractive sentencing option for magistrates, thereby increasing the use of custodial sentences.[5] As one social worker put it, they seemed like a 'credible option':

> I think the magistrates are going to think 'there's a lot of training going on in prisons, it's not a prison sentence any more, it's a detention and training order, and they've got all this going for them', they will use them. The kid's got to fit the criteria, but where you would have put a supervision order in place with specified activities, you'd have got him off a custodial sentence at that point, but if they're fed up of seeing that kid coming through the courts, what they think as getting away with it, then they're going to say, right we've had enough, DTO. (Brian, social worker)

Yet, despite practitioners' doubts about the 'positive' nature of the disposals, the apparent changes to the nature of the regimes ostensibly placed some of their objections to custody at issue. As Mark put it, 'the premises that we worked on before don't apply now':

> Now I mean if the prisons are changing to more child-orientated regimes, and they're actually more intervening regimes, and half their time's spent inside and half their time's outside in the community and the same sort of resources are being made available in both settings, the logic is then that prisons could be quite a positive experience, that's what it's saying isn't it, and the only reason that you're recommending it is really that you need the added security, for protection of the public. Otherwise, there's no difference. (Mark, YOT manager)

Should staff revise the way they think about custody? Tom, a social worker, explained,

> One of the quite interesting things is do we recommend a DTO or not. [. . .] DTOs are quite different, because it's a training order as well, supposedly, it's a more positive order, so do we recommend them or not?

Tom said that despite the supposedly positive emphasis of the order, he would not alter his current practice of trying to deter magistrates from custodial sentences:

> I would personally never recommend one. I'd write in such a way that the magistrates could give everything else.

However, Tom's assertion that he 'personally' would never recommend a DTO allowed for the possibility of a diversity of attitudes among YOT staff. For the first time there appeared to be ambiguity in the defining philosophy of the team. Could their work still be described with certainty as underpinned by an anti-custodial stance?

This uncertainty was further exacerbated by some practitioners' early experiences of the disposals. What if practitioners found that DTOs could actually provide a constructive forum for intervention?

One of the first DTOs to be managed by the team was given to Sharon, a girl aged 15. She had been supervised by Sally, a social worker, for nearly two years, and there appeared to have been little change in her offending behaviour, which was thought to have been aggravated by a violent relationship with her brother. Sally had become frustrated and exhausted at the lack of progress that she appeared to be making with Sharon:

> I'm tired, I've worked with Sharon for a long time and she's really difficult. It's a very intense relationship as there's been so much conflict, I've been upset for and with her, I've been angry with her.

After a series of supervision orders of increasing length over this two-year period, Sharon was eventually sentenced to a four-month DTO. A custodial sentence was expected: Sharon had a history of non-compliance with her orders and had recently reoffended while on a supervision order. The 'training plan' negotiated with Sharon involved a series of regular, fortnightly supervision visits by both Sally and Karen, the health officer, and weekly interventions with a youth and community worker who had close contact with the YOT. Her programme included a series of sessions focusing on her offending behaviour, and the maximum hours of education allowed by the regime. Sharon also had to agree to do 'chores' such as cleaning, and to maintain regular telephone contact with a family member.

Sally was surprised at the progress Sharon appeared to have made during this period in custody. After two years of appearing to have made no impact, Sharon was now 'getting positive feedback from everyone':

> She noticed a change in herself when she came out of custody, the secure estate staff noticed a change in her too, she's better able to deal with situations. She's been back at a youth and community centre one week, and they all said she's really changed. So there has been that positive side of it.

As Sally explained, it was difficult to draw a firm connection between the programme of work in the DTO and the apparent change in Sharon's feelings and behaviour. Any progress may unconnected to the disposal:

> Who knows if its part of her growing maturity, who knows if she'd be here without the DTO.

There also remained a strong likelihood that she would reoffend:

> I said will we be seeing you in court again and she said no, but she also said if someone hits her, she'll hit her back.

However, Sally also felt that this apparent positive change could not be wholly unrelated to Sharon's experience in custody: 'It must be the DTO, it must be.' She thought the disposal had allowed her to carry out an individualised programme of work in an environment where, as she put it, she and the secure unit staff literally had 'a captive audience':

> It's being in an environment where there's constant conflict, the staff have challenged her, then talked it though with her as well [. . .] her self-esteem has gone up, she says its us not giving up on her, continuing with her.

Sharon said that the period of the order in secure accommodation gave her 'a bit of peace from the constant chatting' from her violent brother, or as Sally explained, 'she felt safe, it gave her time to reflect'.

In this way, despite her strongly felt opposition to custody, Sally felt that the regime offered by the DTO may have contributed to the positive change widely perceived in Sharon. In this one instance, 'I think we have to see it as a positive thing'. Yet as Sally explained, this introduced an irreconcilable conflict with the values she felt integral to her occupational identity as a social worker:

I still have problems advocating DTOs. I've *never* recommended custody. It goes against all my values. I don't work for the police, I don't work for the CPS, if I did, I might think, yeah, OK and I might recommend custody. But I work for social services, my values are entirely different.

In other words, while Sally's anti-custodial stance remained firm, her experience of this DTO implied a new ambiguity in a defining principle of the team. It thus introduced an element of uncertainty into the ethos that Sally had previously felt was both unambiguous and fundamental to her work.

Becoming a YOT

In this way, membership of the YOT now seemed to be characterised by change and ambiguity. Important aspects of team life seemed to be in a state of constant flux. Yet as practitioners came to perceive the boundaries of practice, composition and values as increasingly permeable, and their relationships with their colleagues increasingly detached, the identity of the YOT became at issue. The team could no longer be demarcated by the claims of similarity and difference – of 'us' and 'them' – that had previously enabled practitioners to construct a feeling of a shared culture and identity in the Youth Justice Team. What, then, was a YOT? And what did it mean to be a YOT member?

Some practitioners felt the development of a distinctive team identity was now vital. Yet this was far from straightforward. Firstly, the nature of this shared identity was problematic. It was evident that YOT membership must accommodate the ambiguity and flux of team life that was no longer masked in the team, but had become a central part of members' experiences. And as discussed in Chapter 5, it must also allow staff to retain some degree of distinct identity to avoid compromising the membership of those who did not want to 'become social workers'. In other words, the crucial aspect of YOT identity paradoxically was the incorporation of difference. But in addition, despite practitioners' desire to develop some shared sense of team membership, the new diffuse nature of the team made this difficult to achieve.

Many staff thought the establishment of an inter-agency identity could only be developed through discussions among the team as a whole.

Until we all sit down, and talk things through, we're never going to develop as a team. (Julie, social worker)

In this context, team meetings again took on particular importance. Their position as the only site at which the team met as a whole in a formal setting, their function as an accountable forum for 'constructive negotiation' (Crawford and Jones 1995: 31) and their status as a 'sense-making forum' in which the YOT could be made visible to its members were crucial for practitioners to discern and negotiate the identity of the developing team. As a result, regular team meetings were reinstated. They followed an agenda to which team members could contribute in advance. Minutes were taken and circulated after the meetings. There thus seemed to be an end to the repeated cancellations and unaccountable procedures that had characterised the management of team meetings in the previous months.

However, meetings no longer appeared to function. Staff no longer seemed willing to contribute to discussions but would sit in silence for the duration of the meeting. As one practitioner explained:

Everybody contributes after the team meeting. The fag after the meeting is like the meeting. (Andy, probation service assistant)

As a result, practitioners no longer appeared to find the meetings valuable. Attendance dropped: there were often between seven and ten staff present out of a total of 35. As Cath put it:

They're [team meetings] crap, I'm going to stop going to them. They're dull, nobody comes, nobody contributes. They're not useful.

The change in tenor of the meetings appeared to be a consequence of the new experience of membership in the YOT. The team had expanded to such a size that it could no longer accommodate discussions involving all its staff. As Tom, a social worker, explained:

Team meetings will have to change to suit the size, team meetings in the past have been half a dozen. The team's so big, it's like a conference isn't it.

But further, the apparently decreasing importance of team meetings may have been a reflection of the detachment and loss of 'team feeling' that many practitioners described as a feature of YOT membership. Without a strong sense of membership of the team, participation in the activities seen as a core part of the team may have become less important. In other words, practitioners' sense of obligation and commitment to the team may have decreased with their sense of belonging. The sense of detachment that characterised the YOT was particularly likely to be manifested in its meetings, which, as Schwartzman puts it, 'are the organization or community *writ small'* (1989: 39, and see Chapter 7). Thus while many staff felt the lack of a feeling of a shared identity made team meetings important, it may also have made them unlikely to attend. In this way, the aspects of team life that appeared to disrupt the feeling of cohesion in the team also seemed to obstruct the development of a shared identity.

Team building

As an attempt to resolve this dilemma, Mark, the YOT manager, instigated a two-day 'team building' training session. He explained that the training days had the express purpose of developing a team-wide approach:

> That's why we're doing some team building, that's really going to focus on the culture [. . .] it's really to try and expose some of the concerns, the issues, and bring them to the surface.

The sessions were held at an external site and all practitioners were required to attend.

This was the first occasion at which the YOT had met together as a whole. For the first time, therefore, the entire organisation was made visible to its members. Some practitioners felt that this in itself brought home the extent to which the team had changed:

> The fact that we were all sat together, and it was a massive group, we'd never all been together, and there was 28 of us, and there was four missing and two to come. (Denise, admin manager)

It also demonstrated the task facing the team in developing a sense of a shared identity:

> It gave people an opportunity to meet the whole team and give a profile of yourself, it was quite interesting, there were people I didn't know much about. The frightening thing about it is that it's so bloody big, I don't know how you can keep a proper team ethos, it's an incredible size. (Tom, social worker)

The team-building days also revealed the extent to which some social workers still harboured unhappiness and resentment at the change to their professional identity. The facilitator explained that the sessions represented an opportunity for practitioners to 'let go of the past'. Or as Louise, the probation officer, described it, staff were told to 'put everything to rest, speak now or forget it'. Yet it was clear that many social workers were unwilling to abandon their social work identity, and this remained a source of considerable anxiety:

> Mark said 'youth justice is dead', Graham said he wasn't prepared to forget the past. (Louise, probation officer)

> Mark kept saying we have to leave the old behind. I felt he was saying the past ways of working were disregarded. (Sally, social worker)

> We've got to move on from the old ways, and I suppose I'm old fashioned, and I want to keep a part of what I had before. There are new people with new ideas, but I think I've seen it all before and it didn't work. I'm worried about putting a damper on people's enthusiasm. (Tom, social worker)

Some staff were surprised at the discontent that was unearthed. Graham described the team as 'this amorphous moaning mass':

> After the first day I was quite despondent. There was no feeling of support, no recognition of how far people have come, how far they've changed. [. . .] It felt as if we were earlier on, just before Duncan died, just after.

However, over the course of the two days many staff felt they were able to identify crucial questions facing the team: as one practitioner put it, 'we really started thrashing things through'. Some of these questions concerned the way the team functioned. What were the roles of each team member? How should staff work together? But practitioners also started to raise key questions underlying the work of the team. What was the nature of young people's responsibility towards their offending behaviour? How far could young offenders be considered 'victims'? Should the practitioners aspire to early intervention with young people, or should they adopt a non-interventionist strategy? What did it mean to develop a professional YOT identity?

In other words, the same underlying questions anticipated to be a focus of conflict since the beginning of the team's transition to the YOT remained at issue nine months later. Of course, many of these reflected fundamental tensions at the heart of the youth justice system and had been sources of ambiguity underpinning the work of the youth justice team well before the arrival of staff from partner agencies. It was therefore clearly impossible for the team to arrive at a consensus on any of these complex issues in just two team-building days. However, it was also clear that, despite an increasing acceptance of ambiguity and flux, the notion of consensus over key issues retained its potency as an indicator of team identity. Practitioners were not yet ready to abandon attempts to come to a shared view about the purpose and values underlying their practice. Team meetings retained their potency as a site at which a YOT identity could be developed. Practitioners agreed that they would become more collaborative, more 'dynamic', 'discussing real issues'. However, the obstructions to effective negotiation inherent in the nature of team membership continued to render the meetings impotent. They remained similar in character to the meetings before the team-building days, much to the frustration of some team members:

> We need to take it [issues raised] away and work at them. But we don't. I get so frustrated, it seems so obvious. I think it gives us the potential to change things, but . . . [laughs]. (Cath, education officer)

Staff were disappointed that the sessions appeared to have made little tangible impact on the sense of team feeling in the YOT. As Denise, the admin manager, explained:

> Since it happened, it hasn't been discussed, certainly not in here. It's been like something that you had to do, and business as usual on Monday.

In July 2000, therefore, the team remained grappling with the problem of creating a shared identity for a team now characterised by ambiguity, change and difference. As discussed in the following chapter, these questions put at issue the nature of inter-agency working at the heart of Labour's youth justice reforms.

Notes

1 Some practitioners in the team also saw Graham's adoption of a caseload as a demotion. One described it as a sign that Mark recognised that 'things haven't been running the way they should': in other words, that Graham had been incompetent as a manager and thus had his duties removed.

2 This was not entirely true. The social work staff continued to be employed by the DSS and could be redeployed elsewhere in the social services if they chose: they were seconded to the YOT. Graham's own position was less clear. His post was funded jointly by the social services and the YOT and he was unsure whether he remained a social services employee:

I'm presuming that if I'm ever wanting to jack this in I have nowhere to go, I couldn't go back to social services, end my secondment so to speak, but apparently I can, but to go back as what, I don't know.

3 Anti-Social Behaviour Orders and local child curfews had already become available to the courts but at this stage – and contrary to the now apparently inexorable rise in interest and employment of ASBOs – they were not anticipated to be a frequently used sentencing option. At the time of this study neither had been used in the YOT area.

4 The DTO replaced the two previous primary custodial sentences: the Secure Training Order for 12–14 year olds, and Detention in a Young Offender Institution for 15 year olds and above. A DTO can be given to 15–17 year olds for any offence serious enough to warrant a custodial sentence, and those 12–14 year olds who are 'persistent offenders'. The Crime and Disorder Act provided the discretionary power for the Home Secretary to introduce the DTO for ten and eleven year olds if this became 'necessary' or 'desirable' at a later date (Home Office 1998a: para. 73).

5 Custodial rates in England and Wales did in fact rise from 7,414 in 2000 to 7,595 in 2001, although as a proportion of all sentences of 10–17 year olds in these years this represented a very slight reduction from 8.10 per cent in 2000 to 7.96 per cent. The total number of custodial disposals fell in subsequent years: in 2002 there were 7,416 (7.85 per cent of all sentences); there were 6,200 in 2003 (6.70 per cent); and 6,325 in 2004 (6.58 per cent) (*source*: Home Office, criminal statistics England and Wales).

Chapter 9

Occupational identity and cultural change

In this book I have adopted a different approach to most writing on contemporary youth justice measures. My primary focus has not been the ideological and theoretical underpinnings of the new Labour government's strategies for youth justice, or an evaluation of the implementation of its measures, but their underside in the everyday lives and experiences of those professionals whose task it was to enact them. What was the impact of this transformation of the youth justice system on practitioners' working lives? And what were its effects on their sense of occupational identity and vocation? As these questions can only be explored through close observation, I have adopted a relatively micro-level approach. I have followed one group of actors in one locality over a determinate period, as they attempted to carry out the delivery of youth justice services in the context of organisational change. This close study of the ordinary, lived experience of practitioners undergoing the reconfiguration of youth justice services reveals the complexity of its effects. Not only did the formation of multi-agency YOTs bring about a period of intense disruption for practitioners, they also brought with them a series of problems about membership, identity and loss.

This chapter draws together some of the arguments in this book. What were the effects of organisational change on those practitioners working within it? What are the implications for wider questions of occupational culture and identity in contemporary organisations? What does it suggest about the purpose and nature of inter-agency working, in particular in relation to the government's central rationale of developing a shared culture among youth justice practitioners? And how can questions of culture and identity inform an understanding of the relationship between policy and practice?

Transforming youth justice social work

The processes that the Crime and Disorder Act set in train were received as profoundly unsettling by youth justice social workers. The tone of repudiation and disdain in the communications surrounding the implementation of the Crime and Disorder Act and the radical reorganisation these set in train were understood by social workers as a dismissal of their previous practice. They were confronted with the criticism that their practice was inactive, collusive and ineffective and in need of fundamental change. Social workers said they felt 'hurt', 'we're being told we've failed'. Their professional experience and expertise now appeared to count for nothing.

Every aspect of their working lives was felt to be under attack. Even the daily administrative routines, such as the way they filled out their paperwork, were now open to scrutiny and thus susceptible to abrupt change. Yet it transpired that these routine tasks, however mundane, were integral to practitioners' sense of occupational identity. Some practitioners explained that the shape of their routines had developed to reflect important working assumptions and values in youth justice social work. For example, the way they filled in their paperwork was said to reflect the organisational learning from the Pindown Enquiry, a particularly difficult moment in the recent history of social work (Levy and Kahan 1991). But these routine tasks also appeared to be associated in a more deeply embedded way with the profession itself. Performing their accustomed routines appeared to reinforce practitioners' sense of being a youth justice social worker, and the values and traditions this was felt to represent. In this way, attacking the mundane aspects of team life seemed to go right to the core of what it was to be a youth justice social worker.

This perceived attack was particularly unsettling as the nature of the change was as yet intangible. The shape, structure, practice and ethos of both the YOT and the wider youth justice system were unformed and indiscernible. Practitioners were thus being asked to put aside their occupational identity in place of something that was not yet clear.

But further, the nature of youth justice social work made it hard for practitioners to defend. As described in Chapter 3, staff explained that the methods they used, the values underlying them, the purpose and scope of their interest and the outcomes they could effect were complex and ambiguous. While they shared a strongly-felt common orientation to their work, an understanding of its overarching purpose, and comparable experiences and problems, these common themes accommodated multiple and diverse meanings. Such 'normal ambiguity' (Meyerson 1991) was an essential cultural cue of their practice. It reflected shared working assumptions, for example, about the complexity of the nature of human behaviour and social problems and the centrality of notions of individualisation and subjectivity to the work of the team. However, it also made the work of the team difficult to articulate. If practitioners could not easily describe the technologies of their practice or demonstrate its impact, how could they defend themselves against accusations of inactivity and failure? This issue became particularly salient in the context of the increasing priority given to actuarial techniques in the management of youth offending. The refocusing of the youth justice system towards particular notions of risks, outcomes and evidence meant that practitioners' accounts of what they did could no longer satisfy. At the same time, the ambiguity inherent in their practice made the team vulnerable to encroachment from other agencies. The difficulty in delineating the unique expertise and technologies of youth justice social work – its 'functional territory' (Huntington 1981) – made it hard for staff to defend the boundaries of the team by claiming ownership of their central tasks.

In this way, the reconfiguration of youth justice services left practitioners anxious and uncomfortable. It appeared to strike at the core of their practice and professional identity, at the same time leaving them with no easy defence.

Transforming occupational identity

But further, the restructuring of youth justice services was responsible for a series of profound shifts in practitioners' self-image. By disrupting the ways in which staff had been able to construct a sense of shared identity and culture, the formation of the YOT put in question what it was to be a youth justice worker.

Social work members of the Youth Justice Team had described themselves as part of a tightly cohesive team, bound together by shared aims, values and practices. These aspects of working life were seen to define the identity of the team, and thus of the practitioners within it. They were therefore crucial to practitioners' sense of what it was to be a youth justice social worker. Although these key elements of occupational identity were inherently ambiguous, this ambiguity could largely be masked by the construction of a series of 'us and them' claims (Parker 2000) which delineated the boundaries of the work and values of the team by placing them in opposition to those of other agencies and of other areas of social work. So, for example, by contrasting their work with the punitive orientation of other criminal justice agencies, staff described their own 'welfarist' approach; differentiating their working style from the apparently rigid outlook of agencies such as the police clarified the espoused importance of flexibility and discretion in their work. In other words, such claims about similarity and difference enabled practitioners to eliminate and clarify the ambiguities of their experiences. By describing the ways in which the team was not like others, staff could both delineate the boundaries of the team and describe its shared identity.

However, the development of the YOT placed these boundary constructions in question. First, the absorption of practitioners from partner agencies into the team blurred the boundaries between agencies. It became increasingly difficult to delineate who constituted 'them' and 'us'. Practitioners were suddenly deprived of a clear demonstration of what was distinct about their occupational identity. Second, the formation of the YOT required the development of new, multi-agency practice and administrative routines. This explicitly placed in question the values and purpose of youth justice interventions. Practitioners now had to become engaged in discussions about the underlying aims, scope and beliefs that shaped their work. As a result, it brought into focus the ambiguities of their practice that had previously been masked by the routinised conventions of the team. The diversity, disagreement and confusion among team members about the scope and purpose of their work now became exposed.

At the same time, the team became severed from the Department of Social Services and the YOT was established as a distinct stand-alone entity. The formal separation of the team from the social services was experienced as removing the legitimating authority of their professional body. The removal of these clarifying and legitimating supports of their professional identity brought about a consequent loss of a sense of occupational belonging.

Fragmentation

These developments brought about a fundamental change in the dominant perception of the team. It became increasingly difficult for practitioners to construct a sense of the team as a strongly cohesive unit. Instead, the ambiguities underlying the experiences of team membership were brought into focus. The shift in their professional self-image and their experience of team membership was experienced as deeply unsettling by many practitioners. Practitioners felt the team had 'disintegrated', 'fragmented', that they were 'working in isolation'. Or as one newly arrived member of staff put it, 'it feels like I'm coming to a place where there's people working, but I don't think it feels like a team'.

The confusion and uncertainty that pervaded the team left many team members anxious and bewildered. Moreover, there appeared to be no resolution to these anxieties. Practitioners were unable to identify the problems they faced, their solutions or a source of direction. As described in Chapter 7, this confusion appeared to pervade all levels of the youth justice system. Like the practitioners in the developing team, their managers in the YOT and the newly formed Youth Justice Board at the centre were all in a similar process of creating a service from scratch, with few resources on which they could draw. As the YOT manager put it, 'you don't have a right to anything ... you don't actually belong anywhere ... you're not part of anything'. Further, the emerging structures of governance between the YOT and the YJB were proving difficult to negotiate. The concurrent devolving of autonomy to the YOT and tightening of supervision at the centre was experienced as simultaneously overwhelming and constraining. There thus seemed to be no source of guidance or certainty that could resolve the ambiguity experienced among team members. Practitioners described a vacuum of direction in the team. As Martin and Meyerson (1988) explain, such an overpowering sense of free-floating anxiety can lead to paralysis: 'When a situation is ambiguous, it is difficult to know if action is called for, which actions would be appropriate, and what their consequences might be. The frequent result is inaction.' The team appeared to be trapped in a state of inert anxiety.

However, the absence of guidance and direction in the team also appeared to have encouraged creativity. Staff could determine the shape of their roles, adopting positions of greater responsibility and developing new tasks. Martin and Meyerson (1988) argue that ambiguity brings with it a sense of safety: a work environment infused with uncertainty and confusion makes it difficult to detect and evaluate negative outcomes in work. It therefore provides the freedom to experiment. For example, before the appointment of the operations manager, Graham commented on his role as acting in both operations manager and team leader positions, saying 'whatever I want to do, I'm going to do, because no one will notice any difference'. Thus while many practitioners felt the team was paralysed through this period, the innovation it encouraged was also shaping the form the YOT would take. As Weick (1985) argues, 'If an organisation continues to act even though it doesn't know for certain what it is doing, there is a chance that the organization will emerge from its confrontations with ambiguity in slightly different shape than when it started to cope' (1985: 125). Or as Graham put it when the new calm after the launch of the YOT allowed space for reflection: 'We're still floundering, but it's moved on a lot, and people are doing things they weren't doing before.' In this way, although the apparent vacuum of direction in the early stages of the YOT was experienced as incapacitating, it also was a source of innovation and creativity. In the light of the increasing centralised control of services and the new evidence-based culture heralded by the new arrangements for youth justice, these early months may ironically have represented a brief period of freedom in the team's practice.

This period of free-floating anxiety appeared to have become resolved by a series of explicit statements about the beginning of a new team, and by a move towards a more directive form of management which seemed to fill the vacuum of direction. It was perhaps surprising that team members' unease appeared to become resolved so suddenly. As discussed in Chapter 8, the sudden calm among team members may reflect a feeling of resignation: the changes they had resisted had now irreversibly taken place. However, it may also reflect a feeling of relief. The move from a tightly cohesive team into a more loosely defined structure with less clearly defined obligations of membership may have been experienced as liberating. The new detachment among team members allowed practitioners a freedom of diversity that had previously been constrained by the felt need to present the team as a tightly cohesive unit.

Occupational culture and identity revisited

The development of the team therefore brought about a series of profound shifts in the way practitioners perceived their identity as youth justice professionals, and their experience of team membership. How then do the experiences of the developing YOT relate to wider questions of occupational culture and identity in contemporary organisations?

Firstly, the developments in the YOT demonstrate the complexity and flux of organisational experiences. They suggest that even when occupational members have a strong sense of a shared, cohesive occupational culture, organisational life can also be understood as characterised by incompletely understood or irreconcilable conflicts, inconsistencies and contradictions (Martin 2002). This in turn indicates the importance of thinking about organisational cultures in a way that can accommodate these aspects of organisational life, even when they may not appear to be central to members' experiences. As Martin and Meyerson argue (Martin 1992, 2002; Martin and Meyerson 1988; Meyerson and Martin 1987), while a particular way of looking at an organisational culture may seem particularly appropriate or accurate, and may be considered so by its members, other perspectives remain available and may produce particularly useful insights. Thus, although social workers presented the Youth Justice Team as a remarkably cohesive, settled entity, conflicts and ambiguities were also important elements of their experiences of team membership and it was these that became particularly important in the context of organisational change.

Secondly, the changes in the way that the team was perceived and experienced by its members indicates the fluid and dynamic nature of organisational cultures. As Parker (2000) argues, cultures should be seen as 'processual' (2000: 89): the claims about unity and division that members use to describe the boundaries of the organisation are in a constant state of dispute and flux. 'Organisation is a contested process, a continually shifting set of claims and counter-claims, and there is not place or time from which it can be finally captured and presented as the truth' (2000: 225). Yet practitioners' experiences also show how the external contexts of organisational life have a profound effect on the way these claims are made. The intense politicisation of youth justice, the radical reconfiguration of youth justice services it set in train, the negotiation of the new relationships between the local delivery of crime control and its central management, and the pressure of administration and workload that these developments produced were all paramount in bringing into focus the ambiguity experienced by these practitioners and the ensuing shifts in the way they understood their organisational world. The development of the YOT therefore indicates the potency of the external context in shaping the way that members perceive and construct their internal culture.

However, the importance of the impact of the external context on the internal cultures of organisations is largely neglected in organisational culture research. As Jelinek et al. describe, research on organisational cultures tends 'to stress the internal, rather than to look to the external, societal, cultural context within which organizations are embedded' (Jelinek et al. 1983: 338; see also Martin 1992: 113). Recent critical writing on organisational culture (e.g. Jermier 1991; Martin 1992; Parker 2000) has addressed this issue by showing how the power relations that structure the environment in which an organisation is situated also structures the organisation itself. An organisation is understood as a 'microcosm of the surrounding societal culture' (Martin 1992: 111): external cultural influences such as race, gender and class permeate the boundaries of an organisation and are enacted within it. Organisations are thus closely grounded in the broader culture both through the extra-organisational identities of their members (Jermier 1991; Martin 1992) and in the way these wider power relations structure the differing status and legitimacy bestowed upon various occupational members, actions and beliefs (Parker 2000). In this way, 'The sense members make of their organization ... is therefore bounded by the context of understood power relations – between men and women, the old and the young, managers and workers, professionals and administrators and so on' (Parker 2000: 226).

Yet while this writing enlightens a crucial understanding of the inextricability of the cultures and identities of organisational members from their wider social environment, the developments in the Midlands YOT suggest that this understanding could be expanded in two ways. Firstly, the social environment in which organisations are situated have primarily been conceived as those aspects of power relations (such as race, gender and class) which are deeply embedded and thus relatively stable. The experiences described in this book show that the dynamic, unstable aspects of the external context of organisations – such as the political climate, organisational change and pressures of workload and administration – also have a powerful impact on internal culture. Secondly, it indicates something about the nature of this impact. The external context in which an organisation is situated can permeate into organisational cultures not just through the pervasive enactment of broader power relations, but can also have an instrumental effect in the way that internal cultures are perceived, bringing about fundamental and widespread shifts in members' experience of their organisation.

Further, the development of the Midlands YOT revealed the fragility of the construction of an occupational identity. The ambiguities of their experiences and the ease with which their self-image was disrupted indicates something of the complexity of what it means to be a member of an occupation. These complexities were perhaps revealed most clearly by the experiences of staff from partner agencies who found themselves suddenly dislocated from their home agency and without a role yet established in the YOT. The development of an appropriate role and way of working therefore required new staff to consider what it was be a member of their home agency. It became evident that this was far from straightforward. Staff neither had a clear understanding of the principles and practices of their occupation, nor a straightforward or unproblematic attachment to them. Instead, their understanding of their occupational identity was often complex and contradictory, characterised by a fluctuating sense of disjunction from their home agency.

Culture, policy and practice

The understanding of culture and identity discussed here is therefore very different from that currently dominant in criminological writing about occupational cultures. As I have outlined in the introduction to this book, much of the interest in the occupational cultures of criminal justice professionals has concerned the relationship between culture and practice, and its implications for questions of justice and legitimacy. So, for example, the attention to police culture derived largely from research which showed how policing among rank and file staff in particular was shaped less by legal rules than by informal values, beliefs and working assumptions (e.g. Banton 1964; Skolnick 1966; Van Maanen 1978). Research has explored the nature of such working assumptions, beliefs and values, how they might be shaped by the distinctive tasks or working environments of particular occupations, how they might influence what practitioners do, and thus how they might mediate outcomes for service users. Perhaps partly because of this focus, a series of common themes has come to dominate the way that occupational cultures are presented in much of this work. Cultures are largely understood as aspects of members' experiences which are generated by the distinctive pressures of particular occupational environments. They are those aspects of organisational life which are shared by their members, and common only to those other occupations which experience similar pressures. While there may be important variations in the culture across different parts of the profession due to different pressures (e.g. Fielding 1995; Reiner 2000; Reuss-Ianni and Ianni 1983; Shapland and Vagg 1988), and members may vary in their understanding of and orientation towards their occupational culture (e.g. Reiner 1978; Shearing 1981; Walsh 1977), such variations have generally been presented as static, discrete and distinct.

As I have argued, this dominant view of culture cannot capture the flux, ambiguity and complexity that are essential parts of occupational experiences. But in addition, it leads to a particular framing of the relationship between culture, policy and practice. As Waddington (1999) and Chan (1996) have pointed out, discussions of police culture in particular tend to have normative connotations. As far as police culture has an impact on practice, it is generally seen as a negative one: informal values and beliefs are understood as producing discriminatory and unjust outcomes, reinforcing traditional ways of thinking and acting and promoting a resistance to change. 'Culture' is thus often presented as an aspect of organisational life that obstructs innovation and impedes reform. Yet the developments in the Midlands YOT suggest a different understanding of the way that culture can affect the implementation of policy. Questions of culture and identity were indeed of crucial importance in a dissonance between policy and practice in the establishment of the team. First, practitioners' anxiety and dismay at the radical restructuring of the youth justice system resulted in some attempts to resist and undermine the changes with which they were confronted. Such resistance was most clearly brought into focus over particularly overt and uncomfortable indicators of change, such as the development of new multi-agency practice with the introduction of groupwork. However, practitioners' resistance did not appear merely to reflect an antipathy to change itself, as some of the newer team members had assumed. Nor did it seem to reflect an intractable, conservative occupational culture. Instead, practitioners' resistance to the changes set in train by Labour's reforms reflected the potency of their effects: they appeared to strike at the core of their sense of identity and vocation.

But further, the developments in the team put in question the feasibility of the emergence of a 'common approach to youth justice work' (Home Office 1997a: 10, 1997d: 8.9) which was at the heart of the transformation of the youth justice system. As outlined in Chapter 1, the new Labour government had argued that the way the youth justice system had previously been organised perpetuated a fundamental confusion about its purpose. The dispersal of responsibility for youth offending across different government departments and different agencies had led the delivery of youth justice services to become incoherent and inconsistent. The consolidation of work with young offenders into single structures was intended to resolve these tensions and bring about a shared approach.

Writing about multi-agency work highlights problems of occupational identity and culture in the implementation of such strategies (e.g. Crawford 1997; Crawford and Jones 1995; Gilling 1994; Pearson et al. 1992; Sampson et al. 1988). It is a central theme of this work that conflict is inevitable in inter-agency partnerships due to the competing interests of participating agencies. As Crawford and Jones explain: 'As a consequence of their different histories, cultures, and traditions, organizations engaging in multi-agency community crime prevention work pursue conflicting ideologies, strategies, and practices' (1995: 20). In other words, because agencies inhabit 'different assumptive worlds' (Gilling 1994: 251), staff from these agencies are likely to have different conceptions of the problems at hand and thus the appropriate approach to them. Gilling argues that 'It is naïve to expect them to act otherwise, or to cede to some higher mutual rationality' (1994: 251). The problems of cultural conflicts between practitioners from different agencies – in particular between police staff and social workers – and how these might affect co-working has also been a feature of writing about the formation of YOTs (e.g. Burnett and Appleton 2004; Holdaway et al. 2001; Bailey and Williams 2000). Indeed, as described in Chapters 3 and 4, these questions were a source of considerable anxiety among social work members of the Youth Justice Team, who felt there were fundamental conflicts with the working styles and assumptions of the police.

However, this research puts in question the assumption that conflicts between agencies will be played out among individual staff. Such a notion is founded on the assumptions that firstly, occupational members understand what the 'ideologies, strategies and practices' of their home agencies are, and, secondly, that these are accepted. The experiences of staff in the Midlands YOT put in question the existence of clear occupational 'agendas' which are understood by all agency members and wholly and unambiguously accepted and carried out by these practitioners. Conflicts were rife in the YOT, but these were transitory, issue-specific disagreements that did not fall neatly along inter-agency lines.

Yet despite these complexities, inter-agency conflicts appeared to take on considerable significance in the early stages of the team. Indeed, because of their concerns about a punitive and inflexible working culture in the police, social workers effectively ostracised police staff from the core functions in the team. For a while, therefore, perceived conflicts between agencies threatened to compromise the membership of agency staff and thus prevent the YOT from cohering. Given the complexities of occupational identity, why should this have been the case?

In part, the perception of conflict between agencies demonstrates how claims about similarity and difference – or 'us' and 'them' – results in stereotypical perceptions across occupational boundaries. Thus contrasting central aspects of their practice and orientation with those of the police eliminated the ambiguities and similarities of experience. Ironically, therefore, social workers' articulation of the ambiguity and flexibility deemed central to their work with young offenders resulted in an uncompromisingly rigid view of the police.

But in addition, inter-agency conflicts may have become particularly salient in the early development of the YOT as a means through which practitioners could position themselves against uncertain and unwelcome changes. The intense politicisation of youth offending and the punitive rhetoric accompanying the reconfiguration of the youth justice system had been clearly received by social work staff, who were concerned that they were on the brink of a more punitive climate in youth justice. As one social worker put it, 'it seems we're moving to be a statutory agency whose bottom line is preventing crime, not looking at the well-being of [young people]'. The introduction of police staff into the YOT appeared symbolic of this shift towards a more punitive ethos. Moreover, the perceived shift in climate signalled by the new measures brought into focus the tensions inherent in social workers' own roles, where the aims of 'helping' and 'enabling' young people took place within the context of the administration of punishments. The elements of control intrinsic to their roles now appeared more overt. In this context, claims about opposition with the police became of crucial importance. They allowed social work staff to clarify their 'welfarist' orientation and delineate the boundaries of the team accordingly. In other words, the construction of inter-agency conflicts became a channel through which the team could regroup against the perceived threat to the way they worked. Yet this could only be an effective strategy of resistance for a limited time. The appointment of a police officer in a senior managerial position made it evident that boundaries between agencies could no longer clearly be drawn.

However, the development of the Midlands YOT raised a different set of questions about the possibility of a shared working culture in inter-agency YOTs. Firstly, it put at issue the assumption that the absorption of practitioners from diverse agencies into the same structure is able to bring about consistency in the aims and principles of youth justice work. It was the introduction of staff from partner agencies that brought about the crisis of identity and purpose in the team. It disrupted the 'us and them' distinctions that clarified the ambiguity of youth justice social work, and brought into question the accustomed routines and underlying purpose and values. In this way, instead of bringing about the emergence of a shared approach to youth justice work, the formation of an inter-agency team brought into focus the confusion about the goals and principles of youth justice work among professionals from all agencies.

Practitioners' confusion about the principles that governed their work appeared in part to reflect the fundamental confusion at the heart of the youth justice system, as indeed Labour had claimed (Labour Party 1996). As discussed in Chapter 3, practitioners' uncertainty about how, why and when to work with young offenders to some extent mirrored a persistent confusion about the overarching rationale of their work. In other words, there is an important connection between practitioners' understanding of the philosophy underlying the aims of youth justice work and the delivery of youth justice services. As Haines and Drakeford argue:

> It is crucial that professionals within the youth justice system understand the aims of their work, and in order to do so it is essential to be explicit about this philosophy and its importance [. . .] philosophy gives purpose to action: philosophy shapes the way in which we use knowledge and skills to achieve certain outcomes. (Haines and Drakeford 1998: 68–9)

Yet while the reconfiguration of the youth justice system brought practitioners' confusion about the principles of youth justice work into focus, it provided little resolution. Despite its espoused intention of bringing coherence to the objectives of work with young offenders, the Crime and Disorder Act and its surrounding communications provided little insight into what such objectives might be. As discussed in Chapter 1, Labour's ambitious programme for youth justice was defined not by a particular philosophy of justice or welfare, but by an 'all-pervasive political pragmatism' (Muncie 2000: 32). The elasticity of the overarching aim of 'crime prevention' allowed for the absorption of a range of diverse strategies and practices, founded on diverse and potentially conflicting principles. Rather than providing a framework for such consistency in broad aims of the youth justice system, therefore, this 'pick and mix' approach to youth justice (Muncie 2000: 31) instead allowed for the persistence of its central ambiguities. This had important consequences for service delivery. The lack of philosophical and ideological coherence underlying the Act and the tensions incorporated within its measures gave practitioners little indication about the principles that should govern the way they worked. Instead, it allowed for the absorption of diverse and conflicting approaches in the delivery of youth justice services.

Secondly, an understanding of the complexity of what it is to be a member of an occupation puts at issue the purpose of inter-agency work. What does it mean to represent an agency on an inter-agency team? The type of inter-agency relations required of YOT membership indicates that practitioners' contributions are envisaged as transcending the professional skills they bring with them. Staff are to some extent required to put aside their accustomed roles and take on new tasks defined by the YOT. Indeed, some staff are unable to carry out the core tasks of their home agency at all. Thus, in the case of the police staff in the Midlands YOT, what Mike and Bob *were* as police officers was necessarily divorced from what they *did*. Yet at the same time, the complexities of occupational identity put at issue the notion of a distinctive occupational outlook or ethos which might be contributed by collaborating staff. Practitioners' fluctuating and contradictory understanding of what it was to be an occupational member was brought into focus by the 'ambiguous organizational position' (Crawford 1997) that they were required to adopt. These issues are further complicated by the atypicality of those staff who feel able to take on work in structures of this kind (Chapter 4 and see also Crawford and Jones 1995). What, then, do collaborating staff embody of their home agency?

Further, what does it mean to work in an 'inter-agency way'? At the time I left the field, practitioners were starting explicitly to address these questions. While a sense of transition remained and it seemed that these issues would not be quickly resolved, it seemed that the nature of any shared identity would be more complex than merely a consistency in the purpose and principles of its work. Practitioners' sense that a common team feeling could emerge in the YOT was only made possible by an acceptance that team membership was now characterised by constant change, overt ambiguity and diversity in approach and identity among practitioners. In this way, it seems that the development of a shared approach to youth justice in an inter-agency team paradoxically is dependent on the acceptance and incorporation of difference.

There is inevitably something arbitrary about the moment at which the researcher quits the field, and by the time of my departure the sense of disquiet and transition in the Midlands YOT had only very partially been resolved. Nearly a decade later, the roles and practice of YOTs have become prescribed in increasing detail and some of the ambiguity experienced by the Midland's team may now have been resolved. Yet at the time of writing YOTs are surrounded by further change and insecurity. In the last few years alone, the formation of Local Criminal

Justice Boards, the development of the National Offender Management Service, the establishment of Children's Trusts, the creation of Local Area Agreements and the recent proposals to strengthen and restructure local authorities are among a myriad of developments that are fundamentally altering the local environments in which YOTs and their statutory partners work. Further, youth justice retains its political potency. The media continues to resound with stories of serious offences and juvenile nuisance, and the government's 'Respect' agenda reaffirms their espoused commitment to tackling youth crime and anti-social behaviour. Youth justice is a topic that, for the present, politics seems unable to leave alone. It seems inevitable therefore that practitioners will continue to have to struggle with the consequences of changes that electoral competition periodically mandates. What I take to have been important in the way of understanding that I have sought to develop here is that amongst our means of taking account of the effects of such recurrent and sometimes drastic upheavals, we must make space for an account of their underside in the everyday lives and experiences of those whose task it is to enact them. This is something more than a matter of 'implementation'. It is also a matter of the very identity of youth justice as an arena of social practice and hence of the identities of those who deliver it.

Appendix

Researching a Developing YOT

The following pages explore some of the strategies, problems and dilemmas involved in conducting research in a developing team during a period of conflict and uncertainty, and one in which questions of identity and membership became at issue. How did I fit into the team? What was my role, and what were the implications of it for my research? Relations in the developing team were often unstable, fraught and conflictual. How did this environment affect my research? How did I affect the dynamics of the team? And what were the challenges of researching a context in which ambiguity and confusion was pervasive?

Joining the team

My research began when Graham, the then team leader, approached my Department. He mentioned that he was keen to forge links between the Youth Justice Team and the university, and thought that my research might be one such link. He quickly became my 'sponsor' (Hammersley and Atkinson 1995: 60), introducing me to the team, inviting me to their meetings, giving me free access to their offices, providing the security codes I needed to enter the building, organising police security clearance necessary to have access to young people and case files, and so on. Graham's enthusiastic sponsorship raised some questions: why was he so keen to support my research? What did he think I could offer? These questions became more salient as my fieldwork progressed and are discussed below. But official permission to proceed with my research was only one aspect of the process of negotiating access to the field. I needed to ensure I had the consent and cooperation of the rest of the staff. As Hammersley and Atkinson (1995) argue, the negotiation of participation is an ongoing issue throughout the research process (see below), but is particularly acute in the first few days of entry into a setting. Researchers need to build the trust of informants fairly rapidly, or they may refuse access in a way that they would not later on in the fieldwork. And as Sparks et al. say, gaining the cooperation of inform-ants has moral as well as practical implications: '. . . the entitlement to ask certain types of questions (which may be personal, painful, taxing, incriminating) cannot be taken for granted' (1996: 351). Instead, they argue, this entitlement must be negotiated through a series of undertak-ings by the researcher. These include assurances about confidentiality and uses of the data, asking for time and cooperation, and answering questions about your own purposes and identity. Only then can the researcher begin to ask questions in return.

It was therefore particularly important to spend an initial period on the team giving my own account of myself and my research. This involved introducing myself to practitioners, making sure I emphasised my independence and discretion and what I hoped they would be able to contribute if they wished to participate. It also involved quickly learning an appropriate manner of approaching practitioners, and of chatting, making jokes and asking questions so that I could put practitioners at ease. It was important to talk to all members of the team: as Mason (1996: 67) argues, it is impossible to maintain a 'completely neutral stance' in the development of relationships in a setting and a perception that I was favouring some alliances and neglecting others would have risked cutting off research opportunities.

Practitioners were invariably warm and welcoming: this was a first-hand experience of the friendliness later described as an essential part of the team experience and remarked upon by staff from partner agencies when they joined the YOT. Part of this friendliness was manifested in the teasing or 'abuse' which practitioners described as an integral part of the team experience. Yet while the banter directed towards me seemed to signify the acceptance of me as part of the team, it also indicated some of the problems about my membership. The teasing to which I was subject was clearly gendered: male practitioners would make flirtatious jokes, press their faces up against the windows and blow kisses when I was conducting interviews, and so on. This was typical of the nature of the banter in the team as a whole, sometimes described as sexist, which reflected the predominantly male membership of the team. As a woman in the team this sexist teasing was to be expected: as Hammersley and Atkinson state, 'The researcher cannot escape the implications of gender: no position of genderless neutrality can be achieved' (1995: 92). I was teased about being middle-class and Southern ('she thinks we're all rude and rough in the North'; 'what's a nice posh girl like you doing in a place like this?'). I was also teased about the work I was doing. One practitioner saluted every time I walked past, saying 'look out, it's the Thought Police'; I was a 'honey-trap', 'never trust a girl with a tape-recorder'.[1] This teasing didn't seem aggressive, but it was clearly pointed. It revealed real concerns about me – my difference to the team in terms of background and class, and suspicion about my work. This was useful: it enabled these issues to be aired in a friendly, unthreatening way and allowed me to respond.

A few weeks later, Graham invited me to present my research plans at a team meeting. This 'official' introduction to the team represented a formal request for participation after the informal individual approaches I had already made. The meeting began with two very long, very boring presentations by outside speakers during which the impatience of the team became evident. After the speakers left, there was a sigh of relief from team members and an outpouring of frustration. There were suggestions of making coffee or having a drink before the 'rest' of the meeting – the business of the team – took place. This was similar to the 'backstage' informality described by Goffman (1959):[2] the polite performance to those outside the team was over. Allowing me to witness this transformation appeared to be an acknowledgement that I was included in the 'backstage' life of the team, an 'insider'. That this transformation had occurred before my presentation indicated that my research was seen as part of the business of the team. I understood this as an indication that I now had the practitioners' permission to proceed.

Becoming educated

My first months on the team were spent experiencing as much of the practice and daily life of the team as I could, so that I could begin to familiarise myself with the setting and identify useful sources of data. This was greatly facilitated by the friendly interest of the team members. Practitioners offered me access to their places of work, young people and case notes. They invited me to accompany them on prison visits and court duty. They offered me books and explained the details of their work. In this way (and no doubt reflecting their perceptions of my middle-class status and gender) practitioners appeared to be fitting me into the role of a 'student' whom they were helping to 'educate'. This role was one that was familiar to the team, many of whom had undertaken professional and postgraduate qualifications, some in the same university department as myself. It was a very useful role to adopt. It allowed me to start to see how practitioners understood their work. It gave me an excuse to be in the team offices and observe the interactions and routines of the team. But above all, it was educational, and I needed to be educated. When I began my fieldwork, I knew very little about the work of a youth justice worker. As well as being unfamiliar with their daily practice, I was faced with a new technical language which I did not understand. The widespread use of abbreviated terms such as PSRs, TWOC and PACE seemed mystifying. This problem mirrored that faced by practitioners from partner agencies who came to join the team. As the health officer put it: 'It's almost like a different language to me you know, because they use a lot of abbreviations don't they.' This process of acclimatisation was thus similar to that of the new practitioners, which may have helped me better understand their experience. It also created similar anxieties about competence. The new practitioners worried about being deskilled; I worried about being fraudulent. It is argued that a lack of foreknowledge is an essential part of ethnography. As Sparks et al. put it, 'if a research project is genuinely directed towards new knowledge then there are limits to the kind of foreknowledge the researchers can have. Hence, the research would have to begin in an exploratory, even naïve, spirit' (1996: 343). However, this naiveté must also be balanced with credibility. As they argue, researchers need to become 'sufficiently knowledgeable for people to think it worthwhile speaking to us' (1996: 347). My 'student' persona helped reconcile this dilemma, allowing me to admit my ignorance without too much damage to my credibility, while providing the means for me to become more knowledgeable.

Creating a membership role

As I became more established in the team, my initial role of 'student' developed into a more sustainable, involved role of 'team member'. The nature of the team in May 1999 made the adoption of some sort of membership role inevitable. Youth justice workers represented themselves as members of a clearly defined team. Team membership and loyalty was described as a highly valued feature of the work environment: the team was unusually 'cohesive', 'gelled', 'sociable'. I was forming a long association with the team, was based in the same offices and subject to the same banter – all elements associated with the experience of being a team member. Consequently, I was seen to be entering into a membership role: practitioners described me as 'part of the team'.

An important consequence of adopting a membership role and being recognised by the group as such is that it provides access to the routine activities of the group (Adler and Adler 1987). My acceptance as a team member meant that I was automatically invited to team events such as meetings and facilitated my inclusion in the mundane activities, banter and gossip described above. This inclusion in turn reinforced my position as a team member. As Adler and Adler argue, membership allows researchers access to 'secret' information known only to the group, and 'this information, known only to members, ratifies the solidarity and continued existence of the group' (1987: 34).

However, there were important differences between my team membership and that of the other members. Most obviously, I was not a practitioner. I couldn't participate in the specific activities of the group. In this way, my role was similar to that described by Adler and Adler as a 'peripheral membership role', where researchers 'interact closely, significantly, and frequently enough to acquire recognition by members as insiders. They do not, however, interact in the role of central members, refraining from participating in activities that stand at the core of group membership and identification' (1987: 36). Instead, I developed my own 'researcher-member' role (Adler and Adler 1987: 37), where I was labelled and accepted by the team as a researcher. Practitioners often asked me about the progress of my research, reassured me that they were happy to answer my questions as 'you've got a job to do, haven't you', and so on. Yet the role of a peripheral researcher-member is more complex than Adler and Adler appear to suggest. Rather than forming a new, unproblematic role, the dual roles of researcher and team member are in constant tension. There is thus an inherent ambiguity in the position. This emerged in two ways in the research process.

The researcher-member role

The boundaries of team membership

Firstly, the limitations to my membership of the team were not always clear. Adler and Adler (1987) argue that peripheral membership researchers' episodic presence and participation leads members to develop limited expectations of them. But was my understanding of the boundaries of my involvement the same as that of the practitioners? An engagement with these questions was important to ensure practitioners' continued participation. As discussed earlier, access is a problem that persists throughout the data collection process (Hammersley and Atkinson 1995). Appearing to overstep the appropriate limitations of my role might have seemed intrusive or disruptive, and could have compromised my relationships with practitioners, thereby risking their cooperation. But what were the appropriate limitations of my role, and how were they perceived by the team?

These questions were made more complex by the ambiguity of my position as both a team member and a researcher. The boundaries of access to data differed according to which of these roles was seen to have more prominence in particular contexts. This became at issue in December 1999, when Duncan, a social worker, suddenly died (see Chapter 7). He was a key member of the team, playing a prominent part in the team's banter and well respected and very well liked by his colleagues, including me. His funeral took place in early January, and it was announced at a team meeting that the whole team was invited to go. As a friend and 'colleague' of the practitioner, I wanted to go. But it was clear the funeral was also an occasion for the team to support each other and reinforce their group membership. My status as a team member was now at issue. Was I seen as a member of the team, in which case my absence would be seen as inappropriate, or offensive?[3] Or was I seen as a researcher, whose presence would be intrusive and unwelcome at an emotional time?[4]

On occasion, my status on the team was called into question by YOT members. In July 2000, the YOT manager organised a two-day session in which the whole team would be involved in a 'team-building' training exercise. The days were an attempt to identify and solve some of the problems practitioners were experiencing and aimed to bring about a greater team cohesion. This meeting would be an interesting and potentially important source of data. Should I attend? As a team member, I was included in the invitation. But as a researcher, I wasn't directly involved in the concerns of the team. Moreover, a researcher might have made the team feel inhibited, and as the occasion was intended to provoke an honest dialogue about the problems of the team this would be obstructive. The team's management disagreed about whether it would be appropriate for me to attend. For Graham, the team leader, as a team member it was right that I should attend: 'You're part of the team, warts and all'. Yet Jeff, the operations manager, saw my role at the meeting primarily to be that of a researcher: he said he was 'reluctant' to for me to be 'sitting there scribing and observing'.[5] This ambivalence among the YOT management appeared to reflect the ambiguity of my dual status as researcher and member.

Membership, disclosure and confidentiality

A second issue resulting from my role as a researcher-member concerned the implications of this dual status for confidentiality. As a researcher, the questions I asked often prompted confidential disclosures. These were more likely to be forthcoming in part because of my difference to the rest of the team: there were different 'rules' regarding confidentiality and impartiality compared to other team members. Such disclosures have the potential for 'costs' (Arksey and Knight 1999) such as feelings of guilt, shame or embarrassment. These potential costs were inflated by my dual status. As a member I had a continued involvement with practitioners: I remained in the same research setting, sharing the same office space. My ability to move between public and private settings, different types of talk and different relationships may have caused concerns about the confidentiality of my research. This was perhaps most clearly at issue in the context of interviewing.

The interview situation creates an intimate environment. Interviews took place in private rooms, and enabled practitioners to talk about their views and feelings in a way that their ordinary work environment is unlikely to have allowed and which may have surprised them. Some practitioners jokingly described the interviews as 'therapy' or 'counselling' which suggested a perception of personal disclosure. The intimacy involved in an interview is usually terminated at the end of the interview, with the termination of the relationship between the informant and interviewer. However, I continued an ongoing relationship with the practitioners: at the end of the interview we both returned to the same research setting. This inevitably caused some anxiety about confidentiality. This was most frequently managed by practitioners making jokes to their colleagues as we came back into the team room after the interview: saying, for instance, that 'she gave me a grilling', 'that were terrible, that', thereby tacitly acknowledging the aspect of disclosure in the interview while preventing any further inquiry about it. It is probably because of this anxiety that most practitioners 'tested' my discretion in some way. This often occurred during the interview. Nearly all practitioners asked me to turn off the tape recorder at some point, to tell me something 'off the record'. Occasionally these disclosures seemed fairly mundane in the context of the interviews and later conversations. Occasionally they were deliberately provocative, such as the practitioner who said while I changed the tape 'this is where I say that I hate fucking probation officers'. It seemed that the purpose of these episodes was to underline to me the practitioner's control over the interview.

Research, power and conflict

A second problem in conducting the research involved the unstable and fluid nature of power within the team. The team members' practice, skills, qualification and status were all at issue. Members of the management staff were jostling for status. New practice was being interpreted and implemented, with implications for practitioners' roles. How did this dynamic of conflict affect my research? And how did my research affect the balance of power within the team?

Research and conflict management

The development of the YOT involved a considerable degree of anxiety, uncertainty and stress for the practitioners. Team members were in a constant state of conflict over their roles and practice. Why were they willing to add to this disruption by participating in the research? What did team members think I was offering?

There may have been particular reasons why Graham, the team leader, played such an important role in my introduction and induction into the team. His interest in my research went beyond granting access to the team and facilities. Before my arrival at the team he acted as 'mediator' in requesting the cooperation of practitioners. Throughout the research period he frequently asked me about the progress of my research and about my findings. He was keen to offer his views on the development of the team, often inviting me to interview him as 'there are some interesting things you should know about'. In other words, he promoted himself as a key figure in my research for the duration of the fieldwork. But why did he want to sponsor my research in this way?

It is possible that the sponsorship of my research was a way for Graham to negotiate his status in the team. In May 1999 when I began my research he presented himself as a key figure in shaping the new YOT. He talked at team meetings about his 'vision' of the YOT, the direction he wanted it to take, the way he saw the new members' roles forming. He talked of valuing and encouraging the team's 'intellectual' approach to the new developments. I appeared to be part of this approach: he explained to the team that my role was to give an 'intellectual insight' into the formation of the YOT. However, at this time Graham was acting up in his post and his status in the team was unstable. He was the only manager dealing with the team on a daily basis and trying to make strategic decisions, yet these decisions could be overruled by the YOT manager. He had applied for the operations manager position but had not yet been accepted for the job. He was aware that he might be unsuccessful and 'the rug could be pulled out from under me': he would be back working alongside his colleagues as senior practitioner. It is possible that by joining the team as a researcher, I was helping form the YOT in the 'intellectual' shape associated with him, which may have raised his profile and thus his position in the contested power relations of the YOT management.

But while sponsorship of my research my have had a particular appeal for Graham, why did the other practitioners agree to participate? Initially, practitioners' cooperation appeared to be fuelled in part by interest and curiosity: they talked of being in 'a fly-on-the-wall docusoap'. However, as the team began to develop, practitioners felt extremely pressured: they were short-staffed, anxious, coping with the death of a key member, in conflict about the development of their roles, and so on. Yet they remained willing to cooperate with my research, taking time out of their working days for interviews, offering to have quick chats and talk about issues they saw as pressing. Why would they want to add to the pressure of their working life by participating in my research?

As Kleinman and Copp (1992) suggest, exploration of reasons why people participate in research reveals something of the nature of power in the setting:

What do they [participants] think we are offering that makes us attractive to them? Do we give them the chance to say things they cannot talk about among themselves (thus indicating a norm in the setting)? Do they want our sympathy (because they think outsiders do not understand them)? Do we provide some legitimacy for the group? (1992: 46–7)

In other words, research can act as an expression or outlet for conflicts. It appears that my research performed this function and was thus directly involved in the conflicts within the team.

As I was leaving the field, several practitioners thanked me, comparing my research to 'counselling' or 'therapy'. When Jeff, the operations manager, formally announced I was leaving at my last team meeting, he introduced me with 'she's been our counsellor and mentor'. It is likely that the analogy with therapy was a recognition that practitioners had been able to talk about issues that were personal to them to someone who listened attentively. But there are further similarities with therapy following from the consequences of this talk.

Kvale (1996, 1999) describes the aim of the therapeutic interview as effecting change in the patient. This often involves new insights in the way the patient understands themselves and their world. Kvale acknowledges that the research interview may encourage quasi-therapeutic relationships, but argues that there are important differences between research and therapeutic interviews. Most significantly, the research interview's goal is 'the acquisition of knowledge' (1996: 154) rather than the therapeutic aim of effecting emotional change. It is true that practitioners did not take part in my research to seek out such emotional change, and I did not intend to bring this about. However, although this was not the intention, it seems likely that by providing a private arena for practitioners to discuss their concerns, my research did effect some sort of new insights or change. This effect can perhaps most usefully be understood in terms of conflict management.

Conflict is an integral part of organisational life (Bartunek et al. 1992). It appears not only in public forms (such as official negotiation, grievance procedures and so on) but in the private spheres of organisations. These are spaces 'behind closed doors' – 'spaces out of public view that provide opportunities for the expression of sentiments that cannot be voiced in public' (Bartunek et al. 1992: 213) – or 'organizational time-outs' (Van Maanen 1992), in which the ordinary constraints of the workplace are suspended. In these spheres, conflict may not be recognised as such: it is often covert, and may be disguised as other activities. In these private spaces, conflict is more likely to take a 'non-rational' form of expression, the 'unconscious or spontaneous aspects of disputing' (Kolb and Puttnam 1992: 20). This may take the form of personalised accounts, bitching, gossiping or venting feelings. By this understanding, research activities such as interviews represent a forum in which the expression of conflict is to be expected. They were held in a private space, removing the practitioner from the rest of the organisation. They also can be understood as an instance of an 'organisational time-out'. For the duration of the interview, the norms of organisational life are temporarily suspended. They seek out personalised accounts, and this often promoted the gossip, bitching and emoting that is characteristic of non-rational disputing. Thus they provided 'the space to act in nonrational ways' (Bartunek et al. 1992: 216).

The understanding of my research as conflict management may explain the practitioners' association of it with therapy. The interviews did bring about resolution, change and insight, though not in the emotional, therapeutic sense described by Kvale. First, the expression of conflict itself may be enough to resolve the conflict and prevent it from emerging in the public arena (Kolb and Puttnam 1992). Certainly, there were many instances where practitioners told me about events or people that had irritated or upset them, and these did not seem to emerge in a public arena. Second, the private expression of conflict may enable the dispute to go public. The informal expression of the dispute allows formal expressions to function smoothly: the gossip, venting feelings and bitching allow the formal meetings to look rational and cooperative.

Research and conflict: becoming partisan

A danger in researching a setting in which there are conflicts between participants is that the researcher may become partisan. As Sparks et al. argue, 'the researcher, whose position is inherently somewhat isolating, may become captivated by his or her involvement with particular individuals or groups . . . and come to take on their point of view to the exclusion of others' (1996: 343). Did I 'take sides' in the conflicts in the YOT? And how was this partisanship manifested?

The risk of forming partisan alliances appears to stem from the development of empathy towards the participants in the setting: this allows the researcher to become 'captivated' and 'involved' with a group as Sparks et al. describe. It is perhaps inevitable that researchers form some degree of sympathetic attachment to their informants. As Becker (1970) argues, it is impossible to do research that is 'uncontaminated by personal and political sympathies' (1970: 99). Indeed, Kleinman and Copp write that part of the job of being a researcher involves developing feelings of this sort. Researchers try to understand the perspective of those they study, which involves developing some degree of empathy towards them: 'If we do not feel what participants feel, we expect at least to feel *for* them' (Kleinman and Copp 1993: 28).

For Becker (1970), the question of empathy in a research setting is inherently involved with becoming partisan. A researcher's sympathies will lead them to 'take sides' in the research setting, adopting one viewpoint to the exclusion of others. Such partisanship is inextricable from issues of power in the research setting. Researchers must take the standpoint of either the subordinates or superiors in a research setting, and we tend to sympathise with those without power – the 'underdog' or 'subordinate'. But as Gouldner (1970) argues, the question of the location of power in a setting is far more complex than this analysis allows: people are simultaneously subordinate and superior to different groups. Such fluidity of power was particularly evident in the YOT. Power was always seen to lie elsewhere. Team members described different and conflicting perceived hierarchies of influence. For example, some described a division between senior practitioners, other practitioners and unqualified staff; others a division along agency lines in which the power was seen to lie with social workers. Most practitioners described feeling powerless with regard to the decisions of the managers, while the managers described being impotent with regard to the demands of the Youth Justice Board and the other management staff. The balance of power between these groups was seen to be in a constant state of flux. The identification of a group or individual as a subordinate or superior changed according to specific instances and particular contexts.

Despite the fluidity and ambiguity of the location of power within the team, it is true that it did dictate my empathic attachments and, as Becker argues is typical of sociologists, my empathy tended to lie with the powerless, the 'underdog'. However, reflecting the balance of power in the team, this empathy was also fluid and ambiguous. I might share practitioners' frustration at a meeting in which the team's management avoided responding to their concerns, and then empathise with the powerlessness and confusion later described by the managers. My empathic attachments were thus constantly shifting and contradictory. In this way, they cannot easily be understood as producing or resulting from a partisan alliance.

Researching ambiguities

Lastly, as discussed throughout this book, an appreciation of the ambiguities and complexities of practitioners' experiences were of crucial importance in understanding the effects of organisational change on team members' working lives. However, there are particular difficulties in researching ambiguity.

As I have argued in this book, to understand culture and change it is important to look at a setting through all three interpretative frameworks or 'perspectives' identified by Meyerson and Martin (Martin 1992; Martin and Meyerson 1988; Meyerson and Martin 1987). These are three very different ways of understanding culture which have come to dominate research about organisational cultures: the 'integration' perspective understands culture as 'what people share' and is marked by organisation-wide consensus; the 'differentiation' perspective views organisational culture as a nexus of competing, overlapping subcultures; the 'fragmentation' viewpoint gives centrality to the ambiguities of cultural experiences and understands culture as a web of loosely connected individuals for whom particular subcultural identities and coalitions become salient at specific moments and over specific issues. Martin and Meyerson argue that all three perspectives are available in any cultural setting. Focusing on one perspective to the exclusion of others may produce a distorted picture of the setting: it 'causes blind spots. If cultural change is perceived and enacted from only one paradigmatic perspective, then other sources and types of change may not be considered' (1987: 643). Consequently, researchers should attempt to consider organisational cultures from all three theoretical viewpoints. For instance, when I entered the setting in June 1999, many of the social workers in the team appeared to have adopted a similar perspective of the developing multi-agency YOT. The previous social work team was described as having clearly defined boundaries, within which there was consensus over clearly defined values. These values conflicted with the equally unambiguous boundaries and values of other agencies, most notably with the police who were portrayed as aggressive, punitive and intolerant of the perceived ethos of help and support in youth justice social work. A critical view of this image of cohesion, consensus and conflict was crucial to discern the diversity and ambiguities that were also prevalent in the setting.

However, there is a considerable amount of internal and external pressure on researchers not to seek out these ambiguities. Meyerson argues that the dominant values of social science research promote the tendency to deny ambiguity at the expense of clarity. Studies that reflect ambiguities may be seen as 'sloppy' or 'incomplete' (Meyerson 1991: 259). This is particularly at issue in ethnographic studies, as the acknowledgement of ambiguities risks the rejection of the ethnography as a 'bad story': 'Without the full authority of science, ethnographies must tell good stories to be convincing. Good stories have clear story lines. Thus ambiguities which cloud a story may fundamentally undermine the authority of an ethnographic text' (1991: 259). But, moreover, ambiguity is unsettling. Conducting this research throughout a turbulent period which appeared to be characterised by chaos and fragmentation was an anxious experience. There appeared to be no order or structure to practitioners' experiences of unfolding events. I felt as confused as the practitioners I was researching: what was happening in the team? What was I looking for? Meyerson (1991) shows that this anxiety tends to result in researchers prioritising clear consistency and inconsistency at the expense of ambiguity: '. . . we tend to notice (and value) that which is clear, stable, and "orderly" (that which we can readily understand, measure and control) and ignore that which is unclear, unstable, and "disorderly" (that which is more fragmented, intractable, and difficult to control)' (1991: 255). In this way, researching ambiguity is a difficult and uncomfortable experience. There is thus a tendency to overlook the ambiguities of participants' experiences in favour of clear patterns and consistency. How can this be overcome?

During my research, there were two potential checks on my tendency to clarify practitioners' experiences. First, the use of observations and loosely structured interviews in which respondents can frame their own concerns allowed ambiguities to emerge. Meyerson argues methodologies that generate 'presentational' data (Van Maanen 1979) such as interviews tend to invoke self-consciousness and social desirability. Consequently, when confusion or contradictions do arise in interviews, respondents may eliminate or resolve them in their responses. However, although some clarification may have taken place, interviews with practitioners' in the YOT appeared to be rife with ambiguities, confusion and admissions of lack of knowledge. Meyerson argues that, as presentational data tend to reflect the norms of a given context, the elimination of ambiguity is particularly produced in contexts which hold strong norms against ambiguities. It perhaps reveals something about the norms of the YOT that this elimination does not seem to have been prevalent.

Second, there appeared to be a change to the 'home perspective' (Martin 1992) of the team which alerted me to the complexity of practitioners' experiences. As my fieldwork unfolded, the dominant presentation of the views of the practitioners appeared to change so that the ambiguities within professional ideologies and individual beliefs became apparent. As I looked back at my earlier interviews and notes, it was possible to see these same contradictions and uncertainties, despite the practitioners' assurances of consensus within their subcultures. It then became clearer that I needed to give my attention not just to the issues presented, but to the presentation itself.

Leaving the field

The point at which fieldwork ends may always seem somewhat arbitrary: deciding when to end a study of a developing team particularly so. I chose to quit the field after the first raft of new orders mandated under the Crime and Disorder Act had become available to the courts and the new YOT appeared to have acquired some degree of stability after a period of apparent crisis. As I left the team, I offered to present some of my research to the team members in a way which might be useful to them. I wanted to give something back to the team in return for their time and participation, the costs of which I was acutely aware. Staff thought that a presentation of my research might enable practitioners to recognise issues that were ongoing or emerging and facilitate some discussion about these. At their suggestion I presented a 'history' of the key events in the development of the YOT during my research period, showing how the team had changed and putting events in a context which would explain why the problems they had experienced had seemed so acute.

This exercise also acted to some extent as a check on my data. I asked the all practitioners individually before and after my presentation for their comments and to tell me whether I had understood what they had told me and what I had missed out. As an exercise in 'respondent validation' (Mason 1996: 151) this was necessarily limited, as concerns about confidentiality and the needs of the team restricted the kind of data I could report to them. However, as far as it went, I was satisfied that practitioners felt I had given an accurate account of the events as they understood them: they described it as 'frighteningly accurate', 'spot on'.

Of course, the account in this book has a rather different focus to that presented to the Midlands staff some years ago, and whether it will seem as accurate is hard to know. I have tried throughout to describe the events and processes that unfolded as they were understood by the practitioners involved. I have tried to refrain from attributing thoughts or beliefs to them, or elaborating or interpreting what they have left unspoken. I have also attempted to maintain a sense of the individual personalities of those involved and the diverse ways in which the unfolding events were experienced. I hope therefore that if any of the Midlands practitioners happen to read this book, they will be able to recognise the account presented here and themselves within it.

Notes

1 These were references to the then high-profile case of the former England rugby captain Lawrence Dallaglio, who at the end of May 1999 was set up in

a 'honey trap' by a female *News of the World* reporter in which he admitted to taking and dealing cocaine, which resulted in him losing the captaincy.

2 Though I am using the concept of 'backstage' to describe the shift into informal behaviour rather than the physical place in which this informality might be associated.

3 Mark, the YOT manager, didn't attend the funeral, and several practitioners later talked of their anger about this. He had caused offence by demonstrating a lack of interest in team solidarity. As the admin manager told me, he told the team 'it was a personal matter, but the team don't see it like that, they thought it was a team matter'.

4 I decided that the harm of being intrusive would be worse than not attending, so I didn't attend.

5 I judged the potential harm of obstructing the session to be too important to risk attending. In the event, practitioners' varying accounts of the session proved to be very useful.

References

Adler, P. A. and Adler, P. (1987) *Membership Roles in Field Research*. London: Sage.

Arksey, H. and Knight, P. (1999) *Interviewing for Social Scientists: An Introductory Resource with Examples*. London: Sage.

Audit Commission (1996) *Misspent Youth*. London: Audit Commission.

Bailey, R. and Brake, M. (1975) *Radical Social Work*. London: Edward Arnold.

Bailey, R. V. and Williams, B. (2000) *Inter-agency Partnerships in Youth Justice: Implementing the Crime and Disorder Act 1998*. Sheffield: Joint Unit for Social Services Research.

Banton, M. P. (1964) *The Policeman in the Community*. London: Tavistock Press.

Bartunek, J. M., Kolb, D. M. and Lewicki, R. J. (1992) 'Bringing conflict out from behind the scenes: private, informal and nonrational dimensions of conflict in organizations', in D. M. Kolb and J. M. Bartunek (eds), *Hidden Conflict in Organizations: Uncovering Behind-the-Scenes Disputes*. Newbury Park, CA: Sage, pp. 209–28.

Becker, H. S. (1963) *Outsiders: Studies in the Sociology of Deviance*. New York: Free Press.

Becker, H. S. (1970) 'Whose side are we on?', reprinted in J. Douglas (ed.), *The Relevance of Sociology*. New York: Meredith, pp. 99–111.

Beetham, D. (1991) *The Legitimation of Power*. Basingstoke: Macmillan.

Biestek, F. P. (1961) *The Casework Relationship*. London: Allen & Unwin.

Bittner, E. (1975) *The Functions of the Police in Modern Society: A Review of Background Factors, Current Practices, and Possible Role Models*. Seattle, WA: University of Washington Press.

Black, D. (1990) 'The elementary forms of conflict management', in Arizona School of Justice Studies, Arizona State University (ed.), *New Directions in the Study of Justice, Law and Social Control*. New York: Plenum, pp. 43–69.

Blagg, H. and Smith, D. (1989) *Crime, Penal Policy and Social Work*. Harlow: Longman.

Brown, A. (1992) *Groupwork*, 3rd edn. Aldershot: Ashgate.

Brown, A. and Caddick, B. (1993) 'Groupwork with offenders: approaches and issues', in A. Brown and B. Caddick (eds), *Groupwork with Offenders*. London: Whiting & Birch.

Brown, S. (1991) *Magistrates at Work: Sentencing and Social Structure*. Milton Keynes: Open University Press.

Brownlee, I. (1998) 'New Labour: new penology? Punitive rhetoric and the limits of managerialism in criminal justice policy', *Journal of Law and Society*, 25 (3): 313–35.

Brunsson, N. (2000) *The Irrational Organization: Irrationality as a Basis for Organizational Action and Change*. Copenhagen: Fagbokforlaget

Burnett, R. and Appleton, C. (2004) 'Joined up services to tackle youth crime: a case-study in England', *British Journal of Criminology*, 44 (1): 34–55.

Caddick, B. (1991) 'Using groups in working with offenders: a survey of groupwork in the probation services of England and Wales', *Groupwork*, 4 (3): 197–214.

Cain, M. (1973) *Society and the Policeman's Role*. London: Routledge.

Canton, R., Mack, C. and Smith, J. (1991) 'Handling conflict: groupwork with violent offenders', in A. Brown and B. Caddick (eds), *Groupwork with Offenders*. London: Whiting & Birch.

Carlen, P. (1992) 'Pindown, truancy, and the interrogation of discipline: a paper about theory, policy, social worker bashing . . . and hypocrisy', *Journal of Law and Society*, 19: 251–70.

Chan, J. (1996) 'Changing police culture', *British Journal of Criminology*, 36 (1): 109–34.

Chan, J. (1997) *Changing Police Culture: Policing in a Multi-Cultural Society*. Cambridge: Cambridge University Press.

Chan, J., with Devery, C. and Doran, S. (2003) *Fair Cop: Learning the Art of Policing*. Toronto: University of Toronto Press.

Chapman, T. and Hough, M. (1998) *Evidence Based Practice: A Guide to Effective Practice*. London: HMSO.

Chatterton, M. R. (1989) 'Managing paperwork', in M. Weatheritt (ed.), *Police Research: Some Future Prospects*. Aldershot: Avebury.

Cohen, S. (1975) 'It's all right for you to talk: political and sociological manifestos for social action', R. Bailey and M. Brake (eds), *Radical Social Work*. London: Edward Arnold, pp. 76–95.

Cohen, S. (1985) *Visions of Social Control*. London: Polity Press.

Commission for Racial Equality (2003) *Racial Equality in Prisons*. London: CRE.

Crawford, A. (1994) 'The partnership approach: corporatism at the local level?', *Social and Legal Studies*, 3 (4): 497–519.

Crawford, A. (1997) *The Local Governance of Crime: Appeals to Community and Partnerships*. Oxford: Clarendon Press.

Crawford, A. (2001) 'Joined-up but fragmented: contradiction, ambiguity and ambivalence at the heart of New Labour's "third way"', in R. Matthews and J. Pitts (eds), *Crime, Disorder and Community Safety*. London: Routledge.

Crawford, A. and Jones, M. (1995) 'Inter-agency co-operation and community-based crime prevention: some reflections on the work of Pearson and colleagues', *British Journal of Criminology*, 35 (1): 17–33.

Crawford, A. and Newburn, T. (2003) *Youth Offending and Restorative Justice: Implementing Reform in Youth Justice*. Cullompton: Willan.

Crawley, E. (2004) *Doing Prison Work: The Public and Private Lives of Prison Officers*. Cullompton: Willan.

Denman, G. (1982) *Intensive Intermediate Treatment with Juvenile Offenders*. Lancaster University.

Douglas, M. (1986) *How Institutions Think*. Syracuse, NY: Syracuse University Press.

Downes, D. (1998) 'Toughing it out: from Labour opposition to Labour government', *Policy Studies*, 19 (3/4): 191–8.

Elias, N. and Scotson, J. L. (1994) *The Established and the Outsiders: A Sociological Enquiry into Community Problems*, 2nd edn. London: Sage.

Etzioni, A. (1995) *The Spirit of Community: Rights, Responsibilities and the Communitarian Agenda*. London: Fontana Press.

Farrington, D. (1996) *Understanding and Preventing Youth Crime*, Social Policy Research Findings No. 93. York: Joseph Rowntree Foundation.

Farrington, D. and West, D. (1990) 'The Cambridge study in delinquent development', in H. J. Kerner and G. Kaiser (eds), *Criminality: Personality, Behaviour and Life History*. Berlin: Springer-Verlag.

Feeley, M. and Simon, J. (1992) 'The new penology', *Criminology*, 30 (4): 452–74.

Feldman, M. (1991) 'The meanings of ambiguity', P. J. Frost, L. F. Moore, M. R. Louis, C. C. Lundberg and J. Martin (eds), *Reframing Organizational Culture*. Newbury Park, CA: Sage.

Ferguson, K. (1984) *The Feminist Case Against Bureaucracy*. Philadelphia: Temple University Press.

Fielding, N. (1995) *Community Policing*. Oxford: Clarendon Press.

Fionda, J. (1999) 'New Labour: old hat. Youth justice and the Crime and Disorder Act 1998', *Criminal Law Review*, January: 36–47.

Fischer, J. (1973) 'Is casework effective? A review', *Social Work*, 18 (1): 5–21.

Foster, J. A., Newburn, T. and Souhami, A. (2005) *Assessing the Impact of the Stephen Lawrence Inquiry*, Home Office Research Study 294. London: Home Office.

Garland, D. (1985) *Punishment and Welfare: A History of Penal Strategies*. Aldershot: Gower.

Geertz, C. (1973) *The Interpretation of Cultures: Selected Essays*. New York: Basic Books.

Gilling, D. J. (1994) 'Multi-agency crime prevention: some barriers to collaboration', *Howard Journal*, 33 (3): 246–57.

Goffman, E. (1959) *The Presentation of Self in Everyday Life*. New York: Doubleday.

Goldberg, E. M. and Warburton, R. W. (1979) *Ends and Means in Social Work: The Development and Outcome of a Case Review System for Social Workers*. London: George Allen & Unwin.

Goldblatt, P. (1998) 'Comparative effectiveness of different approaches', in P. Goldblatt and C. Lewis, *Reducing Offending: An Assessment of Research Evidence on Ways of Dealing with Offending Behaviour*, Home Office Research Study No. 187. London: HMSO.

Goldblatt, P. and Lewis, C. (1998) *Reducing Offending: An Assessment of Research Evidence on Ways of Dealing with Offending Behaviour*, Home Office Research Study No. 187. London: HMSO.

Goldson, B. (2000a) ' "Children in need" or "young offenders"? Hardening ideology, organizational change and new challenges for social work with children in trouble', *Child and Family Social Work*, 5: 255–65.

Goldson, B. (2000b) 'Whither diversion? Interventionism and the new youth justice', in B. Goldson (ed.), *The New Youth Justice*. Lyme Regis: Russell House.

Goldson, B. (ed.) (2000c) *The New Youth Justice*. Lyme Regis: Russell House.

Goldson, B. (2002) *Vulnerable Inside: Children in Secure and Penal Settings*. London: Children's Society.

Goldson, B. (2005) 'Beyond formalism: towards "informal" approaches to youth crime and youth justice', in T. Bateman and J. Pitts (eds), *The RHP Companion to Youth Justice*. Lyme Regis: Russell House.

Gould, P. (1998) *The Unfinished Revolution: How the Modernisers Saved the Labour Party*. London: Little, Brown.

Gouldner, A. W. (1970) 'The sociologist as partisan: sociology and the welfare state', reprinted in J. Douglas (ed.), *The Relevance of Sociology*. New York: Meredith, pp. 112–48.

Graham, J. and Bowling, B. (1995) *Young People and Crime*, Home Office Research Study No. 145. London: Home Office.

Haines, K. and Drakeford, M. (1998) *Young People and Youth Justice*. London: Macmillan.

Hammersley, M. and Atkinson, P. (1995) *Ethnography: Principles in Practice*, 2nd edn. London: Routledge.

Hazel, N., Hagell, A., Liddle, M., Archer, M., Grimshaw, R. and King, J. (2002) *Detention and Training: Assessment of the Detention and Training Order and Its Impact on the Secure Estate across England and Wales*. London: Youth Justice Board.

Holdaway, S., Davidson, N., Dignan, J., Hammersley, R., Hine, J. and Marsh, P. (2001) *New Strategies to Address Youth Offending: The National Evaluation of the Pilot Youth Offending Teams*, Research, Development and Statistics Directorate Paper 69. London: Home Office.

Home Office (1997a) *New National and Local Focus on Youth Crime: A Consultation Paper*. London: HMSO.

Home Office (1997b) *Tackling Delays in the Youth Justice System: A Consultation Paper*. London: HMSO.

Home Office (1997c) *Tackling Youth Crime: A Consultation Paper*. London: HMSO.

Home Office (1997d) *No More Excuses: A New Approach to Tackling Youth Crime in England and Wales*. London: HMSO.

Home Office (1997e) *Preventing Children Offending: A Consultation Document*. London: Home Office.

Home Office (1997f) *Community Safety Order: A Consultation Document*. London: Home Office.

Home Office (1997g) *Getting to Grips with Crime*. London: Home Office.

Home Office (1998a) *Summary of the Government's Response to the Home Office Comprehensive Spending Review of Secure Accommodation for Remanded and Sentenced Juveniles*. London: Home Office.

Home Office (1998b) *Preventing Offending by Young People: Final Report of the Youth Justice Task Force*. London: Home Office.

213

Home Office, Department of Health, Welsh Office and Department for Education and Employment (1998) *Establishing Youth Offending Teams*. London: HMSO.

Home Office, Lord Chancellor's Department and Youth Justice Board (2000) *Circular: The Detention and Training Order*, 9 February.

Hood, C. (1991) 'A public management for all seasons?', *Public Administration*, 69 (1): 3–19.

Huntington, J. (1981) *Social Work and General Medical Practice: Collaboration or Conflict?* London: Allen & Unwin.

Jelinek, M., Smircich, L. and Hirsch, P. (1983) 'Introduction: a code of many colours', *Administrative Science Quarterly*, 28 (3): 331–8.

Jermier, J. M. (1991) 'Critical epistemology and the study of organizational culture: reflections on street corner society', in P. J. Frost, L. F. Moore, M. R. Louis, C. C. Lundberg and J. Martin (eds), *Reframing Organizational Culture*. Newbury Park, CA: Sage.

Jones, D. (1989) 'The successful revolution', *Community Care*, 30 March.

Kleinman, S. and Copp, M. A. (1993) *Emotions and Fieldwork*. London: Sage.

Kolb, D. M. and Puttnam, L. L. (1992) 'Introduction: the dialectics of disputing', in D. M. Kolb and J. M. Bartunek (eds), *Hidden Conflict in Organizations: Uncovering Behind-the-Scenes Disputes*. Newbury Park, CA: Sage, pp. 1–31.

Kvale, S. (1996) *InterViews: An Introduction to Qualitative Research Interviewing*. Thousand Oaks, CA: Sage.

Kvale, S. (1999) 'The psychoanalytic interview as qualitative research', *Qualitative Inquiry*, 5 (1): 87–113.

Labour Party (1996) *Tackling Youth Crime: Reforming Youth Justice: A Consultation Paper on an Agenda for Change*. London: Labour Party.

Leacock, V. and Sparks, J. R. (2002) 'Riskiness and at-risk-ness: some ambiguous features of the current penal landscape', in N. Gray, J. Laing and L. Noaks (eds), *Criminal Justice, Mental Health and the Politics of Risk*. London: Cavendish.

Lemert, E. (1970) *Social Action and Legal Challenge: Revolution Within the Juvenile Court*. Chicago: Aldine.

Levy, A. and Kahan, B. (1991) *The Pindown Experience and the Protection of Children: The Report of the Staffordshire Childcare Enquiry 1990*. Stafford: Staffordshire County Council.

Liebling, A. (1992) *Suicides in Prison*. London: Routledge.

Lukes, S. (1974) *Power: A Radical View*. London: Macmillan.

Manning, P. (1980) *The Narc's Game*. Cambridge, MA: MIT Press.

Martin, J. (1992) *Cultures in Organizations: Three Perspectives*. New York: Oxford University Press.

Martin, J. (2002) *Organizational Culture: Mapping the Terrain*. Thousand Oaks, CA: Sage.

Martin, J. and Meyerson, D. E. (1988) 'Organizational culture and the denial, channelling, and acknowledgement of ambiguity', in L. R. Pondy, J. R. Boland, Jr and H. Thomas (eds), *Managing Ambiguity and Change*. New York: John Wiley.

Martinson, R. (1974) 'What works? Questions and answers about prison reform', *Public Interest*, 35: 22–54.

Mason, J. (1996) *Qualitative Researching*. London: Sage.

Matthews, R. and Pitts, J. (2001) 'Introduction: beyond criminology?', in R. Matthews and J. Pitts, *Crime, Disorder and Community Safety*. London: Routledge.

May, T. (1994) 'Transformative power: a study in a human service organisation', *Sociological Review*, 42: 618–38.

May, T. (2001) 'Power, knowledge and organizational transformation: administration as depoliticization', *Social Epistemology*, 15 (3): 171–85.

McWilliams, W. (1987) 'Probation, pragmatism and policy', *Howard Journal*, 26: 97–121.

McWilliams, W. (1992) 'The rise and development of management thought in the English Probation Service', in R. Statham and P. Whitehead (eds), *Managing the Probation Service: Issues for the 1990s*. Harlow: Longman.

Meerabeau, L. and Page, S. (1998) 'Getting the job done: emotion management and cardiopulmonary resuscitation in nursing', G. Bendelow and S. J. Williams (eds), *Emotions in Social Life: Critical Themes and Contemporary Issues*. London: Routledge.

Meyerson, D. E. (1991) ' "Normal" ambiguity? A glimpse of an occupational culture', in P. J. Frost, L. F. Moore, M. R. Louis, C. C. Lundberg and J. Martin (eds), *Reframing Organizational Culture*. Newbury Park, CA: Sage.

Meyerson, D. E. (1994) 'Interpretations of stress in institutions: the cultural production of ambiguity and burnout', *Administrative Science Quarterly*, 39: 628–53.

Meyerson, D. E. and Martin, J. (1987) 'Cultural change: an integration of three different views', *Journal of Management Studies*, 24: 623–47.

Moore, S. (2000) 'Child incarceration and the new youth justice', B. Goldson (ed.), *The New Youth Justice*. Lyme Regis: Russell House.

Morris, A. and Giller, H. (1979) 'Juvenile justice and social work in Britain', in H. Parker (ed.), *Social Work and the Courts*. London: Edward Arnold.

Muncie, J. (1999) 'Institutionalized intolerance: youth justice and the 1998 Crime and Disorder Act', *Critical Social Policy*, 19 (2): 147–75.

Muncie, J. (2000) 'Pragmatic realism? Searching for criminology in the new youth justice', in B. Goldson (ed.), *The New Youth Justice*. Lyme Regis: Russell House.

Muncie, J. (2002) 'A new deal for youth? Early intervention and correctionalism', in G. Hughes, E. McLaughlin and J. Muncie (eds), *Crime Prevention and Community Safety: New Directions*. London: Sage.

Muncie, J. (2004) *Youth and Crime*, 2nd edn. London: Sage.

Munro, E. (2004) 'The impact of audit on social work practice', *British Journal of Social Work*, 34: 1077–97.

Nellis, M. (1995a) 'Probation values for the 1990s', *Howard Journal*, 34 (1): 19–44.

Nellis, M. (1995b) 'The "Third Way" for probation: a response to Spencer and James', *Howard Journal*, 34 (4): 350–3.

Newburn, T. (1998) 'Tackling youth crime and reforming youth justice: the origins and nature of "New Labour" Policy', *Policy Studies*, 19 (3/4): 199–212.

Newburn, T. (2002) 'Young people, crime and youth justice', in M. Maguire, R. Morgan and R. Reiner (eds), *The Oxford Handbook of Criminology*, 3rd edn. Oxford: Clarendon Press, pp. 531–78.

Parker, M. (2000) *Organizational Culture and Identity: Unity and Division at Work.* London: Sage.

Parton, N. (ed.) (1996) *Social Theory, Social Change and Social Work.* London: Routledge.

Payne, M. (1996) *What is Professional Social Work?* Birmingham: Venture Press.

Pearson, G., Blagg, H., Smith, D., Sampson, A. and Stubbs, P. (1992) 'Crime, community and conflict: the multi-agency approach', D. Downes (ed.), *Unravelling Criminal Justice.* London: Macmillan, pp. 46–72.

Pitts, J. (1999) *Working with Young Offenders,* 2nd edn. London: Macmillan.

Pitts, J. (2000) 'The new youth justice and the politics of electoral anxiety', in B. Goldson (ed.), *The New Youth Justice.* Lyme Regis: Russell House.

Pitts, J. (2001) 'The new correctionalism: young people, youth justice and New Labour', in R. Matthews and J. Pitts, *Crime, Disorder and Community Safety.* London: Routledge.

Pitts, J. (2005) 'The recent history of youth justice in England and Wales', in T. Bateman and J. Pitts (eds), *The RHP Companion to Youth Justice.* Lyme Regis: Russell House.

Platt, A. M. (1969) *The Child Savers: The Invention of Delinquency.* Chicago: University of Chicago Press.

Pratt, J. (1989) 'Corporatism: the third model of juvenile justice', *British Journal of Criminology,* 29 (3): 236–54.

Reiner, R. (1978) *The Blue-Coated Worker.* Cambridge: Cambridge University Press.

Reiner, R. (2000) *The Politics of the Police,* 3rd edn. Oxford: Oxford University Press.

Reuss-Ianni, E. and Ianni, F. A. J. (1983) 'Street cops and management cops: the two cultures of policing', in M. Munch (ed.), *Control in the Police Organization.* Cambridge, MA: MIT Press, pp. 251–74.

Rojek, C., Peacock, G. and Collins, S. (1988) *Social Work and Received Ideas.* London: Routledge.

Rutherford, A. (1986) *Growing Out of Crime.* Harmondsworth: Penguin Books.

Sampson, A., Stubbs, D., Smith, D., Pearson, G. and Blagg, H. (1988) 'Crime, localities and the multi-agency approach', *British Journal of Criminology,* 28 (4): 473–93.

Schein, E. H. (1985) *Organizational Culture and Leadership.* San Francisco: Jossey-Bass.

Schein, E. H. (1991) 'What is culture?', in P. J. Frost, L. F. Moore, M. R. Louis, C. C. Lundberg and J. Martin (eds), *Reframing Organizational Culture.* Newbury Park, CA: Sage, pp. 243–53.

Schwartzman, H. B. (1989) *The Meeting: Gatherings in Organizations and Communities.* New York: Plenum.

Schwartzman, H. B. (1993) *Ethnography in Organizations.* London: Sage.

Seebohm, F. (1968) *Report of the Committee on Local Authority and Allied Personal Social Services,* Cmnd 3703. London: HMSO.

Senior, P. (1991) 'Groupwork in the probation service: care or control in the 1990s', in A. Brown and B. Caddick (eds), *Groupwork with Offenders.* London: Whiting & Birch.

Shapland, J. and Vagg, J. (1988) *Policing by the Public*. London: Routledge.

Shearing, C. (1981) 'Subterranean processes in the maintenance of power', *Canadian Review of Sociology and Anthropology*, 18 (3): 283–98.

Shearing, C. and Ericson, R. (1981) 'Culture as figurative action', *British Journal of Sociology*, 42 (4): 481–506.

Sims, D., Fineman, S. and Gabriel, Y. (1993) *Organizing and Organizations: An Introduction*. London: Sage.

Skolnick, J. H. (1966) *Justice Without Trial: Law Enforcement in Democratic Society*. New York: Wiley.

Smith, D. (1998) 'Social work with offenders', R. Adams, L. Dominelli and M. Payne (eds), *Social Work: Themes, Issues and Critical Debates*. Basingstoke: Macmillan.

Smith, R. (2003) *Youth Justice: Ideas, Policy, Practice*. Cullompton: Willan.

Sparks, J. R. and Bottoms, A. E. (1995) 'Legitimacy and order in prisons', *British Journal of Sociology*, 46 (1): 45–62.

Sparks, J. R., Bottoms, A. E. and Hay, W. (1996) *Prisons and the Problem of Order*. Oxford: Clarendon Press.

Thomas, T. (1986) *The Police and Social Workers*. Aldershot: Gower.

Van Maanen, J. (1978) 'The asshole', in J. Van Maanen and P. Manning (eds), *Policing: a View from the Streets*. New York: Random House.

Van Maanen, J. (1979) 'The fact of fiction in organizational ethnography', *Administrative Science Quarterly*, 24: 539–611.

Van Maanen, J. (1992) 'Drinking our troubles away: managing conflict in a British police agency', in D. M. Kolb and J. M. Bartunek (eds), *Hidden Conflict in Organizations: Uncovering Behind-the-Scenes Disputes*. Newbury Park, CA: Sage.

Vennard, J. and Hedderman, C. (1998) 'Effective interventions with offenders', in P. Goldblatt and C. Lewis (eds), *Reducing Offending: An Assessment of Research Evidence on Ways of Dealing with Offending Behaviour*, Home Office Research Study No. 187. London: HMSO.

Waddington, P. A. J. (1999) 'Policy (canteen) sub-culture: an appreciation', *British Journal of Criminology*, 39 (2): 287–309.

Walsh, J. L. (1977) 'Career styles and police behaviour', in D. H. Bayley (ed.), *Police and Society*. Beverly Hills, CA: Sage.

Weick, K. E. (1985) 'Sources of order in underorganized systems: themes in recent organizational theory', in Y. Lincoln (ed.), *Organizational Theory and Inquiry: The Paradigm Revolution*. Beverley Hills, CA: Sage.

Weick, K. E. (1991) 'The vulnerable system: an analysis of the Tenerife air disaster', in P. J. Frost, L. F. Moore, M. R. Louis, C. C. Lundberg and J. Martin (eds), *Reframing Organizational Culture*. Newbury Park, CA: Sage, pp. 117–31.

Worrall, A. and Hoy, C. (2004) *Punishment in the Community: Managing Offenders: Making Choices*. Cullompton: Willan.

Youth Justice Board (2000) *Youth Justice Board News*, Issue 3, March.

Youth Justice Board (2006a) *Youth Justice Board News Supplement*, Issue 32, January.

Youth Justice Board (2006b) *Practice and Performance*. Online at: http: //www. youth-justice-board.gov.uk/PractitionersPortal/PracticeAndPerformance/ Performance/

Index

Adler, P. A. and P. 198–9
aims and values 52–5, 125–9
ambiguities *see* Youth Justice Team
    and subheadings; Youth
    Offending Team *and*
    subheadings
Atkinson, P. 195, 196
Audit Commission, criticism of
        system 13–16
    efficiency/effectiveness 15–16
    objectives 13–14
    offending behaviour, addressing of
        14–15
    risks, outcomes and evidence
        18–19

Bailey, R. V. 19
banter and team membership 36–7,
        41–4
Becker, H. S. 204, 205
behaviour, offending 14–15
boundaries 164–5
    practice 169–70
    team membership 166–9, 199–200
    values 171–5
Bowling, B. 18
Brown, A. 117–19, 127
Brunsson, N. 151
Bulger, James 11

Caddick, B. 117, 127
Canton, R. 127
Chan, J. 5, 189

change
    and cohesion 37–9
    and occupational cultures 5, 181,
        189–90, 206
    practice 64, 111–13, 125–9
cohesion
    and change 37–9
    of team 36–7
confidentiality 200–1
conflict management 201–4
Copp, M. A. 203, 204–5
court officers 34–5
Crawford, A. 19–20, 23, 24, 73–4, 144,
        146, 190
Crime and Disorder Act 1998 1, 11
    effect on social workers 182–3
    inclusionary measures 22
    national/local structures 19–21
    objectives 16–17
    prevention of offending 17–18, 21–2
    punitiveness 54
criminal justice system, role of youth
        justice teams 50–2
culture, organisational *see*
        occupational cultures

detachment 110–11
    and team membership 163–4
detention and training orders (DTOs)
        165–6, 169–75
disclosure and confidentiality 200–1
Douglas, M. 80
Drakeford, M. 192

Elias, N. 93
exclusion/disjunction 93–8

fragmentation 184–6

Gilling, D. J. 24, 190
Goffman, E. 197
Gouldner, A. W. 205
Graham, J. 18
groupwork
    introduction 116–20
    and professional expertise 119–20
    and team membership 123–5

Haines, K. 192
Hammersley, M. 195, 196
Huntington, J. 56, 58, 59

identity see occupational identity
inclusionary measures 22
individualisation 58
inter-agency conflicts 49–50, 190–2
inter-agency teams 23–4, 193–4
    at YOT 98–106
    multi-agency benefits 16
interpersonal relationships 58–60
interpretive frameworks 39–40, 206

Jelinek, M. 187
Jones, M. 24, 73, 74, 144, 146, 190

Kleinman, S. 203, 204–5
Kolb, D. M. 145
Kvale, S. 203, 204

labelling theory 15
Labour government approach
    ambiguities 22–3, 192–3
    criticism of system 12–13 see also
        Audit Commission
    inclusionary measures 22
    inter-agency teams 23–4
    national/local structures 19–21
    prevention of offending 17–18, 21–2
    reforms 16–21
    restructuring of system 21–5
    risks, outcomes and evidence 18–19
Leacock, V. 18

Martin, J. 6, 10, 39–41, 72, 118, 128,
    143, 185, 186, 206
Mason, J. 196
May, T. 120, 136
Meyerson, D. E. 6, 39, 40, 62, 118, 128,
    143, 185, 186, 206–7
monitoring and evaluation 65–7
multi-agency benefits 16
Muncie, J. 21–2, 23
Munro, E. 66

national/local structures 19–21
Nellis, M. 68
new public management 15–16
No more excuses (White Paper) 11, 84

occupational cultures 2–6
    as aspects of organisational life 3–4
    and change 5, 181, 189–90, 206
    and criminal justice agencies 2–3,
        188–9
    and occupational identity 4–5
    organisational cultures 39–40, 206
    unique aspects 4
occupational identity
    and occupational cultures 4–5
    transformation 183–4, 186–8
    and YOT 106–8, 113–16, 160–1,
        175–9, 183–4, 186–8
    and youth justice system 183–4
offending behaviour, addressing
    14–15
officers of the court 34–5
organisational cultures 39–40, 206

Parker, M. 35, 120, 186–7
partisanship 204–5
Pitts, J. 50, 56, 60
police
    and occupational cultures 3–4
    and social work 46–9
        background 70–1
    and social workers 63–4
police, role in YOT 70–87, 103–6
    atypicality of role 78
    contradictory position 84–7
    development of role 75–8

freedom from core police activities 75–8
and harder/stricter guidelines 79–84
and police culture 71–4
practice
changes 64, 111–13, 125–9
changing boundaries 169–70
development 101–3
education 197–8
and outcomes 60–2
tradition and identity 113–16
prevention of offending 17–18, 21–2
punitiveness 53–5
Puttnam, L. L. 145

Reiner, R. 3, 77, 81
research methods see Youth Offending Team (YOT), research methods
restructuring of system 21–5
risks, outcomes and evidence 18–19
Rojek, C. 58

sabotage 122–3
Schein, E. H. 39
Schwartzman, H. B. 147, 148–9, 177
Scotson, J. L. 93
Seebohm, F. 33
sexist banter 42–4
Sims, D. 37
social justice work see Youth Justice Team and subheadings; Youth Offending Team and subheadings
social work ethos 103–6
Sparks, J. R. 18, 196, 198, 204
specialist practitioners/expertise
YOT as established team 98–101
Youth Justice Team 32–4
structures, national/local 19–21

team meetings, management 145–51
teams see Youth Justice Team and subheadings; Youth Offending Team and subheadings
Thomas, T. 53

values
and aims 52–5, 125–9
changing boundaries 171–5
Van Maanen, J. 7

Waddington, P. A. 3, 189
Weick, K. E. 153, 185
what works agenda 16
White Paper, No more excuses 11, 84
women, and sexist banter 42–4

Youth Justice Board (YJB) 19–21
Youth Justice and Criminal Evidence Act 1999 22
youth justice system
challenges to orthodoxy 23
fragmentation 184–6
inter-agency teams 23–4
occupational identity, transformation 183–4
orthodoxy 15
restructuring challenges 23–5
Youth Justice Team 27–31
aims and values 52–5
change and continuity 28–31
interpersonal relationships 58–60
as transition process 27–8
Youth Justice Team, and ambiguities of social work 46–68
aims and values 52–5
background 46
and changes in practice 64
functional aspects of social work 58–60
functional differentiation 67–8
importance of conflict 63–4
inter-agency conflicts 49–50
monitoring and evaluation 65–7
normality of ambiguities 62–4, 182–3
police and social work 46–9
practice and outcomes 60–2
punitiveness v enabling role 53–5
role in criminal justice system 50–2
standardising practice 65
understanding offending behaviour 55–7

Youth Justice Team, experiences/
    problems 32–44
  background 32
  banter and team membership 36–7,
    41–4
  cohesion and change 37–9
  cohesion of team 36–7
  consensus, conflict and ambiguity
    40–1
  as officers of the court 34–5
  and organisational culture 39–40,
    206
  and other social work staff 32–9
  similarities/differences 35–6
  as specialist practitioners 32–4
Youth Offending Team (YOT)
  atmosphere change 161–4
  background 155, 156
  change and ambiguity 89–90
  changing boundaries 164–5
  changing boundaries of
    membership 166–9
  changing boundaries of practice
    169–70
  changing boundaries of values 171–5
  detachment and team membership
    163–4
  and DTOs, introduction 165–6,
    169–75
  fragmentation 184–6
  management style changes 157–8
  occupational identity,
    transformation 160–1, 175–9,
    183–4, 186–8
  police role *see* police, role in YOT
  rellocation 156–7
  team building 177
  team changes 159
Youth Offending Team (YOT), as
    changing team 109–29
  aims and values 125–9
  ambiguity and innovation 116–20
  background 109
  changing/developing practice
    111–13, 125–9
  detachment 110–11
  practice, tradition and identity
    113–16

resistance to change 120–5
sabotage 122–3
Youth Offending Team (YOT), as
    established team 91–108
  background 91
  common practice, development
    101–3
  exclusion/disjunction 93–8
  identity 91–3
  inter-agency role 98–106
  and professional identity 106–8
  and social work ethos 103–6
  specialist expertise, definition
    98–101
Youth Offending Team (YOT),
    managing ambiguity and
    change 131–54
  autonomy and isolation 139–43
  background 131–2
  deferring decisions 151–2
  disintegration possibility 152–4
  legitimacy, authority and resistance
    134–6
  management appointments 132–6
  management team developments
    137–9
  paralysis and creativity 143–52, 185
  postponing change 151–2
  power and powerlessness 136–9
  team meetings, management 145–51
Youth Offending Team (YOT),
    research methods 6–8, 195–208
  ambiguities 205–7
  boundaries of team membership
    199–200
  and conflict management 201–4
  disclosure and confidentiality 200–1
  interpretive frameworks 39–40, 206
  invitation to join team 195–7
  and partisanship 204–5
  practice education 197–8
  presentation of fieldwork to team
    208
  researcher/member role 198–201
youth offending teams (YOTs) 1–2
  further changes 193–4
  national/local structures 19–21